Cedar.

The Life and Music
of Cedar Walton

Ben Markley

Number 18 in the North Texas Lives of Musicians Series

University of North Texas Press
Denton, Texas

Permissions:
University of North Texas Press
1155 Union Circle #311336
Denton, TX 76203-5017

The paper used in this book meets the minimum requirements of the
American National Standard for Permanence of Paper for Printed Library
Materials, z39.48.1984. Binding materials have been chosen for durability.

Library of Congress Cataloging-in-Publication Data

Markley, Ben, author.
  Cedar : the life and music of Cedar Walton / Ben Markley.
    Pages cm
  Includes bibliographical references and index.
  ISBN-13 978-1-57441-897-2 (cloth)
  ISBN-13 978-1-57441-904-7 (ebook)
  1. LCSH: Walton, Cedar. 2. Pianists—United States—Biography.
3. Jazz musicians—United States—Biography. 4. LCGFT: Biographies.

  ML417 .W24 M37 2022
  781.65092 [B]–dc23
                    2022055951

Cedar is Number 18 in the North Texas Lives of Musicians Series.

The electronic edition of this book was made possible by the support of
the Vick Family Foundation.

Typeset by vPrompt eServices.

Contents

Foreword

C edar Walton is my first cousin with our dads being brothers. Cedar being the son of the oldest brother and I being the youngest son of the youngest brother, there was an 18-year gap in our ages. It took me awhile to come of age and become aware of my cousin the Jazz Piano Musician. At family gatherings, my father, uncles, and aunts would always ask my Uncle Cedar and Aunt Ruth how Billy (Cedar Jr.) was doing among the things they all caught up on as a family. From what I remember there were some trials and tribulations early on. He was doing ok but that at times he needed and received assistance from my aunt and uncle. The first time I got a chance to hear how well he played was when an album showed up in the household that was one of those albums that labels put out that highlighted several of their artists. One of the tunes was of J. J. Johnson's band and right there on the label it said piano, Cedar Walton. I can't tell you how excited that made me. I listened to it over and overpaying special attention to the piano. I always loved music and that love grew over the years as I played drums and percussion with some thoughts of taking it to the next level. I'm sure my parents were a bit relieved when I ended up going to pharmacy school because they knew of some of the challenges my cousin Billy had to overcome. After getting my Pharmacy license I ended up working in Dallas, Cedar's hometown. It was there I started to develop a closer relationship with my older cousin as he would come back home to see his mom and dad. In the end, I became his favorite cousin (his words not mine), which meant so much to me because he sure was mine. I cherish the times and conversations we had and am so proud of the musical legacy he left.

When my cousin Carl, Cedar's oldest son, called letting me know about someone writing a biography about his father and asking was it ok for him to share my contact info, I cautiously agreed. I let it be known that I would have to vet anyone doing such a project to make sure that (1) their motivation for doing it was coming from a good place and (2) they were up to the task, before I'd lend my support or offer my personal participation. You see, for me, my cousin Cedar, who was called Billy by close family, was not only a world class musician, but more importantly, he was family. My first contact with Ben, I had more questions for him than answers, approval or support. After the initial phone conversations, I got the impression fairly quickly that Ben had a genuine love for Cedar, the artist and his compositions. I could also tell, after some internet research, that he was quite an accomplished and talented jazz pianist himself. Soon after receiving a copy of Clockwise, a recording of Ben's Big Band performing some of Cedar's compositions, I realized how much of a talented and gifted arranger he is. Still, I wanted a face-to-face meeting to finalize agreement to any participation or help that I could possibly be in aiding him in the pursuit of his project. That opportunity presented itself soon after as we would both be attending that year's JEN conference in Dallas. Ben would be there with his big band featuring Terell Stafford performing his arrangements of Walton tunes and I would be there pursuing my passion for photography. We met for lunch, and it was there that I could see how excited and personally invested he was to the project. That's when I decided to share any information and connections that would maybe help.

Later, at the conference, I asked if I could attend the band's sound check/ rehearsal to maybe get some shots. It was there I experienced one of those moments in jazz that I'll never forget. Ben was quickly going through the things you do at a sound check. Moving quickly thru sections he wanted to go over knowing time was tight as others are coming in after him. Terell Stafford had gotten to the conference late as he had flight delays because of bad weather. The musicians were all really talented and were sounding great. Things were going along swiftly as Ben would start songs or sections and being satisfied quickly get their attention stopping them to go to the next thing. I was taking a few photos and enjoying the mini concert when they went into a song as before and got to a section where Terell would be soloing and man I tell you, he went beast mode erupting into a cascade of melodious extemporization. It was like a hungry cheetah bursting into full speed after a swift antelope. You could tell something special was happening as the other musicians began to turn in amazement. It was as if he was releasing all the pent-up frustrations of the travel issues the days before. Ben, sitting behind the piano, was still in business mode looking down at the charts, held up his hand as he had before but the band did not stop. Terell had his eyes closed as an explosion of improvisation burst from his horn. Ben, after giving the cutoff sign a couple of times from behind the piano, all the while studying large sheets of charts in front of him finally stood up as to get back the control of runaway band. He tried once more before finally giving up and letting the moment run its course. When finally winding down, Terell opened his eyes and gave a very casual smile as if nothing had happened. The rest of us or at least I was in awe and amused at what had just happened. The night of the performance I took a big emotional hit as the essence of Cedar and Freddie Hubbard were very strong in the room.

As my awareness of jazz artists expanded over the years, when I would mention to any artist that I was most recently fascinated with to my cousin, I was always amazed that the vast majority of time he would have a personal story of him interacting with them. That would be the case no matter how high profile or famous the artist was. I would often, while reading liner notes, see his name and even a couple of times notice that he was part of the session for a movie. While I would be totally in awe and star struck, when I would call and ask him why he never mentioned them, he would just speak of them rather matter of fact, with little of the amazement that I felt. After my cousin Cedar passed, I took the time to use online resources that were now available to do a deeper dive into his career. I must admit I found out much more than I ever knew. So much so, it was then I learned I never really understood just how much my cousin contributed to this American born art-form we call Jazz. He was a true Jazz Master in every sense. He walked among giants because he was a giant. I am so excited about what Ben's research and interviews bring to light about this American Jazz treasure I knew as my cousin Billy.

—*William Walton*

Preface

Black American Music has been an important part of my life for many years. During the formative period of my musical development, the sounds of Oscar Peterson, Miles Davis, and Wynton Kelly made me fall in love with jazz and ultimately pursue a career in music. I grew up in the rural farm town of Chapman, Kansas. As you can imagine, there haven't been many jazz pianists coming from the 1,200-person farming community. The history of jazz has countless stories of musicians making the trek to New York to be at the forefront of the music and to have the opportunity to hear and play with the best musicians doing it. The stories of the legendary Charlie Parker (my Kansas City adjacent neighbor) made it apparent to me that New York City was the place and I wanted to have this experience for myself.

After graduating from Fort Hays State University with a piano performance degree (and playing jazz any chance I could), my wife, Abby, and I packed up our few belongings and headed East. I enrolled at New York University and went to class each day to get as much out of school and the city as possible. It was only a few weeks before I spent most of my money going to shows and trying to hear everyone. Two of the most influential teachers I had during that time were David Hazeltine and Brian Lynch. Our lessons would often include a phrase like, "Cedar does it like this." That was enough for me to realize that I needed to get deep in Cedar Walton's music. As my studies of Cedar's playing and writing continued, I realized there was a depth in the esthetic of his playing and writing that captured all the best parts of the music. This understanding continued to grow as I learned that Cedar and the many groups he played with captured the very essence of the African esthetic found in Black American Music. What an epiphany for me! The playing of the iconic trio of the Magic Triangle or the equally special trio Cedar, Sam Jones, and Louis Hayes remain quintessential examples for me to which all other trios are measured.

One of the absolute best jobs I had while in New York was working as an intern at Dizzy's Club Coca Cola for legendary club owner, manager, and record producer, Todd Barkan, and club manager, Roland Chassagne. The opportunity for me to be around musicians on a nightly basis was amazing. I got to see the entire package—how they rehearsed, how the music evolved from night to night, and how they treated fans, the staff, and each other.

Barkan had deep ties with jazz musicians dating back to his time as the club owner of the Keystone Korner in San Francisco. His knowledge and passion for music and its history is unwavering. The Keystone Korner was a "who's who" of jazz musicians that included Dexter Gordon, Art Blakey, McCoy Tyner, and of course, Cedar. Todd brought much of this atmosphere to Dizzy's. When I started at Dizzy's I realized that this club was much more than a business transaction between musicians and the club. It was a family. And none more so than with Cedar. During Todd's time at Dizzy's, Cedar held a two-week residency in August almost every year. This time also coincided with Todd's birthday. I was so impressed by the sheer number of jazz musicians who came out to hear Cedar during these runs—a true sign of admiration and respect. My study and dedication to Cedar's music solidified in part because of my experiences at Dizzy's.

In 2017, I released a big band album of my arrangements of Cedar's compositions. For me, this project was a tribute to a jazz giant. Different from other tributes, however, I wanted to present Cedar's compositions in a unique setting than he was accustomed to playing in (a big band), with the goal being to bring more recognition to his works by having more people play his music. *Clockwise: The Music of Cedar Walton* was very well received and consequently, many contemporaries and family members of Cedar reached out with messages of congratulations. It was during this time that I met Cedar's wife, Martha. I was so flattered to hear her kind words about the recording saying that "Cedar would be so pleased." During our conversations, Martha let me know that she had kept much of Cedar's archives and memorabilia from over the years. After soaking all of this in, I got up the nerve to ask Martha if I could write a biography on Cedar. She agreed, and I started the process of reviewing the materials she had as well as the large task of interviewing family, friends, and contemporaries of Cedar. The results are my humble offering to remember a man who has had such a profound impact on jazz and so many musicians.

My research for this project was multifaceted. One of the most valuable resources and the impetus for this book was Martha's private collection. They were indispensable and included everything from tour itineraries, personal pictures and awards, as well as correspondence. Among the most impressive correspondence saved was Cedar's letters to his mother, Ruth. These letters spanned the late 1950s to the early 1980s and offer an intimate look into his life at the time of each writing. They discuss his time in the military, touring life, and family. They also address current events of the time, including integration.

In 2010, Cedar Walton was recognized as an NEA Jazz Master. One of the benefits from this award is that Cedar participated in an in-depth interview that was conducted over two days and covered his entire life. Having Cedar's own words to describe his life is extremely informative in creating an accurate picture of his experiences.

Thanks to the help of many, I was able to conduct over 80 interviews of people who knew Cedar as a friend, family member, and musician. From the start it was clear that each person had a love and deep respect for Cedar. Every effort was made on my part to compile and complete the most comprehensive interview list possible. Unfortunately, there were some musicians who were not available for an interview and thus are not included in this book the way I would have preferred.

Cedar's discography is extensive. Liner notes from these albums provide valuable information that aided me in my pursuit to paint a picture of Walton's life as a musician. When an album title appears in this book, I have chosen to include its most recent offering so that fans can easily access these recordings to learn more about the master.

To the reader: I have written this book as a musician and fan of Cedar Walton. It is written in the way I would want to learn about someone— with stories and interviews from people who really knew Cedar—and from

Cedar's own accounts. While the interviews provide information about different periods in Cedar's life, they more importantly offer a personal look into each person's relationship with Cedar. For me, conducting and collecting interviews was the most enjoyable part of this process. The interviews helped me to understand Cedar and his music on a deeper level. The sole purpose of this project is to create a document that others can use to learn more about this jazz giant so his legacy can live on.

Chapter 1

Firm Roots (1875–1934): *The Beginnings of the Walton Family in America*

The journey of the Walton family in America began in the depths of slavery. In time, they become landowners who were eventually able to send some of their children to college. They instilled values of hard work and honor and fostered a close-knit family atmosphere, all of which were the model for future generations of Waltons. Family successors held prominent positions in government, civil rights organizations, education, and the private sector.[1] Cedar's success as a world-renowned jazz musician is rooted in the experiences and lessons of his ancestors, and his contributions to Black American Music continue to influence musicians all around the world.

Before being forced into slavery in America, it is believed that that Waltons were part of the Lyela tribe in what is now the West African country of Burkino Faso.[2] The harsh cruelties of slavery made it difficult to trace the Walton family lineage until the 1800s. However, beginning in the early 1800s, the family's roots in North Carolina are documented by the U.S. Census.[3] Handy and Patience Walton (Cedar's great-grandparents) spent the prime of their lives as slaves working in the apple and tobacco fields of North Carolina. They had five sons. Toward the end of the 1800s (approximately 1875), they packed up their belongings, their five sons, and their niece and migrated west.[4]

Accounts of where exactly the Waltons were initially headed are somewhat conflicting.[5] The family settled in the Brazos River Valley in Texas. During that time, Texas had "seemingly boundless amounts of uncultivated land which had "promises equal to that of the gold rush days."[6] Handy learned about land in this area that could be purchased for $1 an acre. The family used their life savings to purchase "virgin land" around the Brazos River bend. The property they purchased was raw and required the land to be cleared of trees and brush before crops of cotton, corn, and others essential for their survival could be planted. As with many settlers during this time, the Walton's experienced highs and lows in their new undertaking.[7] The program from a Walton family reunion in 1981 described the land around the Brazos River:

> The Brazos River was the reservoir that collected water flow from all the parts of the area of Brazos County. This body of water was held in check at that time by a poorly constructed dam which often gave way overflowing the lowlands destroying crops that were well on the way to harvest. The overflow at other times served as nature's way of fertilization, which caused crops to grow in abundance; these were looked upon as the good years.[8]

Handy and Patience were smart, hardworking, and resilient people. They understood the importance of education. In fact, they were able to send their youngest son, Edward, and niece, Rena (who made the trip with them from North Carolina), to college. By moving their family and establishing themselves as property owners, the Walton's significantly improved their lives and set the stage for success for future Walton generations.[9] The values of hard work as well as a sense of family pride have continually been passed down the Walton line. Patience and Handy endured slavery, became landowners, and sent children to college, a remarkable transition in one lifetime.[10]

William Walton (Cedar's grandfather) was born a slave and was the eldest son of Handy and Patience. He and his wife Elmira had seven children. Cedar Anthony (C.A.) Walton Sr.[11] was the eldest child and was born in 1901 in Wilcox, Texas.[12]

William and Elmira owned a farm near the Brazos River basin and made their living farming. The land was rich and fertile.[13] C.A. learned much about

Walton Family: (l to r) C.A., Eunice, Homer, Erma, Odis, Elmyra, and William,
ca. 1905. *William H. Walton estate*

farming and agriculture as a child. After high school, he attended Prairie
View A&M University and graduated in 1926 with a Bachelor of Science
degree. The next year he began working as the Dallas County agricultural
agent, a position he held for 23 years.[14]

In 1950, he resigned as an agricultural agent and accepted an appoint-
ment by the U.S. State Department International Cooperation Administration to advise the Liberian government on agricultural projects. Walton was
assigned to Monrovia, West Africa. In 1954, he returned to the United States
and worked stateside until his retirement in 1959.[15]

C.A. was a prominent man in the Dallas community and took an active
role in many organizations. He was a board member of the Dallas Black
Chamber of Commerce and served as the chamber's executive secretary.
Other community services' roles included: interim secretary for the Moorland
Branch YMCA, counselor for the Small Business Administration, a member
of the Phi Beta Sigma fraternity, the Progressive Voters League, and Knights
of Pythias of Texas. He was a member of the New Hope Baptist Church for
fifty years.[16]

C.A.'s eventual wife, Ruth Grimstead, was born in 1905 and raised in Beaumont, Texas. Ruth was very active in school and had many talents. She attended Charlton High School and served as the musical editor of the school's yearbook (*The Rice Shock*) in 1921. Her nickname was "Frenchie," and her yearbook quote was, "I intend to be an old maid."[17] Ruth was a talented pianist. The 1921 *Rice Shock* read: "Ruth Grimstead has had the instrumental solo for the school commencements a number of years and her pieces have been received very favorably by the audiences."[18] After high school, Ruth attended Wiley College and graduated in 1926 with a degree in music. She taught arithmetic for the Dallas Independent School District at B.F. Darrell Elementary School for 30 years.[19]

Ruth and C.A. were married in 1932. On January 17, 1934, the couple welcomed their one and only child, Cedar Anthony Walton Jr., into the world.[20]

Chapter 2

Groundwork (1934–1950): *Growing up in Dallas*

Around the Walton household, Cedar was known as Billy. Cedar's cousin William Hunter Walton said, "His mom called him Billy. In fact, growing up, I thought that was his given first name. He was just always Billy to us."[1] C.A. and Ruth Walton provided a very comfortable lifestyle for their son. They also took in Ruth's mother, Louise, who was referred to by most as Mrs. Grimstead. Mrs. Grimstead was described as a "strong woman"[2] who was a wonderful cook. The precedent for the Walton's taking their mother in was one that was modeled by Handy and Patience. After Handy passed and Patience grew older, each of the Walton sons had a room in their house specifically for their mother. This is something that C.A. saw first-hand.[3] Cedar Jr. describes his household growing up:

> I had very loving parents and I was an only child. I came up in a happy home that included also my grandmother, my mother's mother .... Which tells you that, my father accepted a package deal, you know— mother and her mother. But he had no choice because my grandmother's cooking was superlative, to use one way to describe it. Seductive would be another ... he couldn't turn this combination of people down .... We had a very happy life .... We had everything, we had everything on our side of the color line so to speak.[4]

Music was a regular part of Cedar's upbringing. C.A. and Ruth both loved music and played recordings regularly. They also took Cedar to concerts.

Cedar's first exposures to the piano were hearing his mother play.[5] Cedar recalls some of his first musical experiences:

> [My mother] had an affinity for jazz that was uncanny ... uncanny in a sense that she would take me to concerts. That's when I first heard Hank Jones .... That tour, Jazz at the Philharmonic ... my eyes popped when I saw Hank .... I said, "Wow!" .... I was ... pretty young but totally impressionable because I'd been trying to play since I was five .... There was a room in my home [where our piano was] ... in wintertime, they didn't turn on the heat unless we had guests ... so I would put on my overcoat and go in there and tinkle and play what I thought I heard on these records by Louie Jordan and Nat Cole. And I know now I wasn't even close, but at that time I thought I was. [laughs].
>
> [At first I started playing the piano] just from seeing her [my mom] play these pieces that she liked, I possibly could have been emulating her, but I was drawn to the instrument without her. She was working most of the time of the day that I'd selected to go and be with the piano .... She saw my excitement about the likes of Hank Jones and .... Oscar Peterson ... a lot of great people came through that tour. She whispered to me that those guys are great and they don't have any music in front of them, but they can read music, so I suggest that you look into that. [laughs] That's putting it mildly. She said, "You're gonna have to get your act together; you got to stop playing by ear and start learning some music." So that's when she came in and started me with the books.[6]

Ruth showed her son some of the basics, including Hanon studies for finger technique.[7] Eventually, Cedar received keyboard training outside the house, a decision that was preferable to both mother and son as Cedar remembers:

> [My mother and I] ... for lack of a better term, we couldn't get along. [laughs] I mean, we loved each other dearly, but we would fight all the time ... just mother and son differences of opinion. And so when I tried to teach her to drive, for instance, we ended up in a ditch ... we had shouting matches all the time. And for what it's worth, she was a Gemini and I'm a Capricorn .... So I had other teachers she recommended. The other teachers used to come to our home and teach me.[8]

All of Cedar's piano lessons were studying Western Classical music. Jazz lessons were not offered at that time. Anything he learned in the way of jazz was by himself, imitating sounds and styles he heard on recordings.[9] Cedar's parents went to great lengths to find excellent teachers for him. One teacher who was memorable to Cedar was a lady named Mrs. Marble.

> Mrs. Marble who had gone to … some school in Michigan which was quite a distance from Texas, especially to me …. She had been infatuated with the great George Gershwin and I'm sure she had a big crush on him; I mean musically, you know. [laughs] I think she'd even met him once …. I learned "Rhapsody in Blue" as best I could through her. And she was Caucasian, so we had to meet—still in the '40s—in a used church, which was … a natural … rendezvous point … I can remember … quote–unquote auditioning for her to see did she want to teach me, with a piece named "Whatta Ya Say We Go," I think by Charlie Ventura. Somehow, by this time … I could teach myself pieces from recordings … so I had developed from somebody who didn't know what they were doing to somebody who could pick up things by ear and … reconstruct them, shall we say …. So she said, "Oh yeah, I like that." I'm sure she'd never heard it, but I guess my … enthusiasm about this must have convinced her that …. I could be a good student. And we had quite a few lessons together.
>
> Bach, Beethoven, [laughs] Debussy were some of the pieces I worked the hardest on. And you can call Gershwin a classical composer. I spent a lot of time on "Rhapsody in Blue." I was also attracted to … piano concertos … I just couldn't believe that these pianists could remember all that stuff. I mean, the length of a piano concerto was, with an orchestra, for me, humongous, you know. Even though they're not really that long if you consider the performance of a jazz piece sometime, but they seemed longer, you know [laughs] …. Gershwin wrote one, for instance, "Concerto in F," and it features the piano and of course in most of these they'll be the qualities of a piano concerto with orchestra there's always a long period where the piano is alone … before the orchestra comes back in. For me that's a very exciting highlight of a concerto …. My training led me into the total appreciation of some very high-level pieces.

Cedar didn't spend all his time practicing the classics. At a young age, he also tried his hand at composing and arranging, skills he would use his entire life.

In an interview with jazz pianist Ethan Iverson, Walton spoke about when he
first started to compose.

> I always tried to compose—just something I would try to do.
> [My early compositions] They had some of the strangest titles, you
> know, "Trash Can." They weren't that memorable, but I was trying.
> I was just determined to come up with something original. I just never
> stopped trying." "... When I look back, I wasn't writing, but I was
> trying to. My mother used to call out, "Are you making up pieces
> again?" She was a pianist. She couldn't play a note without music,
> but she could play with the sheet music and sing along with the lyrics.
> That was very helpful to me to see someone to do that.[10]

Throughout Cedar's career, his outstanding arranging skills have been on
display. Some of the first recorded examples of his arranging were during his
tenure with Art Blakey and The Jazz Messengers. Cedar got his start by studying simplified arrangements by George Shearing.[11] Walton remembers:

> I would gobble these up ... 'cause they weren't hard. They were
> purposely simplified and so I remember learning how he harmonized
> "That Old Feeling" .... I ended up recording [that tune] with Art
> Blakey but not his version .... By this time, I had ... an ability to have
> my own version of this piece. And that's on *Three Blind Mice*. I sort
> of attribute that, 'cause that's one of the first pieces I learned from
> the George Shearing book which was simplified but very advanced
> to me because this is not something I had been capable of coming up
> on my own.[12]

C.A. and Ruth's home was in South Dallas. In that area in the '40s and
'50s, most black students attended Phyllis Wheatley Elementary School.
Roger Boykin, Cedar's childhood friend, remembers Cedar attending
Phyllis Wheatley. Cedar's mother Ruth taught arithmetic at B.F. Darrell
Elementary, another all-black school, formerly named Colored School
No. 2, before changing the name to honor B.F. Darrell.[13] For secondary
school, students attended Lincoln High School. Many of the friends
Cedar made in the neighborhood were also school mates. Several of these
people became lifelong friends that he would call and visit whenever he
was in their town.

James Wilson was one of Cedar's dear friends. He was an important figure in the Dallas music scene in his own right. He taught band at B.F. Darrell Elementary School and was known for getting students to play jazz at an early age.[14] He also opened a music shop that offered horn repair. Any musician coming to town in need of a horn repair, including Dallas native and friend, David "Fathead" Newman, would stop by. Cedar would also stop by when he was in town to check up on his old friend. Cedar and Wilson made a pact that they would look in on the other's mother if the other moved away from Dallas.[15] James Wilson recalls his friendship with Cedar:

Cedar and I grew up in Dallas. I lived about five or six blocks from where Cedar lived. His parents were much better off than my family. Cedar had a wonderful grandmother, Mrs. Grimstead was her name.

When I was young, I liked sports, basketball, and whatever else the neighborhood kids were playing. The Walton's lived on the corner lot in a big house and I would go up to the door and Cedar would be inside practicing piano. I wouldn't even make it to the door and Mrs. Grimstead would say, "James, go home." I don't know how she heard me, but that's how she always responded when I came up. I didn't come up too often. [laughs]

As time went by, I remember Cedar would sometimes practice a little bit at the school piano. I remember vaguely when Cedar took his first gig. He slipped off from school and went and played with some local musicians. After that, Cedar slowly started to play out more.

When Cedar and I were teenagers, he could be mischievous. My stepfather had a brand new 1955 Mercury. He would let me borrow it on occasion. One night I picked up Cedar and Leon Henderson, his nick name was Skeebo. The three of us used to pal around together a lot. I remember we were riding somewhere in between Dallas and Fort Worth during the Christmas holidays. Cedar and I were in the back seat and Leon was driving the car. We had some firecrackers somewhere in the car and Cedar lit one up and threw it out the window at the car next to us. I didn't know that he was that mischievous! [laughs] We got back home and of course Mrs. Walton scolded us for being out so long. My mother was there too. She didn't say much.

The three of us thought we were the sharpest people in town. Fort Worth was the closest town and not one of us had a girlfriend. We would dress up, put on a shirt and tie and dress our best and go into a little place in Fort Worth that had some good music on. It was mostly jazz. We would sit there and listen to the jazz and just enjoy our time there.

We thought we were pretty clean. As time went on, Cedar would get
more jobs as a pianist in Dallas.[16]

Howard Hill is another friend from the neighborhood who recalls Cedar's
early experiences with jazz:

Growing up, I lived one block away from Cedar. He lived on the
corner of Oakland and Metropolitan. His dad and mother went to the
same church I did which was the New Hope Baptist Church in Dallas.
His dad was an ambassador, and his mother was a schoolteacher.
Her name was Ruth. Cedar and I went to Lincoln High School in
Dallas. I was a couple grades ahead of him. Cedar graduated with my
brother Raymond Hill in 1951. At school, Cedar played in the concert
band and in the jazz band. His jazz band director was Uncle Dud, and
Uncle Dud was famous for his jazz band. He directed the marching
band too. When we had football games, the stadium was filled with just
as many blacks as whites and they were there to hear the band! Cedar
also played in the same group as David "Fathead" Newman. Cedar was
in South Dallas and Fathead grew up in East Dallas.
    In 1950, we went to the state fair auditorium in Dallas, Texas and
watched Jazz at the Philharmonic. I remember Cedar, myself, and
my brother went backstage at intermission to see Ella Fitzgerald.
She invited us in and talked to us. Cedar told her that he was really
involved in music and Ella told Cedar "make sure you stick to it. Don't
give it up." And he did![17]

Leon Henderson recalls that Cedar was not only a talented musician but also
a smart student.

I remember that Cedar was very smart. When the seniors in high school
had their day, Cedar was chosen to act as principal because he was one
of the class presidents. He wasn't as adept in sports as others but held
his own. I think his mother asked our music teacher to get him involved.
He played the triangle in the band before playing the clarinet. We had
an excellent band director who produced some major musicians.
    We would play a lot in the park after school as well as in the summer.
Cedar would inevitably arrive when we were almost finished because
Ruth, his mother, had him practicing piano hour after hour with the
metronome atop the standalone [piano] .... I came over one evening
and listened to Cedar while he was practicing. He was playing Duke

Ellington's "Satin Doll." He played it over and over and over with the metronome. It seemed like he never stopped. After a long while he said while still playing, "You like that piece, right?"

The summer of our senior year in high school, Cedar's parents took him to New York City. They heard a lot of music and visited some museums too. When Cedar returned, he said, "That's where I want to be." And the rest is history![18]

Lincoln High School and J.K. Miller "Uncle Dud"

The legendary band program of Lincoln High School in South Dallas produced many talented musicians in the '40s and '50s who went on to have notable careers. Bobby Bradford, David "Fathead" Newman, Leroy Cooper, and Cedar were four musicians who attended LHS during this time that had careers in music and had extended tenures with notable musicians, including Ray Charles and Ornette Coleman. Each musician also did extensive recording session work. Band director, J.K. Miller ("Uncle Dud"), created a culture that expected excellence. He also was very encouraging to musicians learning to improvise as well as developing their ear. When marching season was over, Miller would frequently bring in big band jazz charts for the band to read. Before teaching band at Lincoln High School, J.K. Miller played professionally with territory bands as well as the Fletcher Henderson Orchestra.[19] According to Cedar:

> The band director was a good trumpet player, but he decided to teach. I think in one of our formations—you know, during halftime—we were supposed to go straight and Fathead [David "Fathead" Newman] went out. From that moment on, that band director nicknamed him "Fathead."[20]
>
> I was an ear guy. I'll always remember J.K. Miller, who was very tolerant of something like that. He'd also bring in charts arranged by Gil Fuller for the Dizzy Gillespie orchestra for us to try off-season, when it wasn't football season. J.K. Miller had played in bands. In fact, he told me that he played in those bands—they used to call them territory bands—bands in the '40s or even the '30s.[21]

In addition to taking Cedar to concerts in Dallas, the Walton's also took their son to New York City as Leon Henderson mentioned. This trip was very inspiring to a young and impressionable Cedar. Throughout his life he mentioned the trip in interviews and even referenced it in letters he wrote to his mother. During this trip to New York, Cedar met Miles Davis for the first time via Dallas pianist Red Garland. Miles and Cedar connected about J.K. Miller. Cedar recalls:

> I went into the Café Bohemia ... my family stayed about one block away from the Red Garland family. I mean, his father was still in Dallas, and I'd heard all about it and so I introduced myself to Red Garland. He was standin' next to Miles Davis at the bar, and it was an instant. Red was a guy would say, "Oh, oh, hey my man!" You know, he was an instant friend, you know, [laughs] as compared to Miles, [who] was a little standoffish. One reason is because he had a voice impediment .... You must have heard recordings of his voice. It was kinda hoarse. So I think he resisted conversations because of that .... When he found out I was from Dallas, he asked me did I know J.K. Miller, which was ... our high school band director. So imagine my enthusiasm ... at hearing the great Miles Davis talking about my high school band director. I said, "This must be Heaven."

During Cedar's time at Lincoln High School, he played the clarinet as well as the glockenspiel in the marching band. According to accounts of some of his school mates, clarinet was not Cedar's forte.[22] From Cedar's own admission, he struggled to play the clarinet. He primarily played by ear. Sight reading was a challenge. And the ledger lines in the clarinet parts of the marches the band played were difficult for him.[23]

Allison C. Tucker was the band director who succeeded Miller at Lincoln High School. He said that he and Miller "were determined to give students at the predominantly black school an opportunity to make it despite often severe economic disadvantages."[24] Jazz singer and class of '68 Lincoln High School Marlyn Walton (no relation) likens the '40s–'80s at Lincoln High School to the musicians of the Harlem Renaissance in the '20s. "Whatever the reasons, Lincoln's jazz greats have built a record of achievement."[25]

Trumpeter Bobby Bradford was a Lincoln High School bandmate of Cedar's. Bradford is another notable musician to come out of the LHS lineage at that time. His resume includes playing and recording with Ornette Coleman as well as numerous recordings under his own name as a leader. Bradford discusses J.K. Miller and the Lincoln High School Band Program.

First of all, in high schools in Texas, white and black, football is next to religion. Actually, it's above religion. [laughs] We had this football sort of pep thing and a marching band that played at half time. The band would go out on the field, make a formation and then march off. In the football game itself we played the school song and some other things to keep our side of the stadium all hyped up for the games, similar to what all of the marching bands do today. Sometimes during the year we'd have to play parades, but it was mostly a marching band for football. When football season was finished, there was basketball and just a small handful of kids were assembled for a pep band. We didn't have a formal symphonic band program that some schools did.

If you were a freshman at LHS and you decided you were gonna be in the band, the first year you would take Band I and then in the spring take Band II. In your second year, you were in varsity band. No matter how badly or how well you played, everyone had to take Bands I and II. The best players got to be section leaders. If you weren't a very good player, you were just one of a multitude of people who played in the band. We had a pretty good size band, about fifty kids in the band.

We had enough kids to fill out the band. We had sousaphones, trombones, saxophones, clarinets, and Cedar played those bells, the glockenspiel and sometimes he would play the bells with the choir.

By the time you got to Lincoln High School you'd already heard all these stories about Uncle Dud and if you were interested in being in the band, you couldn't wait to take his classes. If you didn't do your part to behave or you do some unruly stuff in the class, Uncle Dud will make you "ride the horse." You'd just get on a chair, and he'd whack you with these boards, not like he was some cruel monster, but he didn't put up with any slack. That was the discipline of the day, but the kids loved him.

Uncle Dud had been a professional trumpet player before he decided to get into teaching. He had had some experience as a professional performer. He was a terrific brass player. By the time I got to him of course this was late in his life, and he was not in good health. In fact, he died while I was in the band.

Cedar had graduated already, but right in that three- or four-year period Miller died. Uncle Dud was legendary, at the very least. He's the one that gave Fathead the name that stuck with "Fathead." I don't think he sat up one day and figured out he was gonna call David Newman "Fathead" but if you didn't play a part right he would say to you instead of saying ... knucklehead or whatever. He'd say, "no, no, no that's not it Fathead!" He called everybody fathead but somehow it came off to David Newman.[26]

Another bandmate and LHS band captain, Herbie Johnson, recalls his time with Cedar, Uncle Dud, and "Fathead" Newman:

Uncle Dud Miller was our band director. Before he started as a teacher, he played trumpet with the Fletcher Henderson Orchestra. After Fletcher Henderson, he came back to Texas and began to teach school. He imparted a lot professional experience that he gained from that band and others he'd played in. He was about, I guess 5'5" or 5'6," but he had a commanding presence that instilled discipline in all of the musicians. I was not there when he named David Newman "Fathead," [laughs] but David was playing first alto when I got in the band and Uncle Dud sat me down by Fathead and said, "You learn all this stuff that he's playing."

I sat right next to Fathead until he and Cedar graduated. At that time, a guy by the name of James Gray was captain of the band and when James graduated, Uncle Dud assigned me to be captain of the band. Unfortunately, that summer Uncle Dud took seriously ill and passed away. Uncle Dud instilled a certain culture in the band that was very challenging. We had some great players come out of that band. James Gray, who I mentioned was the first principal at the Booker T. Washington High School for the Visual and Performing Arts. Later on, he became Superintendent of a school district in South Carolina. We had David Fathead Newman as well as another great saxophonist by the name of James Clay, and Bobby Bradford .... Clay and Bobby played with Ornette Coleman out in California. Cedar was somewhat more advanced than us because his mother was a piano teacher. Uncle Dud created an atmosphere that promoted our desire to play jazz and to love the music.

A number of students tried to get a football game going across the street across from Cedar's house. We always needed one more player and would send someone over to Cedar's house to see if he could join us. Every time we came over, Cedar would be running those arpeggios. He couldn't come out to play football. We can see why now! [laughs] Cedar also had the experience of travel as his dad was an official with the Department of Agriculture. He visited New York City at a very early age. His mother took him to the plays and other cultural events in New York City, and I believe he went on to Europe with his dad once or twice. He had a wide range of experiences even before he finished high school.

At that time there were three college bands that had great stage or jazz bands in the state of Texas: Wiley College Collegians, Sam Houston Collegians, and Prairie View. All three had monster jazz bands and they would come to Dallas and play for us at Lincoln High School. We would constantly be comparing the bands and who was the worst. At that time, Sam Houston always came out on top. Consequently, the guys who finished Lincoln and wanted to major in music generally gravitated toward Sam Houston.

Clay and Bobby, James Gray and Thomas Roth went down there. There were a whole host of guys who went to Sam Houston and either became band directors in Texas or professional musicians.

That group of students went to the Majestic Theater in downtown Dallas to hear music quite a bit. It was segregated at the time. We'd go there and see the movies up on the roof balcony. When Duke Ellington or Cab Calloway came through, the room was integrated. Those bands wouldn't play for a segregated audience. We'd go to hear Cab Calloway, Duke Ellington, Count Basie, and Lionel Hampton. We got to hear some good music during the '50s.[27]

As Herbie Johnson mentioned, Dallas had a strong music scene that brought many touring acts to town. There were also many opportunities for young aspiring musicians to attend jam sessions. Cedar was a little younger than LHS bandmate David "Fathead" Newman. Newman would invite the young pianist to jam sessions. Walton said, "I was a Walton kid from down the street. [laughs] give him a shot, you know, and they would see how happy I was, how hungry I was to be a part of this movement."[28]

Cedar remembers a gig he played at a place across the street from his house:

There was a guy named Robert Moss ... and I was able to play with his band. In fact, in a joint across the street from where I lived, they had a band in there and I played with them ... whenever the door opened— they [my folks] could hear me in there with these guys. [laughs] But I was younger to them .... They had to ask Ruth and Louise "could I come and play with them."[29]

C. A. Walton, ca. 1980. *Dallas Public Library.*

Ruth Walton. *Dallas Public Library.*

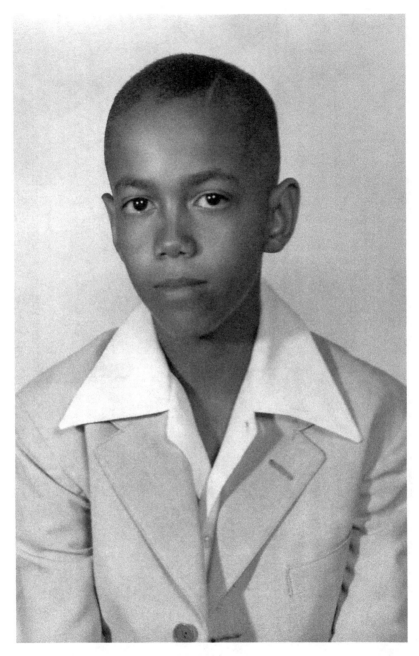

Young Cedar Walton. *Martha Walton collection.*

Cedar Walton at Lincoln High School, front row standing seventh from left, glasses on, holding the bells, ca. 1947–1950. *Martha Walton collection.*

According to Walton he played "well enough to get my feet wet
[laughs] ... I did a significant amount of that around Dallas, but they
were all usually musicians older than me. So that represents me being a
little, precocious .... I know what I didn't have ability-wise, I certainly
had enthusiasm-wise. I know that got through to ... the older musicians."[30]
These gigs early in Walton's development laid the foundation for
Walton's career as a musician.

Chapter 3

Something in Common (1951–1958): *College Days, the Move to New York, and the Army*

Dillard University (1951)

Cedar enrolled at Dillard University in New Orleans after graduating from Lincoln High School at midterm of the fall semester of 1950.[1] Cedar recalls, "I graduated high school on a Friday and my folks shipped me out that Monday to New Orleans."[2] Cedar's parents wanted to keep him busy and preferred he enroll in college immediately. Cedar's time at Dillard was short, but he did have some positive memories of his time there. He befriended pianist Ellis Marsalis and multi-instrumentalist Harold Battiste. Both Battiste and Marsalis had significant careers in music, and each kept in touch with Walton throughout their lives. Cedar also had two professors in particular who made an impression on him.[3] Walton reflected on his time at Dillard in his 2010 NEA Jazz Master interview:

> The New Orleans experience was ... very good. I had a great science teacher ... it was maybe sixty people ... in this great big room. This guy, he was so intense ... he was an eccentric ... and he would ... drive his points home in a ... almost comedic way, but it made a lot of sense ... I joined the choir. I was a music major.... Everybody went to the college choir ... the choir director was named Henry Booker ... and he was an absolute genius .... He could play those pieces ... and

look up like he was in ecstasy, you know without even [looking at the
music] .... Evidently ... he could scope it, which the great readers can
scope a whole two pages and not have to look at it ... they may glance
down and then they got it. I've met people like that too. And he was
one .... He would teach us these pieces and we were in a cappella
choir, so we went on tour through the South. That's a great memory
too 'cause he had perfect pitch so he would just whisper the tones to
the sopranos, altos, all the way up, inaudible to the audience, and then
when he would do that, we would just start. I imagine if you were in
the audience, you'd say, "my God, how'd he do that?" That was my
first contact with what I considered real genius .... And we were all
music majors so we could read the notes; it was just one note for us
to read .... I think I was a baritone by that time ... that was a great
experience ....

   They had a ... military band that rehearsed on campus there, and
... they were playin' jazz charts, and that was my first experience of
being that close ... hearing that .... Why they rehearsed on the Dillard
campus, I still don't know .... There was a guy named Harold Battiste
I became friendly with, and all of the things.[4]

NEA Jazz Master jazz pianist, Ellis Marsalis, recalls his memories of Cedar
and their time together in New Orleans:

   Cedar and I first met when he was a freshman at Dillard. I was a high
   school senior and on my way to Gaudet High School, I would get off
   the bus at Dillard during that Spring semester and hang with Harold
   Battiste and Cedar on campus.
      I wasn't at the university until the following year. Cedar was already
   gone by then. The year prior, I would shoot hooky and get off the bus
   and go to Dillard and hang out with Harold and Cedar because the bus
   route took me right past Dillard, but there wasn't so much time that we
   had, anyway, because Cedar had classes he had to go to. I don't know
   how to really describe it because at that time, none of us really knew
   what we were going to become anyway! [laughs]
      There was no jazz inside the school. As far as Dillard went, the
   best thing that happened for me at Dillard was Harold Battiste. That's
   where I learned in the very early stages things like reading chord
   symbols and voicing chords. But other than that, nothing. The school
   offered nothing but grief and misery. I talked to other people who
   attended HBCUs during my day and they all had the same story.
   It was the way of the world that we lived in at the time.

In the country, invariably all of the different ramifications affected the situation of music. In New Orleans, the segregation laws didn't permit fraternization of black and white musicians, not until after 1964. Now some of us knew each other and after 1964, people who were interested in the more modernistic part of music could get together very easily then because all the laws had changed.[5]

Denver University (1952–1955)

Denver had boasted a healthy music scene since before the turn of the century. During the '50s and '60s, some referred to it as the Harlem of the West. For gigging musicians heading West, Denver was the last stop to play before California. During this time, the city had an impressive number of jazz venues that hosted some of most prominent musicians of the time, including Charlie Parker, Duke Ellington, Dizzy Gillespie, and Art Tatum.[6]

It's not clear why Cedar left New Orleans after one semester. However, it could have been that he was in search of a stronger jazz music scene, one that was more welcoming for African American musicians. The segregation Marsalis mentions left many African American musicians not wanting to play in the South. Denver, on the other hand, had an exciting and well-established jazz scene that welcomed black artists.

In the Fall of 1952, he enrolled at Denver University. He took classes in music education. The curriculum required education students to study multiple instruments. In addition to piano, Cedar studied bass. He remembers his teacher commenting on his large hands.[7]

By the time I'd gotten to the University of Denver ... I took bass. Of course, we were obliged to take a second instrument, so I was with the first chair of basses in the Denver [University] Symphony, and he [his bass instructor] complemented me on the size of my hands. He said, "You could be a bassist," which was encouraging.

The Five Points area in Denver was the heartbeat of the jazz scene. Walton had a regular gig at Lil's, which was an after-hours club. The after-hours "clubs were the best place to go to meet musicians and hear touring musicians sit in after their gigs,"[8] Denver saxophonist, Freddy Rodriguez, recalled. "It wouldn't be uncommon to see Lester Young or Dexter Gordon walking around town."[9] The task of balancing school and a late gig was difficult. "I enrolled at the University of Denver to major in music and landed a gig at an after-hours club called Lil's Chinese Restaurant near Five Points. I never went to work until around midnight, so it was difficult for me to make those early morning classes that I stupidly scheduled for myself,"[10] said Walton. In addition to Walton on piano, the house band at Lil's included Charlie Burrell (bass), Charlie Sanborn (tenor saxophone), Shelly Rhym (drums), and Beatty Hobbs (alto saxophone).[11] Touring musicians regularly sat in with the Lil's house band. Walton recalled one of the most memorable nights when legendary saxophonist Charlie Parker sat in:

I'll never forget that night. Charlie Parker sat in with my group .... That night Bird only wanted to play in the key of C. I really have no idea except that maybe he just wanted to work out tunes in a different key that night. All he said to me was, "Do you want to play in C?" I was glad because that made it easy for me. One of the songs was "Dancing on the Ceiling." I can't remember the other two. Then by the fourth song, he had nodded off to sleep in his chair. I felt fortunate to have played with the great Charlie Parker, although he had been drinking quite a bit. I didn't care that he wasn't on top of his game, but shucks, I was just amazed to be inches away from him on the bandstand. Parker was a very friendly guy, and I've been told he would sit in everywhere he traveled.[12]

According to Walton there was someone in the audience that evening who recorded Bird and the band that night. Unfortunately, it was erased. "I wanted to hear it, but he erased it. So I was goin' after him with a chain saw," said Cedar.[13]

Through his gig at Lil's, Walton met many musicians from New York who encouraged the young pianist to move East. In an interview with Dr. David Schroeder, Walton recalled meeting John Coltrane and Richie Powell.

I also met John Coltrane who was playing with Johnny Hodges's band at the time. Hodges occasionally left Ellington's band to go out on his own. In fact, he had one hit record as a leader named "Castle Rock" that allowed him to travel with his own band that included a young

John Coltrane and Richie Powell, Bud's little brother. Richie sat at the piano for hours teaching me about harmony; I wouldn't let him leave the bandstand till the sun came up.[14]

The night life of the Denver music scene was where Cedar was receiving his education. The schedule of a jazz musician was not conducive to his studies at Denver University. On August 27, 1954, a letter from Dean of Students at Denver University informed Walton that his petition for readmission was denied.[15] The letter also stated, "the terms outlined in the letter which was sent to you on August 11, 1954 must stand."[16] Given how Cedar spoke about the music scene and playing into the early hours of the morning, it is reasonable to speculate that Cedar's school issues were related to gig life and school life not mixing. The combination of school abruptly ending and the urging of touring musicians encouraging Cedar to move to New York most likely had much to do with his decision to make the pilgrimage like so many before him.

Cedar at Denver University, ca. 1952–1955. *Martha Walton collection.*

Chapter 3

BACK ROW
Lynn Lommatsch
Vince Tagliavore
Don Bury
Cliff Maddox
Jim Knudson
Jim Craig
Max Peterson
Alvin Henry
Lynn Higbee
Fred Orrino
Bill Shultz
Hal Rarick
Cornelius Pittman

MIDDLE ROW
Gary Nicloy
Bill King
Elbert Morton
Cliff Vidger
Don Thompson
Lawrence Brewster
Don Kramer
Jerry Hughes
Gordon DeBroder

FRONT ROW
Gene Zumalt
Cedar Walton
Kenny Beard
Rodger Fee
Jack Wheaton
Raoul Tayon
Alex Campbell

Cedar at Denver University, Phi Mu Alpha (front row, second from left), ca. 1952–1955. *Martha Walton collection.*

Cedar at Denver University. *Martha Walton collection.*

Move to New York (1955–1956)

In 1955, Cedar left Denver and moved to New York. He packed up his car
and headed for the city. From his 2010 NEA Jazz Master interview, it seems
Walton first intended to enroll at Manhattan School of Music. His intention
did not come to fruition. Perhaps going to school was how he was able to
sell his parents the idea of moving New York. Cedar describes his early
days in New York and how he began to meet other musicians.

> I had a couple of phone numbers, Ed Thigpen, comes to mind [anyone]
> who had [played at] Encore, I tried to get their number. So I had a
> plan in mind to enroll in Manhattan School of Music. But realistically,
> I wasn't quite ready because I hadn't worked diligently enough on
> certain pieces that were required. Not that there was a list of pieces
> that you needed to play, but you needed to play a complete work of
> something, and I wasn't ready. And you could hear the other applicants
> while you were waiting and I said, "No, I gotta get outta here." And
> that was the end of that idea …. I'll never forget how relieved I felt
> when I went back out into the city. You know, the life of the city. I said,
> "This is why I'm here—to breathe this life, New York City." I was in
> love with the city.
>
> I went to people's rehearsals, I had to take day jobs, of course ….
> I took a room in the YMCA that's located on West 34th Street. Sloan
> House it was called. [The room cost] about $11 dollars a day. I managed
> to work that out by working places like Macy's and Horn & Hardart.
> [I'd call home and Mom would say] "Bring your butt home." I was
> determined and finally, man, fast-forward, quite a while, she was able
> to tell her friends that she'd been to New York to hear her son play
> Carnegie Hall ….
>
> [I worked] day jobs and I was goin' out to all the gigs I could see
> and all the jam sessions all over, rehearsals I could muster …. There
> was a piano in the balcony of the gym in the Y. So I was able to work
> out often. That was a plus.
>
> The musicians I took up with were basically unknown in the jazz
> world, but they played, they had gigs …. New York was so vast,
> Brooklyn gigs, Bronx gigs, people who take you sincere: "Come with
> us, we want to take you to Canarsie." I said, "Canarsie? Okay. Sounds
> interesting." And then we met Phil Woods and I asked him could I sit in
> and he said, "Yeah, come on up." Like in a movie would be, "Come on
> up, kid." [laughs] But he just said, "Come on up." [laughs]
>
> The same with Jackie McLean. I went, sought him out, and his
> pianist was takin' a little too long at the break. Jackie was doing

like this, I asked him could I sit in. Same thing: "Could I sit in?" Same
thing: "Come on up, kid." .... I was everywhere .... Both Phil and
Jackie had recorded but they hadn't made their big move yet .... I was
lucky in that sense to locate them ....

[The jam session scene] was quite strong. There was one place in
Harlem ... Connie's on Seventh Avenue. That's where the musicians
jammed. And I wouldn't miss that .... That's all they did there was jam,
you know, every night. That was the show. So I got a chance to sit in, as
I recall, a couple of times. And I met some of the people that I'd met in
Denver there .... I remember saying to Richie Powell, "You probably
don't remember me, but ...." You know, the usual thing. I hear people
tellin' me that now. I say, "Yes I do, I remember you." Sometimes
I'm truthful and sometimes I'm not. Doesn't matter. I think it means
more to them to say, "Yes, which probably was in the case of Richie
Powell, too. [laughs] .... We spent quite a few hours together that night
in Denver, so ... he might have remembered me."[17]

Walton was starting to make a name for himself in New York. In addition
to meeting Phil Woods and Jackie McLean, he was also starting to work a
little as a musician. One of the most interesting gigs during this period was
with the legendary singer Billie Holiday on Easter Sunday at the Magnolia
Ballroom. By the late '50s, Holiday was not in good health. "She needed help
getting up and down the stairs,"[18] said Walton.

She was quite a challenge to be around. Even though it was a Sunday,
she sent me out for a bottle of gin. [laughs] I was young and very
impressionable .... Anyway, it was a segregated audience in those
days. The piano was horrible, it was unplayable. It was fit for a
fireplace more than [to be] played. I got through it, the keys were
brown .... She wanted to do one of her pieces that's named "Strange
Fruit." I just didn't know it. She didn't have the music so she did it a
cappella. I'll never forget that day.[19]

The time Cedar spent going to jam sessions and meeting people was prov-
ing to be very fruitful. Many musicians were aware of Walton and his
excellent playing. However, his musical career would have to be put on
hold. In 1956, Cedar, at the age of 22, was drafted into the Army. For a
moment before starting his time in the Army, Walton thought he may have
a way out. Drummer Art Blakey with whom he made a positive impression as a player indicated he could get Walton out of his commitment. Walton

recalls his conversation with Blakey. "The night before I went to the military." I told him [Art Blakey], "I'm goin' into the military." He said, "Oh, call me in the morning and I'll tell you have you can avoid the military. But of course he didn't answer. So, I went in."[20] For the next two years, Walton was committed to the U.S. Army.

Army (1956–1958)

Cedar joined the Army in 1956. For six months he was stationed in Fort Dix, New Jersey. Before shipping out, the base was graced by a performance from none other than the Duke Ellington Orchestra. Duke was one of Cedar's heroes and it must have been a thrill to not only hear Ellington but sit in with his band. In an interview with Ethan Iverson, Cedar recalled the time he asked the maestro to sit in.

> The [Ellington] band was playing in the afternoon in what looked like a big armory, but they had what could pass for a dance floor. It was a huge place but there weren't many people: it was afternoon at an army base—the army having duties, of course.
>
> I was about to ship out to Germany, and my buddy was shipping out somewhere, too. And we were there in our uniforms. And we dared ask him to sit in. And he said, "Yes." He had a spinet: I have a feeling he wanted to escape that for at least a few minutes.
>
> It was a high bandstand and on the way up he said, "Now go easy on those keys, young man." Such an elegant person ... "Duke Elegant." So we played "What Is This Thing Called Love?" My friend sang. I can remember, the bass was here, the band was straight ahead of me from saxophones out. And down there was my man singing at the mic. And they made up an ending. When we got close to the ending it sounded sort of like what we used to call the "clambake ending." And on the way back down, Duke, in his Duke-ish way, said, "I thought I told you to go easy!" That's an experience that just stays alive in your system.[21]

For the remainder of his time in the Army, Cedar was stationed in Stuttgart, Germany. Initially, Cedar was assigned to the Calvary where he worked as a wireman.[22] He would connect the officer's command post to the outer post. If there was ever a problem, he was called day or night to fix the issue. One night Cedar was woken by a young lieutenant who woke him by kicking him in the head. "Luckily I had my helmet [on],"[23] said Cedar. By Walton's own account he wasn't very adept with the skills required of his job. "I heard some of the people as I was pretending to be asleep, talking about me," said, "That Walton, he can't even splice a wire." Which I said to myself, "You got that right." [laughs][24]

Eventually, Walton found a job that suited him much better. He found a home in Special Services. Special Services had bands that performed variety shows for the troops and throughout Germany. The groups backed various artists such as Gary Crosby (Bing Crosby's son).[25] Saxophonist Lanny Morgan was also stationed in Germany and remembers the Special Services bands. "The 7th Army had a great program called the 7th Army Symphony and Soldier Show Company. It had a 110-piece symphony orchestra that was really, really world class. They got people who had already been playing in symphonies."[26]

While the Army was formally integrated, there were still divisions socially. White and black soldiers did not generally mingle together and would often gather at different bars after hours. On one tour Walton and some of him fellow black soldiers entered a "redneck bar,"[27] and there was a "furious mistake,"[28] as Cedar described it. "Bottles started being thrown and oh man, I was hiding under the table, you know—stealthy animal that I was—and made it back to the bus."[29] Walton was aware of integration issues on a broader level too. In a letter he wrote to his mother, Ruth, dated September 18, 1957 he wrote:

> Uppermost in my mind right now is the integration issue. Just finished reading a disgusting series of articles in Time magazine about the first day-of-school incidents throughout the southern part of the country. Arkansas's Faubus must be insane. In Charlotte, N.C., a poor girl, age fifteen, was harassed by a mob of young-sters spurred on [by] an old white woman, the wife of some truck driver. The mob marched on either side of her on the street, a bottle was thrown at her, she was even spat upon full in the face! But the moving part of the article stated that "she walked right on, head high." Also noticed that Dallas "might" integrate after Christmas holidays. How will this affect you? Why is Dallas slow? Or is the somewhat belated date regarded by the local elite as being slow? Write me and fill me in on the facts, will you?[30]

Although there were still racial obstacles to overcome, music would be the pianist's focus. Cedar spent the remainder of his two-year enlistment with Special Services in Stuttgart, in a role that eventually allowed him to lead a jazz band. Once the jazz band was formed, Cedar's duties were very different. In addition to leading the band, he also practiced and wrote music as part of his daily activities. The group Cedar lead was called Jazz One (later there were Jazz Two and Jazz Three). During this time, there were many musicians who were drafted into different divisions who were also in Germany, including Eddie Harris, Leo Wright, Lanny Morgan, and Don Ellis. The Army also allowed Cedar to recruit players for Jazz One. "We were able to requisition different players from different places,"[31] said Cedar. The number of American musicians in Germany at this time was very impressive and made for some excellent bands. In a letter to his mother dated July 8, 1957, he writes:

> The jazz festival here was well received by all. Our orchestra had criticisms in the German news, and our saxophone soloist even made the cover of the leading Jazz magazine here! (Down-beat counterpart) With all these achievements, plus more, in mind, we still can't convince the top brass that we deserve to be sent to France, England, etc. to perform for troops and countrymen there. After they promised us these journeys at the outset, they have backed down for some reason or other. As a last resort we are writing the fellow in the state department, who was so instrumental in sending the Dizzy Gillespie orch. to the Far East.[32]

On weekends, musicians would frequently gather in Heidelberg for jam sessions. Cedar befriended saxophonist Eddie Harris during these meetings. This musical association would yield recorded work after the two got out of the Army. Other musicians who frequented this session were Philadelphia drummer Lex Humphries, and saxophonists Leo Wright and Houston Person.[33] Person was in the Air Force during that time but recalls meeting Cedar and the kindness he showed him as well as the jam sessions in Heidelberg.

> I met Cedar in Heidelberg, Germany around 1956–1957. I was in the Air Force, he was in the Army. He was there with special services.

He was in the jazz orchestra, in the Stuttgart with the 7th Army Jazz Band. They did a lot of good-will jazz tours throughout Germany.

I was just starting out in music. Cedar was already an accomplished musician. There were a bunch of accomplished musicians in that band. We'd get together on the weekends to play. I always had a knack for finding gigs and getting to places.

Cedar was a great composer and a great player. We played every chance we got to in Germany. I can't describe how much he helped me. We were friends throughout. We were big friends. There was a bond there that we had from our experience in Germany.

During that time, many musicians in Germany established a friendship while they were there that continued to keep up long after. Guys like Don Menza, Lanny Morgan, and all of them. I still see them out in California when I go out there. We kept our relationship up and that was good. We always rooted for each other.

Cedar and I talked about music a lot and he was a stickler. He'd stay on my butt. And Eddie Harris too. We all would doodle, especially in Germany. When someone new came over on assignment, that guy would bring the latest, hip tunes. Cedar would learn them on the piano and show us how to play them. We experimented with tunes and that was a great time for me. Each guy who came over from the states was contributing. We met a lot of the musicians who were coming over to Germany, and Europe. I met Chet Baker, Gerry Mulligan, the Lionel Hampton Band, and the Basie Band. It was a lot of fun. There were a lot of opportunities that I had at that time, that I wouldn't have had in the states.[34]

As Person mentioned, there were many bands coming through Germany at that time. Walton first heard the Modern Jazz Quartet during his service in Germany. The meeting struck up a friendship and musical association with vibraphonist Milt Jackson that would last their entire lives. In an interview in 2003 with WEAA FM Baltimore, Walton recalled their meeting:

Mr. Jackson was just so encouraging. I [first] met him, I was in the armed services and the Modern Jazz Quartet first formed. We were instant friends. We hung out. He went back [to the U.S.], I found out that he mentioned me more than a few times. I was 21 or 22 then. Instant friendship, especially musically. He encouraged me and used me as often as he could which was quite often after I left Blakey.[35]

Toward the end of Walton's two-year commitment, he could have become an officer. "I didn't want to be any part of the military after my required time. I wanted to get back to the city and ... explore."[36] The next period in the young pianist's life would see him working with the some of the greatest musicians in music.

Chapter 4

Hand in Glove (1958–1961): *First Gigs upon Returning Stateside*

C edar left Germany in March of 1958 and finished the last month of his service stateside.[1] Thanks to folks like Milt Jackson and others spreading the word, Cedar began to work quickly after his discharge. In a letter to his mother dated May 22, 1958, Cedar wrote:

> I'm still enjoying the convenience of my own piano and I still can't get over the importance of having one that you can wake up with if you want to. I'm slowly but surely getting my fingers together. Still working enough not to have to disturb my traveler's [sic] cheque [checks] for the moment, which is right according to plan because I want to stay in and practice and perhaps do some writing.[2]

Cedar's fingers seemed to be working very well. On July 7, he recorded on trumpeter and fellow Texan Kenny Dorham's album *This Is the Moment*.[3] This is the first known recording of Cedar. From the moment Cedar was back in New York, his career started to take off. He began working with jazz royalty, the likes of whom would shape his career for the rest of his life.

In many ways, *This Is the Moment* foreshadows playing characteristics that would define Cedar's playing for the rest of his life. Kenny Dorham was primarily known for his trumpet playing, although for this recording he would sing and play trumpet. In the rhythm section Cedar was joined by Sam Jones on bass while G.T. Hogan and Charlie Persip would share drum set duties. Trombonist Curtis Fuller was also on the session. Cedar would go on to work frequently with both Fuller and Jones.

Many of Cedar's first employers were impressed with his excellent comping skills. He was a masterful accompanist. His comping was an ideal balance of swinging rhythmic propulsion, support, and responsiveness to the soloist, as well as harmonic contributions that were subtle yet interesting. From Dorham's session, the medium swinging "This Is the Moment" subtly highlights Cedar's propulsive and supporting comping behind Dorham's voice and trumpet. Cedar interjects soulful bluesy responses between Dorham's phrases on the slow blues "Since I Fell for You" that tell Dorham and the listener he was listening to each note the trumpeter played and had the perfect response. The blues was a major part of Cedar's musical makeup and present in every note he played from this recording to his last. While *Moment* didn't feature many piano solos, there are small glimpses into what listeners could expect from him soloistically. The up-tempo "From This Moment On" starts with a Bud Powell like introduction. Cedar follows Dorham's solo with a full chorus of his own. Even at a faster tempo, there is a weight and solidity to the notes Cedar plays. His ideas are strong and deliberate. His lines are melodic and precisely timed. Cedar played the piano in a way that made the entire band lock in rhythmically with what he was playing. His playing would continue to strengthen and develop as his career progressed.

As Cedar mentioned in the letter to his mother, he was working enough to make ends meet. Cedar frequented a jam session at Birdland led by Johnnie Gary. Early on, Birdland would be very significant for Cedar's career. He made many connections that would lead to musical associations that would last his entire lifetime as well as being part of some of the most influential recordings in jazz.[4]

One Birdland gig during this time was led by saxophonist John Coltrane. Cedar recalled, "I played with a group coordinated by John Coltrane that included Wayne Shorter, Freddie Hubbard and Elvin [Jones]."[5] After this gig, Cedar recorded with Coltrane, Shorter, and Hubbard within in the next two years.[6]

J.J. Johnson

Cedar also caught the attention of trombonist J.J. Johnson at Birdland. Johnson was a virtuosic player, an innovator of the trombone. In the '40s he worked with the most iconic names of the time, including Benny Carter, Count Basie, Charlie Parker, and Dizzy Gillespie. In the late '40s and early '50s, he led recording sessions with Bud Powell, Max Roach, Clifford Brown, and Sonny Stitt. By the late 50s he began touring as a leader with his own group.

Cedar and drummer Albert "Tootie" Heath entered Johnson's band at the same time and replaced pianist Tommy Flanagan and drummer Elvin Jones.[7] Cedar would stay in Johnson's band for two years. During this period the band recorded two albums, *Really Livin'* in 1959 and *J.J. Inc.* in 1960.[8] Much of the personnel from these recordings were people with whom Cedar would go on to play and record with regularly. In addition to Johnson and Tootie Heath, *Really Livin'* featured Nat Adderley (cornet), Bobby Jasper (tenor saxophone and flute), and Spanky DeBrest (bass). Cedar and Tootie would play and record frequently in the years to come. In addition to Johnson and Tootie Heath, the band for *J.J. Inc.* included Freddie Hubbard (trumpet), Clifford Jordan (tenor saxophone), and Arthur Harper (bass). Jordan and Hubbard would be some of Cedar's most frequent collaborators for the next several decades.[9]

Johnson's band was a touring band where the musicians were required to wear band uniforms, with the exception of the leader. According to Cedar, playing with Johnson "was a great experience, [he had] impeccable artistry and was miraculous."[10] Johnson was 10 years older than Walton and very established by the late '50s. He was a regular poll winner for best trombonist. The experience of working in Johnson's group with outstanding musicians was very impactful on Cedar and would influence him later in his career when he started to lead groups of his own.

John Coltrane

In 1959, Cedar also recorded with saxophonist John Coltrane. During the late '50s Cedar and Coltrane lived fairly close to each other on the Upper West Side.[11] Coltrane's recording *Giant Steps* is a landmark recording that has had a significant impact on jazz musicians since its inception. The initial release of the recording was titled *Giant Steps* and featured pianist Tommy Flanagan on piano,[12] Paul Chambers on bass, and Arthur Taylor on drums. Cedar, however, was Coltrane's first choice to play piano on the recording. Years later, Cedar's playing with Coltrane on Coltrane's iconic tunes were released on an album titled *Alternate Takes*. Along with Cedar on piano, the recording featured Lex Humphries on drums and Chambers again on bass. *Alternate Takes* is yet another example that Cedar was at the center of innovative music with the best musicians during this time.

Cedar first heard Coltrane's iconic tune "Giant Steps" when the saxophonist came over to his apartment. Cedar remembers:

> John stopped by my apartment one day in 1959 to show me things related to a new song he had written, "Giant Steps." John was very friendly and seemed impressed with my playing .... I had an upright piano and John played "Giant Steps" for me. I thought the song and John's playing were wonderful .... I was watching, listening and absorbing what he was doing. I also tried to write down what he was doing. I can't recall if he was standing at the piano or sitting but he said, "Here's how this tune goes." His playing style was so orchestral. It sounded like "Blue Train," with trumpet, trombone, and tenor sax. John would play a lot of things with three notes. It was amazing because the notes he chose would fit the voicings of three horns. Just being around him, period, was extremely instructive.[13]

After Coltrane showed Cedar "Giant Steps," Cedar played it for Coltrane. Cedar worked on the tune on his own before getting together with Coltrane and drummer Lex Humphries. "Lex and I would go over there [to Coltrane's place] unannounced, and each time we could hear him practicing before we rang the bell," said Cedar.[14] He continued:

> When I sat down to play "Giant Steps," he was sitting on his couch behind me with his saxophone. Hearing that sound emanate from right behind me was so moving and awe-inspiring. I felt like I was in the presence of God. That's without exaggeration. It was so perfect, and his sound went right to my heart.[15]

"Giant Steps" was a very modern tune for its time. The harmonic rhythm of the first 8 measures of the tune was something that jazz musicians had not dealt with until then. This harmonic progression would come to be known as "Giant Steps changes" or "tri-tonic changes" and would change jazz improvisation forever.[16] "The way John conceived of the harmonies," said Cedar, "they were totally original. Those harmonies aren't easy to manipulate on any instrument, let alone the piano."[17]

About a month after that fateful visit, Coltrane called Cedar and asked if he and Lex Humphries could record "Giant Steps" and some other Coltrane tunes on a session to take place on April 1, 1959. Coltrane, Cedar, Humphries, and bassist Paul Chambers were in the band for this session. Although the takes were recorded, this date was intended to be a rehearsal session only.[18] The group rehearsed Coltrane originals "Naima," "Countdown," "Like Sonny," and "Giant Steps."[19] When the group played "Giant Steps," Cedar declined to solo. "The song was too hard for me. But you just didn't do that. I was young. I should have done what Flanagan did—take a solo .... I know now you just don't do that."

Unfortunately, Cedar and Lex Humphries couldn't make the actual *Giant Steps* recording session on May 4, 1959.[20] Cedar was with J.J. Johnson and Lex Humphries on tour with Dizzy Gillespie. Cedar's tour with Johnson lasted about a month. When he returned to New York he called Coltrane to inquire about the session. According to Cedar, "John told me on the telephone that that kind of thing was fairly normal. He was probably under pressure by Atlantic to record." He [Coltrane] said, "Sorry Cedar, we couldn't wait for you. I had to do it with Flanagan. It broke my heart."[21]

Alternate Takes (recordings of the rehearsal takes with Cedar) would eventually be released in 1975 and then included on a 50th anniversary reissuing of *Giant Steps* on March 3, 1998.[22] when Cedar learned of these recordings he said, "When someone played me the alternate takes in the late '90s, I couldn't believe it. I had no idea they were still around."[23] It's interesting to think about what might have transpired further between Cedar and Coltrane had he been around to play on the original session. Coltrane's desire to have Cedar play on this landmark session speaks to Cedar's stature in New York during this time. Despite this session, Cedar's career continued to ascend.

Jimmy Heath

Saxophonist Jimmy Heath also met Cedar in the late '50s. During that period, Heath signed a deal with Riverside. These recordings were Heath's first as a leader who started an extensive recording career as a saxophonist. Cedar played on three of Heath's records titled *Really Big!, The Quota,* and *Triple Threat,* all recorded in the early '60s.[24] Heath reminisced about his work with Cedar and the recordings they played together on.

I met Cedar in New York around 1959 when he was playing with J.J. Johnson. My brother (Albert "Tootie" Heath) was playing drums. Clifford Jordan and Nat Adderley were in the band too.

I had just gotten my recording contract with Riverside. I had made one record, *The Thumper,* with Wynton Kelly on the piano. I had just left Miles's band. Wynton was on the road all the time and Cedar was around. I was about to make my second recording for them. After I met and heard Cedar, I knew how wonderful he was as a player and a writer. The next three albums I made for Riverside were: *Really Big!*—a 10-piece thing, *The Quota,* and *Triple Threat.* Cedar was the guy that I wanted to use for those dates. I used him because I liked the way he comped and the way he soloed. He was a very competent performer. To be playing with J.J., he had to be right. I recorded with J.J. in 1953 (*Jay Jay Johnson,* Blue Note 5028). We also recorded together with Miles (*Miles Davis Vol. 2,* Blue Note 5022) around that time. Over a period of time Cedar played on about five of my recordings. He's also on a lot of the ones I made with Milt Jackson. Bags liked Cedar a lot and he used him on a lot of his recording dates, too. The recordings Cedar did with Milt and the ones he did with me are all precious to me.

Cedar was a funny guy. He had a lot of quips going. You know? Do you remember the show *Mission Impossible*? Cedar told me a story once where a guy called to book him on a gig. The guy said, "I can pay you this and I can pay this. Oh! I forgot. I gotta get my commission." Cedar said, "Commission impossible!" JH: [laughing] I always liked that. The guy was offering such a small amount of money to Cedar and then asking for a commission too? [laughs][25]

Art Farmer/Benny Golson Jazztet

After two years, Cedar left J.J. Johnson's group for the Art Farmer/Benny Golson Jazztet.[26] Saxophonist and composer Benny Golson is yet another iconic figure who Cedar worked with. Golson is regarded as one of the most influential composers in jazz. Trumpeter Art Farmer worked and recorded with Gigi Gryce (who would start a publishing company with Benny Golson), Horace Silver, Gerry Mulligan, and George Russell before starting the Jazztet with Golson.[27] In the Jazztet, Cedar received a ten dollar raise from what he was making with Johnson. "You know, back in those days that ten dollars was that important,"[28] said Cedar. Cedar and J.J. Johnson bandmate drummer Albert Heath both joined the Jazztet at the same time. Cedar replaced pianist McCoy Tyner.[29] Although the group was co-led by Golson and Farmer, Golson wrote all the music and was very insistent that the music he wrote was to be played exactly as he notated. In an interview with Rhonda Hamilton on WBGO radio, Walton recalled his experience with the Jazztet:

> The atmosphere over there with him [Benny Golson] was quite challenging because we had a lot of music to read. He wrote everything out for piano. He wanted everything a certain way. And I kind of balked against it for a while. Benny said, "If you balk too much, Cedar, you might be out, so maybe you better try this." I ended up really liking it. It was quite a challenge …. It was physically heavy to carry this book of music he had. [laughs] [The music was] spread out across the piano you know like six or seven feet. So that was good too and inspirational, like a role model to be around him and playing his music. That was a good relationship.[30]

The Jazztet recorded three albums during Cedar's tenure with the band: *Big City Sounds, The Jazztet and John Lewis*, and *The Jazztet at Birdhouse*. Saxophonist and Jazztet coleader Benny Golson spoke about his time working with Cedar:

> [I met Cedar] because of Gigi Gryce. Gigi and I became good friends. He was my best man when I married my second wife. We had a publishing company together. He formed a group called the Jazz Lab. Wade Legge was the pianist. Wade was a good piano player, but he wasn't well known as someone like Mulgrew Miller. Cedar had just come to town and he was gigging, and he fit right into that [Wade's] piano slot. That's when I met him. I heard him playing, and I said, "Man, this guy can play." He came with a lot to say and impressed me right away. That's why eventually, down the line, he became the piano player for the Jazztet.

There was never a clash of personalities or wanting to run ahead. And although we never talked about composition, playing and improvising is a kind of composition, because you're doing the same thing there that you do as a writer only you're not putting it on paper. You're making it come to reality in the moment and what you're doing is you're creating things when you improvise that never have existed before. That's what you do when you write, but we do that in a different way when we play.

Cedar didn't have to say a word about his ability. When he sat down to the piano, that said everything. That's all it takes; you don't have to tell anybody anything. They can hear what you can do. That impressed me, he was always so humble, and always willing to listen. We don't go to school telling the teacher what to do. We learn by listening. Cedar was a good listener, he never rejected anything because nobody knows everything. All these things were probably intuitive, but that's what helped to make Cedar the way he was, a very humble and kind young man.

Cedar Walton? Yes indeed. He's one of the geniuses, but did he ever go around telling people, "I'm a genius?" I never heard that. He just did what he did, and if you want to assess anything, you'd sit down and listen to him.

I remember when Tadd Dameron died, Cedar was the only pianist that played at the church on Broadway and 94th street, and it was something. He played not only with his fingers, but man he knew how to play symbolically with his heart. That's what you have to do. It takes more than the head and the fingers, it takes the heart. That's where the lasting things are.

Cedar had all the things that had nothing to do with music. He was a nice man. I never heard him put anybody down about what they were doing or were not doing. That's important, because when musicians come together, they should come together as a family. We're all there trying to accomplish the same thing, make the music sound as good as we can. The piano player is listening to the bass player and the drummer, and I'm listening to the bass player, and the others are listening to me. When we get on that band stand, we're a family, and Cedar knew that. He knew how to mesh things together within the band. Sometimes when that happens, the band plays things that are so in tune that you would have thought that they'd rehearsed those things. But they're looking at each other with nods of their heads, and their eyes, and things like that. He was a part of that.

Cedar was always ready. He did his homework, that's why he was ready. He didn't go around patting himself on the back. You close doors when you do that. His personality had no doors, his life was an open door. What he knew, he was always willing to share. He had no secrets. That's important, too. Mercifully share vestiges of yourself. When we perform, that's what we're doing, we're sharing vestiges of ourselves, musically. That's it. We're in tune with the audience. We're not entertainers. Entertainers do what they think the audience is going to like. Even though we're not entertainers, we do hope that they like it. If we're good enough, they're going to like it. Yes, jazz is really something.[31]

Along with jazz giants Benny Golson, J.J. Johnson, and Art Farmer, Cedar would work with some of the most influential musicians of the period. In addition to J.J. Johnson, the Jazztet, John Coltrane, and Jimmy Heath, Cedar also recorded with Clifford Jordan (*Spellbound*), Wayne Shorter (*Second Genesis*), and Freddie Hubbard (*Hub Cap*) in 1960 and 1961.[32] From their time together in J.J. Johnson's band forward, Cedar and Clifford Jordan enjoyed a friendship and musical association lasting their entire lives. In the more immediate future, however, Cedar would join forces with Hubbard and Shorter to be part of one of the most significant formations of the Jazz Messengers ever assembled.

Cedar played with the Jazztet for a little over a year. While in Chicago on what would be his last tour with the Jazztet, Cedar would get a call from Art Blakey to join the Messengers. In this group, he'd not only play but contribute to the group's book as a writer and arranger.

Chapter 5

Mosaic (1961–1964): *The Jazz Messengers*

C edar met Art Blakey prior to his time in the Army. Blakey had heard his playing at a session in New York and took note. The two had also recorded together on saxophonist Wayne Shorter's second album as a leader, *Second Genesis*.[1] Lyricist John Hackett remembers a story that Cedar told to him about one of the first times he met Art Blakey away from the band stand:

> Cedar had been in New York about six months. He was hanging with a couple of friends and they said, "Hey, I know a place where there's some women." And Cedar went with them. They went up the stairs of this apartment building and there were three women there, a mother and two daughters.
>
> They were yucking it up and all of a sudden, the bedroom door opened, and Art Blakey came walking out. And Cedar, bewildered, said, "Art Blakey, what are you doing here?" Art said, "I live here, motherfucker. What are you doing here?" Cedar was speechless at that and just took off. It wasn't a friendly welcome to him, but he overcame that impression and eventually played with Art, which shows his determination in a funny way.[2]

The Jazz Messengers was one of the paramount hard bop groups in the history of jazz. From the onset, the group and its many different formations included

Art Blakey and the Jazz Messengers, 1963, (l to r) Cedar, Wayne Shorter, Curtis Fuller, Reggie Workman, Art Blakey, and Freddie Hubbard. *Copyright Riccardo Schwamenthal/CTSIMAGES.*

the best musicians and made numerous classic recordings. Blakey had the ability to recognize exceptional talent and was always on the lookout for the next members for his band. The personnel of the group changed regularly. This was not a band in which a musician would spend their entire career. Part of the success of the group was that Blakey wanted his sidemen to graduate from the Messengers and go on to be leaders. The group consisting of Cedar, trumpeter Freddie Hubbard, saxophonist Wayne Shorter, trombonist Curtis Fuller and bassist Jymie Merritt and later Reggie Workman is considered by many to be one of the consummate formations of the Messengers.

Each person who played in the Messengers became part of a special group. A fraternity of Blakey sidemen who wore their membership in the group proudly. Many members were intimately familiar with the lineage and history of the group. Messenger members Terence Blanchard, Brian Lynch, Steve Turre, and Javon Jackson speak about the classic band with Cedar, and what it meant to them.

Terence Blanchard

That group was special. One that myself and countless others were influenced by. These guys were my heroes. When I was in the Messengers, I got to hear Art tell stories about them that made them real people who were also great musicians. That was great for me. There wasn't anyone who was playing like Freddie Hubbard at that time. He was so powerful. The writing and arrangements of Wayne, Cedar, and Freddie had so much to do with the sound and direction of that group. It could sound like a big band at times.[3]

Brian Lynch

That was always the group, the touchstone, the ne plus ultra of small groups. The contrast in the styles between all the instruments is almost perfect. There's a sense of balance with it. When you listen to the way that Cedar plays behind all the soloists in that band there are always subtle things he does. It's also a matter of how you structure a performance. I think that Cedar as a band leader and as a pianist probably got more than a little bit of that influence from Art [Blakey] and Horace [Silver].[4]

Steve Turre

That group was one of the pinnacles. When I first came to New York, we played at the Village Gate, and Curtis Fuller came by and I got to meet him. Cedar was there, and they were talking about old times and they were reminiscing about Blakey. Cedar and Curtis were already established icons. To hear them talk about the Messengers in the way they did was a big learning experience and gave me something to aspire to. I remember thinking, I want to be like that when I grow up.[5]

Javon Jackson

That particular band means a lot to me. I can honestly say, I played with everyone in that band. Wayne would come sit in. I worked with Cedar's band. I worked with Freddie closely and I know Reggie. I'm fortunate to say, I was involved with all of them at different times. It was a special unit.

I asked Art Blakey about the different Messenger groups on many occasions. Once I remember asking him about Lee Morgan and Wayne and that particular group with Bobby Timmons. Art said, he loved the group and then he said, "But I liked the band when Cedar got in. Because we became more sophisticated."

I actually told Cedar that, and he really was happy to know Art had said that about him. I had spoken to Freddie and Cedar about those groups too. Freddie and Cedar joined the same day. In fact, Cedar was on tour with Jazztet when he got the call from Art Blakey to join the Messengers.

I'm a fan of all the Messenger groups, going back to Donald Byrd and Hank Mobley and all the other great incarnations. But obviously that group with Cedar, Freddie, Wayne, Curtis, and Reggie was pretty special.

For me, getting to meet all those gentlemen during my time with Art was incredible. I feel very fortunate to have had a really close relationship with Freddie, Cedar, and Curtis on and off the bandstand. Each one of them got to know me and my family. I got to know about them on a real intimate level too. It was an honor to know Freddie, Cedar, and Curtis in this way.

All of the Messengers musicians I've been around are connected in a brotherhood. At any time, I can call Benny Golson on the phone and it's just like talking to another family member. I used to do this with Donald Byrd and Jackie McLean. We had that same kind of closeness. We all shared our stories and laughter about being part of Art Blakey's group. I always felt that all those gentlemen had information to help me as a musician and as a person as I'm trying to get through this thing—I mean life and being a musician. It's those kinds of people that helped shape me and allow me to be what I am today.[6]

As Jackson mentioned, Cedar was on tour with the Jazztet when he got the call to join Art Blakey. Cedar and trumpeter Freddie Hubbard joined the Messengers on the same day. Cedar had played with most of the band-members on other gigs or recordings prior to joining Blakey. There was a chemistry and fire with the group that was instant. The atmosphere was different from the Jazztet.

The front line of Hubbard, Shorter, and Fuller were sharp. All were virtuosos on their instruments and excellent readers to boot. Cedar wrote "Mosaic" during his time with Jazztet and tried to have the group record it. After 20 to 30 takes, the band was unable to execute. When Cedar brought this tune into the Messengers, however, the group read it down masterfully and with little problem. "They played it better than I could," I said, "Wait a minute; I wrote this thing here. [chuckles]," said Cedar.[7]

Cedar's tune "Mosaic" became the title track for his first recording with the Messengers. *Mosaic* was recorded on October 2, 1961.[8] The album consisted of five tunes all written by band members. In addition to Cedar's tune, Freddie Hubbard contributed two tunes, "Crisis" and "Down Under." Wayne Shorter and Curtis Fuller each contributed one tune, "Children of the Night" and "Arabia," respectively.[9]

The album *Mosaic* was the blueprint for the group. Blakey encouraged band members to write. "We couldn't write fast enough,"[10] said Cedar.

We'd write four, five, six tunes and we'd go in the studio and record them. For a long time, I thought he [Art] was breaching contracts, but I found out much later, he just had ... one-recording deals with every-body .... He was very smart, smarter than I thought he was, 'cause I thought he was just brazenly .... Okay, I'm with Blue Note but I'm goin' over here and record with Columbia."[11]

Watching Blakey negotiate and navigate recording contracts was something
that impacted Cedar and would help him later in his career when he was
working as a leader and recording under his own name.

Cedar was very fond of his time with the Messengers. As he described the
band atmosphere and working for Blakey, listeners get the sense that for the
most part, the band had as much fun off the bandstand as on. Cedar speaks
on Blakey's leadership.

> Incredible. He [Art] pretended that he was the gentleman and we were
> his officers … it was like we were a team of horses and he was …
> leading from behind …. That's how I always pictured him. There was
> no pain except "Pain" Shorter on sax. [laughs]. No man, we all had a
> great time and Wayne … he was in the moment too … I thought intel-
> lect came from going to college. But after meeting Art Blakey ….
> I found out that you can be very intelligent by … never going on any
> campus [chuckles].[12]

The personnel from *Mosaic* also recorded the classic albums *Buhaina's Delight*
and *Three Blind Mice*. *Buhaina's Delight* was recorded on November 28,
1961, where Walton contributed "Shaky Jake,"[13] a soulful bluesy tune that
swung hard and was driven by Art Blakey's patented shuffle. Throughout
the tune, Cedar demonstrates his grooving propulsive comping that at times
vacillates between riff-based big band figures and call and response with
the soloists. His solo is soulful and swinging. During his solo, Cedar's left
hand is the perfect rhythmic complement to Blakey's beat, akin to how
Red Garland would frequently accompany himself. Cedar's right hand is
bluesy and lyrical and builds as the horn backgrounds join. As is the case
with all the great swinging rhythm sections in the history of the music, each
musician in the rhythm section is so strong and able to generate swing on
their own. When the rhythm section plays together, they create a groove
that in the case of this band makes the listener tap their foot, a hallmark of
all the formations of the Messengers and all the groups Cedar would go on
to play in.

The final recording with Jymie Merritt on bass, *Three Blind Mice,* was
recorded on March 18, 1962. Cedar wrote "Plexus" for the date and contributed his arrangement of "That Old Feeling."[14] Walton was very proud of his

arrangement of "That Old Feeling."[15] This is also an instance of his early studies of George Shearing's simplified arrangements coming full circle.

Cedar's arrangement of "That Old Feeling" is a piano feature that allows Cedar to stretch out as a soloist, something that with a six-piece group was not as common in the Messengers. The elements of Cedar's arrangement of "Feeling" were staples in his repertoire that he would employ in arrangements his entire career. The intro starts out with a written bass line that sets the stage for the groove. The horns join shortly with rhythmic pops that invite Cedar's statement of the melody. Once Cedar starts the melody, he's not just playing the Sammy Fain classic tune, he is playing his interpretation of the tune. Cedar's take on the tune is much more rhythmic. As with all his arrangements of standards, Cedar finds a way to honor the composer's original melody in a way that is still singable and recognizable to the listener while inserting a rhythmic character that embraces the African esthetic that at its core is ultimately what makes jazz, jazz.

Cedar uses the horns to punctuate the melody at the end of the bridge. The brief horn entrance acts as a welcome dynamic and textural change before returning back to the trio for the final eight bars of the melody and ultimately Cedar's solo. In addition to the *Three Blind Mice* recording, there is also a video recording of the band playing Cedar's arrangement in Paris, France in 1963.[16]

Cedar's writing and arranging were no doubt influenced by Horace Silver and Duke Ellington, but just as Cedar would do his entire career, he created a style and identity within his compositions and arrangements that were inherently Cedar.

According to record producer and club owner Todd Barkan, Cedar's time in the Messengers was vitally important.

> Cedar told me that when he started to play with Blakey, he was shy and reticent about playing any solos or really asserting himself. Cedar affirmed to me on many occasions that Art Blakey was absolutely invaluable to Cedar in helping him draw out the full flower of his musicianship, the full expression and forceful delineation of his musical being. Art encouraged him to write, arrange, and to play. Art Blakey was an important catalyst to the full development of Cedar Walton as an artist. Obviously, he had played with people before this. He had a short tenure

in the Jazztet with Benny Golson and Art Farmer, but Art Blakey was the first gig that really got him out there. This gig got him out into the world as an internationally recognized jazz force. The edition with Freddie Hubbard, Wayne Shorter, Curtis Fuller, and Reggie Workman, the *Free for All* gang. Both Cedar and Wayne Shorter flowered into major league composer/arranger/instrumentalists during their time with Blakey.[17]

In 1962, bassist Jymie Merritt had to leave the Messengers to recover from an illness.[18] The Messengers were back in New York City and playing at Birdland. Blakey invited bassists Ron Carter and Reggie Workman to come and play with the group.[19] Their playing that night would serve as the audition for the next bassist in the group. Workman was offered the job and went on to be the bassist in the group for three years.[20] That evening was the first time that Cedar and Ron Carter played together. Even though Carter did not get offered the job with Blakey, (he was asked to join Miles Davis's band in the weeks to come), he and Cedar would gig and record together regularly later down the road.[21]

Bassist Reggie Workman replaced Jymie Merritt after the *Three Blind Mice* recording. He speaks about meeting Cedar and their time together in the Messengers.

> Cedar would breeze in and out and I'd have the opportunity to hang out with him for a minute or two. There were some places we'd meet after gigs and have breakfast together. We'd run into some of the greats and to others that we hadn't seen for a long time. All those times were pleasurable because we had conversations and experiences that others would never have. Sometimes it even turned into a musical situation where we'd have a jam session.
>
> Cedar Walton was a member of the community who was out there trying to get his own thing off the ground as well as working with an established band like Art Blakey.
>
> After that, we worked together in Art Blakey's band. Cedar joined the Messengers a little before I did. Before I was in the band, Jymie Merritt played bass and Curley Russell before him. Art Blakey always kept the band together. If one chair was missing, he would send his manager out to find somebody or he and the band members themselves would find somebody. I don't know exactly how it came about that they found me and asked me to work with them.

First of all, everyone was there to improve their well-being, livelihood, and music. Everyone was making contributions to the band in whatever way they could. I was very young and wasn't much of a composer at that time. I was beholden to most of the guys doing the writing.

During that time, there were a lot of opportunities to work in clubs and travel on the road for long periods of time. Alfred Lion and Frank Wolf were recording musicians a lot. They had a special place that they rehearsed for each record date. We'd meet one day before the record date at 89th and Broadway which was our rehearsal studio. I was there many times for different Blue Note projects that I was invited to play on.

Everybody in that band was so unique. We used to travel across the country in what we used to call the "White Moriah." This was a white checkered van that Art bought to transport the band from one city to another. All six of us were in this band and had their own story and jokes. [laughing] They had their own character and reasons to stop and go and do things. It was colorful. Art was the kind of person who liked to tease each person according to what he learned about them. He would mock people, make fun of people, and make fun with people. He kept a jovial feeling in the band. Cedar fit in well with that dynamic. Everyone in that band had a particular attitude and character that you could remember them by. Being with that band was a special experience.

Everybody who brought in a tune would give as much direction as was needed. If there was something I didn't understand about the tune or something that Cedar wanted to have happen that I wasn't particularly getting, we'd talk about it and he'd explain what he had in mind. In most cases when someone brought in a tune, very little direction was needed. You'd look at the music that was given to you and play what the composition called for. If you're doing something that doesn't work with the band, then naturally someone will say something to you. Namely the composer. The reason why there wasn't much direction given in those days is because you chose people for the band that have the same mindset. That way when you get on the bandstand to make music everyone understands what is supposed to be done.

Cedar is a very intelligent guy. He was a very subtle, talkative person. He admired the politician Buckley for his candid remarks and attitude. He was a well-rounded individual and had his own subtle character. You could bet that Cedar was going to come with something to make you laugh that was in tune with the moment. Something that had a kind of subtlety that caused you to wonder where it came from.

He was a joy to work with. He was very sensitive in the way that he dealt with the music and in tune to the attitudes of musicians around him. He was always giving of himself to make what we were creating happen. He had a great sense of humor, very intelligent, and was a good person to be around. There are times that he could be subtly sarcastic. That was definitely a facet of his character. It was understandable. All of us had something in our character that was uniquely us. His sarcasm was never negative. Sometimes musicians can say something to you and you don't know where it came from. Especially if you were young like I was during those times. You would find out that this was a lesson. Someone would say something that gave you reason to move yourself from where you were to the next plateau. Cedar was a little older and more experienced than I was. He would say whatever was necessary to help me through my growing pains.

Aside from that, he was a personal, private type of individual. He liked his own space and liked to keep to himself and only open himself when it was necessary as far as he was concerned.

What makes a pianist special is that he has a character, voicing, and touch of his own that makes you understand that here's a person whose ears and mind are open to whatever creativity is happening during the moment depending on the positioning of the planets. It's quite evident that there is joy in Cedar's music. There was also joy in how he approached the music.

When you listened to an acoustic pianist in the '50s and '60s and you were aware of what was happening, you could tell who it was from their touch, attitude, phrasing, and comping. If you "went to school" like we all had to do daily as far as growing up in this vast world of great creators, you had to listen to people and know who they were using your ear. Cedar fit right into that category because of his character. He found his own voice. That's one of the things that made him a joy to work with.[22]

Workman's final comments about Cedar's pianistic technique were something that many musicians picked up on. Bassist Christian McBride spoke about the sound coming from the piano the first time he heard Cedar play live.

I met Cedar my very first trip to Europe. I went to Europe with James Williams and his quartet. This was in July of 1990. Cedar was there with David Williams and Billy Higgins. I was standing in the back of the hall, and I was so excited. I said, "Man, I'm gonna go see Cedar Walton!" I went to the concert, and I was in the back of the room. It was in a hotel ballroom. All those hotel ballrooms have similar sounds.

They are not very live rooms. There's a lot of carpet and there's not a lot of bounce in the room. Most of the sound is coming from the speakers. But what I remember, most of all was all this sound was coming from the piano and it wasn't because it was loud in volume. It was just a huge sound coming out of the piano and it looked like Cedar was barely moving. I couldn't believe that so much sound was coming out of the piano with such little effort. [After the concert] I got to meet Cedar, briefly. In fact, there was whole a room full of legends. Billy Higgins, Cedar, and Johnny Griffin were there hanging out. Alvin Queen, Jimmy Woody, and Billy Pierce were there too. I got a chance to speak with Mr. Walton and I said, "Mr. Walton, it's so amazing. I was standing at the back of the room, and you were barely moving and I heard all this sound coming out of the piano!" And he [Cedar] said "That's a skill all piano players develop if they play with Art Blakey." [CM: laughs] And then I realized he was right because the only other person I could think of who could do that was Mulgrew Miller.[23]

Pianist and former Jazz Messenger, Benny Green, is equally adept as a world class jazz pianist and jazz scholar and is intimately aware of how the piano needed to be played when playing with Art Blakey.

When you play any instrument with Art, including and especially the piano, you have to think in a colorful sense, not just in a black and white sense. You have to project your sound. You have to develop the sound. From hearing Art, you can only imagine that if one didn't really have a sound, didn't rise to the occasion, that you'd just become submerged by Art. It wouldn't work.

And, the thing is, that if we listen more carefully to what's going on when Art is playing, it's not that he's playing loud so much. And he did play loud, especially toward the end, but it's not that so much on the great recordings that gives this bigness, and this fullness, and this volume to the sound. It's that he uses dynamics. That's the thing so many people miss with Art. And when you play with Art, he puts dynamics behind you. He puts dynamics up under your soul. He creates these waves. Again, it's not just loud volume going on but waves and undulations in the sound. He embraced the form, the structure of the piece you're playing and the direction your solo is going. Because you may have heard the reference that Art Blakey told all of us when we were improvising solos, it's like writing a letter.

You have some kind of introduction, or heading, or greeting. Then you get to the point of the main body where it develops, and

you get to what it is you want to say. Then there's some kind of closing and that makes way for the next soloist. When you play with
Art you learned, on a survival level, humanly, how to ride those waves.
One classic thing that we can hear Art doing again and again on the
records is, as a soloist is playing numerous choruses, as Art gets to
the end of the form of one chorus, getting ready to come into the top
of the form of the next chorus, Art will play a press roll that has a
crescendo to it, that builds and gets louder, leading right up to the end
of the previous chorus. And then, the soloist has a sense of volume and
projection. They have to play over that.

When Art gets to the top of the next chorus, he'll just come right
back down to the tip that he was playing all along. He'll have that roll
going on. Meanwhile, he's propelled the soloist forward and the soloist
is out there. Then he's back to the tip. And that's a classic thing that
Art does. When you experience that with Art, and you go to play with
any other drummer afterward, it feels like the whole bottom dropped
out. "What happened?" And then you realize, "Wow. Art was carrying
me." Yes. Carrying you on his shoulders because Art's true intentions
for the Messengers are to cultivate leaders. And you get it in you that
it's part of your own swagger, that you become a leader, and that when
you're on the bandstand and you have people playing with you, that
you can impart that sense of flow and shape to the music.

Because you've been to the mountaintop. You've played with Art
Blakey and you've felt that. The point is not just to say, "Wow. Art was
great, wasn't he?" What he intended for us was to spread the message.
Indeed, you developed a sound when you played with Art.[24]

Cedar's work in the Messengers left an indelible mark for all future
Messenger composer/arrangers and pianists. His work along with his
bandmates helped to solidify the group's classic sound. James Williams
and Mulgrew Miller were both pianists in the Messengers after Cedar and
had this to say about his impact on the group's sound:

James Williams

The four people who really established the piano sound for the
Messengers—and defined it right on down to the end—would be
Horace Silver, Bobby Timmons, Walter Davis, and Cedar Walton.
The rest of us are just imitators of what they were doing. They set
the tone for what the piano chair should sound like.[25]

"Mosaic" manuscript. *Martha Walton collection.*

Mulgrew Miller

Cedar has always been one of the most criminally underrated pianists in the world. He's a terrific musician and is gifted in many areas: One, as a melodic improviser, he has few peers; two, out of all the Messenger piano players, he was the best orchestrator. He had the most orchestral approach, which has made him the best post-Messenger trio player.[26]

Chapter 6

Clockwise (1958–1965): *Cedar, Ida, and family*

C edar was establishing himself as one of the foremost jazz pianists in the world. At the same time, his personal life was starting to blossom as well. In the late '50s Cedar would make trips to Philadelphia to play with different groups. On one of these gigs, he met a young Ida Desphy. Ida was a jazz fan and she and Cedar became close. In the early '60s, Cedar and Ida got married and settled in New York in 1960. The couple welcomed their first son Carl Walton into the world. Carl describes his mother, Ida, and how she and Cedar met.

> Ida was one of 7 children. Her father was Filipino, and her mom was a black woman in the Philadelphia area. She was the middle child of 7. She and her brother were considered the comedians of the family. She had a great personality and was a very pretty girl. She had some Filipino features as well. She was a childhood friend of Spanky DeBrest.
>
> She told me this story. She listened to the current music that was being played, like doo-wop and early R&B, but she said, it wasn't grabbing her like it was other people in her neighborhood. So Spanky said, "I want to play something for you." So she went over to his house and he played her some Miles Davis *Kind of Blue* or something like that and she was hooked. She started going to jazz clubs and got

her brother involved and he became just as big of a fan. His name is Alfredo Desphy. It's Fareed now. He lives in Atlanta. He's still a huge jazz fan. He was very close to Cedar through Ida. Ida went to hear Spanky play and that's where she met Cedar. Probably in 1958. At some point they started seeing each other. I think she may have been seeing Lee Morgan before she met Cedar. I'm not sure if they met in '58 or '59. Lee Morgan was a childhood friend of my mother and also became friends with my father. They played together a lot. Spanky played with Lee and was a legitimate jazz bassist. He played with everybody that was playing jazz at the time. Lee was a very popular up and coming player and was very good with the ladies as well. He was a very good-looking guy. My mom was seeing him and all of that. At some point she met Cedar and they started seeing each other. The life of a musician means you're out of town a lot and he [Cedar] wasn't there to begin with. He would come in from New York. She would visit him from time to time. When I was conceived, she knew Cedar was the father, but I don't know if Lee was convinced about that quite yet. She had to break it to Lee before she went on a trip she had planned just after graduating from high school. She had planned and saved up for a trip to Hawaii. So she and I went to Hawaii. I mean I didn't know I was in Hawaii! She went there and knew she was pregnant. This was 1959. She spent a good amount of time there. Maybe a month or two. When she came back, she was showing a little more. She gave birth to me in February 1960 in Philadelphia around her family. Later on that year, she moved into a brownstone on Dean Street in Brooklyn. And the story goes, apparently Lee was in NY and came to visit them, I'm not sure if Cedar was there or not. Really, Lee came by just to take a look at the baby. He looked down and saw Cedar's shaped head on my body in the crib and said, "I know that's not mine." They stayed friends for years.

Ida became a big jazz fan. When she got to Brooklyn, she met up with some of the wives and girlfriends of other musicians. Bobby Timmons's wife Stella was a very good friend. Brenda Hubbard was a very good friend. There were a few others too. Naturally they all loved jazz and were looking to support and promote the music. My mom helped found a club called "Club Jest Us." That was a group that included a number of musicians' wives and girlfriends that would promote and sponsor jazz shows in Brooklyn. Up to that point, most of the jazz shows were in Manhattan, across the river from Brooklyn. That group was focused on promoting jazz concerts in Brooklyn. They would bring in jazz artists based on their connections of their husbands and boyfriends or connections they made themselves by going to jazz clubs and meeting up with folks. They would design flyers and get them printed and would post them around Brooklyn. They would select venues that might not necessarily have been used for jazz shows before that. After a while these same venues became known for hosting jazz shows. They did quite well for themselves for many years. When they first started there must have been about 15–20 women involved with them.

As the years went on, things changed. Not all of the wives stayed together with their husbands and some of the spouses like Bobby Timmons died. Eventually the group was whittled down to just a handful of members until it faded out. This was in the late '60s, early '70s.

Ida was a very wonderful and doting mother. Everything was based around us and supporting Cedar. She had three of us children together with Cedar. She was everything a kid would want in a mom. Very supportive, very funny. We always thought we had the coolest mom. To know here was to love her.

We were all pretty smart kids thanks to her. She emphasized education. She kept the family together as long as she could until it was time for them to not be together anymore. She started another family after that and so did Cedar. He had another daughter. My sister Naisha came with his wife after Ida. They lived together in that apartment on lower east side in Manhattan in the '80s and '90s.

I don't remember too many family vacations. He was on the road quite a bit. I do remember he had this car and he was the only one who had it. After he didn't have it anymore, I never saw anyone else have it. It's called a Morris Minor. It was the family car. After that he didn't even own a car for many years.

We would take that car for trips over the weekend, but there weren't big family vacations. Most of the vacations we took were to places like Philadelphia, and it would be without him. He would always be some place playing. We would go there and stay with my mom's sisters and brothers. We became tight with our cousins in Philadelphia. Later on, we took trips to Dallas and he was with us for those trips.[1]

Ida's brother, Alfredo Desphy (who changed his name to Fareed Mumin) befriended Cedar as Ida and Cedar were courting. Mumin and Cedar maintained a lifelong friendship. Mumin reflected on meeting Cedar, the music scene, and all the musicians he met through Cedar:

I met Cedar in Philadelphia in 1958 when I was about 16 years old. Cedar had come to town, I believe at the time he was playing with

Spanky DeBrest, the bass player who later played with the Jazz Messengers. My sister [Ida] had met Cedar at the club and she was telling me about him. So I asked her, what is his name and she said, Cedar, like cedar wood. That was always Cedar's opening if somebody asked him his name. We became friends and by 1960 my sister and Cedar had gotten married. Carl was born in 1960 and from then on, I would go back and forth to New York. I lived in Philadelphia but I would go and stay with them through the years and we just became the best of friends. Cedar was like the older brother that I never had. I had five sisters.

Just like older brothers do, he was always giving me advice about different things. He would take me all over the place, and I was pretty young. I can't even tell you all the people that I've met through Cedar because I didn't know hardly anybody then. I came to New York and I can only remember some of the names and faces and places that I had seen with Cedar all through those years. We became very close and I can remember a story about when he first started playing with Art.

A few years before he passed, I told him, we were all excited about Art Blakey and the Jazz Messengers at the time Lee Morgan and Bobby Timmons were there, and that whole group was kickin' it, you know? And when he told me, "you know we're gettin' ready to play with Art," I got a little nervous. I even remember the first time he came to Philly with the Jazz Messengers and he introduced me to Freddie Hubbard. He said, he's from Indianapolis and had been on the scene in New York a few years off and on but I hadn't heard of him, or knew of him until then. That made me even more nervous!

So I told him years later, "you know Cedar, when you went with Art I was a little apprehensive. Not that I doubted you Cedar; I knew your work and I knew all the music you had played and all the people you had played with. But Art and them had such a big hit with Lee and Bobby and that particular group, I said, I was a little, you know ..." and he kinda laughed. I told him, "But when I heard you and Freddie and Wayne Shorter hit the bandstand, all my anxiety went out the window. Because you all stepped into that scene and took it to another level."

That's what I saw in Cedar, and that was the beginning of him really blowing up. As far as I know, people really knew them and Cedar had always been the type of person that was right on point with the music. I sat with him many times and met different guys, people like John Lewis at the piano at the house and listening to him going over different music with different musicians, and that happened many, many times through the years. And that was like the beginning.

Now Ida and I were two years apart, she was my closest sister, we were like twins. I followed Ida and Cedar to New York when they got together in 1960, and that was the beginning of a long relationship and of all the knowledge and things that I had learned through them. As a matter of fact, at the time people knew me from seeing me but I was always either Ida's brother or Cedar's brother-in-law. I didn't have a name. But I do remember one time, I happened to be on the train coming from Philadelphia and I ran into Kenny Dorham and he called me by my name. He said, "Hey Alfredo!" And I felt so honored, I said dang, he knows my name!

My sister Ida, she was a promoter. She was an original member of "Club Jest Us," a group of musicians' wives, who promoted and supported jazz music throughout Brooklyn, New York City and beyond, so I got a chance to know all of them. So sometimes when we'd go to the club, I'd be the source of envy because I had all these musicians' wives around me. I was a little younger than them, and I'd come into the club with Brenda Hubbard and Stella Timmons, John Ore's wife Ruby and Lex Humphries's wife Barbara, Louis Hayes's wife Pat, and others I can't recall. And they were high-end affairs, in different places not usually known for jazz but they made it work. And Ida and I were like two peas in a pod, in her eyes, it was like I could never do any wrong. I was her little brother.

Philadelphia was swinging too, man; as a matter of fact, Philadelphia was like the sister city to New York because a lot of the musicians came out of Philly. Somebody mentioned to me recently that when Art was there once, he was speaking to Benny Golson about starting a new band and he told him he needed a trumpet player, and he said well I got Lee Morgan, and he said okay, where's he from? He's from Philly. He said okay, what about a bass player? I got a bass player for you too, his name is Jymie Merritt. Where's he from? Philadelphia. And it goes on, you know. Look, everybody was from Philly then. I mean Bobby Timmons, Jymie Merritt, Reggie Workman, most of the musicians in Art's band at one time were all from Philadelphia. So those are the type of musicians that I grew up around, you know. We grew up in a projects called the Richard Allen homes, and some of them even lived there when they grew up.

So I got a chance to see a lot of the musicians coming through. Again, I was young and it was only years later I was told who I was in company of, but many musicians would come through Philadelphia and they would tell me later that they had been there, people like drummers Philly Joe Jones and Mickey Roker. But Philadelphia itself had a lot of clubs too; they had Peps Showboat, Blue Note, the Clef Club,

I mean, it was really an active city musically. At one time it seemed like every other club was a jazz club.[2]

Cedar and Ida had two more children, son Rodney in 1962 and Cedra in 1967. The two share their memories of their father.

Rodney Walton

I was born in 1962 and grew up in New York City in Brooklyn. And growing up was a lot of fun. Dad was busy coming and going because he was on the road a lot playing with a lot of other cats. Dad and I played a lot of paddle ball when I was growing up in New York. He tried handball a little, but he didn't want to mess with the hands too much, so we got paddles and did a lot of paddle ball. That was how we got a little bit of exercise.

I remember him coming in and composing. Sometimes it would wake me up, him working out chords for tunes he had in his head. I didn't mind it because it was good stuff. He always did that. As a kid, I went to a lot of different concerts that he played. But the music was always exciting. I didn't really know anything other than that, except when I visited my mother's side of the family in Philadelphia. They weren't really big jazz fans. They liked R&B and stuff like that.

Once we asked my dad to play in an auditorium in my elementary school. Billy [Higgins] was there too. I remember him coming and entertaining us in the auditorium and people were really excited like, "Wow, that's your dad?" I was in the second grade. I was in PS 138 in Brooklyn. Dad had no problem playing. He was happy to play, and people really loved it.

In my teenage years, I went to a lot of Jazzmobiles with him in some parts of Brooklyn. Those Jazzmobiles were basically a block party. I remember dad playing a lot at the Grant's Tomb location. He always had Billy [Higgins] on drums, David Williams, and Sam Jones on bass. He didn't always lead a group. Sometimes he played with other people. It was always fun and people enjoyed it. You wouldn't think they're a lot of jazz fans, but people really flocked out for those Jazzmobile concerts. It was a good time.

I'll never forget one time Dad took me down to Left Bank in Baltimore. I remember loading the station wagon with Art's [Blakey] drums. And it was me, dad, and Art. We drove down to Baltimore from New York. I don't think it was the Messengers, it was just a group Dad put together. Man, it was swinging so hard. I was right near the front.

We lived on Utica Avenue in Brooklyn right by Carroll Street. We lived right above a bodega, right by a bus stop. Sometimes he would have jam sessions right there. Him and Billy. Billy left his drums at the house. When they played, I would look out the window and see people passing by looking up like, "What was that? What is that? They jamming up in there!" I had good memories at that place.

Soon after, Dad and my mother divorced around that time. But he still continued on his musical journey. He was always around to help me and Carl get what we needed or whatever. Even if he was away, he would always send money from Japan or wherever he was at. Once, he came back from Japan and got Carl this nice boombox. We were all excited about that boombox, man! It was state of the art straight from Japan. On another trip, Dad also got us these nice leather jackets and some jackets from Iceland. Sometimes he really spoiled us.

The music was always prevalent. If I was dealing with any kind of issue that I couldn't figure out. Dad wouldn't try to figure it out for me, he would tell me how he figured his things out. He said, "Listen, I always gravitated toward the music. If I had any kind of issues that always saved me." That was his mindset. He always had the music. That was his thing. It was a special thing for him to just to get up there and play. He loved to do it and he never really compromised any of that.

Dad was always good for helping family get to the gigs. When he played at the Vanguard around Christmas time a whole contingency of my mother's relatives would come up from Philly. That became a regular thing.

After college I joined the Navy and was stationed in San Diego. Eventually my ship went into dry dock up in Long Beach Terminal Island. Dad moved out to California and was living in West Los Angeles. Eventually, I'd drive up to his place and sometimes to hang out. We played tennis quite a bit out there.

I got out of the Navy in 1988. I was still hanging around in California. Dad and I used to play a little tennis too. He would call up and say, "Come on out and hit with me, man." We would play on courts right on Santa Monica Blvd. And they have some nice courts out there. Dad got to have a decent stroke. We had a lot of fun. He always had a major tennis match on at the house. If there was a match on, he'd always know. He loved Wimbledon and all the majors. I became a big tennis fan through him because he was.[3]

Cedra Walton

There's something really cool about being the daughter of a jazz master. My Dad was one of my best friends, whom I adored. When together, we would always have a great time laughing and making fun of each other and many times making fun of others.

Obviously, with the flip of the letters, I am Cedar's namesake. My sibs may fight me on this, but I was also his fave. Growing up, I was always told by Mom that my brother Carl came up with the idea when he was seven to name me Cedra. Unfortunately, in recent years, I interviewed my brother Carl on camera, and he has no recollection.

I love to flash the name; it's like therapy for me. When I meet or when I'm working with musicians, I always start the conversation. I say my name to see if the person will recognize the resemblance being so close in spelling to Dad's. If I don't get the response I was look-ing for, I keep going. Asking who did they study. It's exciting because seven out of ten people have heard of Dad. If they don't know, then I school them.

This therapy is soothing because I get to talk about my dad and the discussion always alludes to his greatness, and how I come from royalty. The blessing in these very often random meetings is knowing I can hold on to him longer because his name and music live forever. This is an intentional conversation that I spark on any given day; it warms my heart and fills my spirit. I miss him so, and that will never stop!

One of my earliest and fondest memories was when my dad brought home a portable recorder. He was testing it out and asking me questions like "Well, what's your name, little girl?" and "How old are you?" I can still see his face watching my responses as he recorded. I was five when my parents separated.

I had a jaded idea of visiting Dad, I thought it was always time to shop. [laughs] I always liked hanging out with my dad. He took me to the studio a lot.

I remember going with Dad to visit his parents in Dallas. Those were great times. Being with him was great. He traveled the world a lot. When he was gone, I was with my mom. While he was traveling, he always called to check in. He was a great provider. That meant the world to my brothers and me.

One night, I came home from a nightclub a little early with my boyfriend. We had dozed off in my bedroom. We were fully dressed and not doing anything mischievous! [laughs] There was hard knock on an open door. My dad came in and said, "Tell your friend goodnight!"

The next day I was so stiff with fear because he was supposed to give
me a driving lesson. He was extra stern in his teaching. Probably
because of what happened the night before.

My dad always tried to make things nice. He was always giving
and giving and giving. Thoughtful. One of my fondest memories is
going on a jazz cruise he took me on. Everybody was on there. I got to
hang out with Milt Jackson, Dizzy Gillespie, and Joe Williams. And of
course, David Williams and Billy Higgins were there. You know, my
family. Lot of laughs.

Because Dad and Billy and David spent so much time together,
Billy and David were like a built-in godfather type of force. They were
always cheering me on and were a fixture in our family. They just
had a natural way of flowing, I never saw them argue, I'm sure they
probably did, but they were always close-knit and in-sync personally.
On and off the stage. I would see them and say, you guys are married
a long time! [laughs]

We inherited them when Dad joined forces with them to play music.
We were lucky enough to have them in our lives. Billy and I had this
long-standing joke, we'd call each other Mumsie from some Robert

(l to r) Ida (Desphy) Walton, Carl Walton, Cedar Walton,
and Rodney Walton, 1996. *Martha Walton collection.*

(l to r) Cedar, Cedra Walton, Ruth, and C.A. Walton.
Martha Walton collection.

(l to r) Greg Osby, Mike LeDonne, Mulgrew Miller, Cedra Walton,
and John Weber, 1996. *Martha Walton collection.*

Townsend joke. Then David picked up on it and now he calls me Mumsie. Thank God for them.

My dad was a jokester. Kind of was a gossip, he loved good gossip. When my siblings and I talk about Dad sometimes, we were always impressed with how humble he was about his greatness. It took me such time to realize that he was just in it because he loved it, nothing else, nothing more or less. He really loved it. And he's a perfect example of doing what you love and going full force with it. It always felt like he was ahead of the game as far as thinking. He was a forward thinker would get impatient with people who couldn't see what he saw. Dad was a really, really good friend of mine. I was one of his biggest fans.[4]

Chapter 7

Turquoise Twice (1964–1975): *Life after the Messengers*

A fter leaving the Messengers in the summer of 1964, Cedar worked and recorded frequently. His first recorded works post-Messengers were as a sideman with his old Army buddy and saxophonist Eddie Harris. Cedar recorded two albums with Harris at the end of year titled *Cool Sax from Hollywood to Broadway* and *Here Comes the Judge*.[1] The two would record frequently in the mid-to-late '60s. In 1965, Cedar would play on another Harris album, *The In Sound*.[2] This record is significant for a number of reasons. This was the first recording that Cedar and drummer Billy Higgins would play on together. In the coming years Walton and Higgins would have a very special musical relationship and friendship. Bassist Ron Carter also played on this recording. The trio of Cedar, Higgins, and Carter would record more albums with Harris including *Mean Greens* and *Tender Storm*, and Cedar and Carter would work frequently in the years to come as well.[3]

Eddie Harris

Cedar held Harris in high regard. "He's the one who comes closer to reminding me of John Coltrane,"[4] said Walton. In addition to Harris's playing, Cedar also paid close attention the trajectory of Harris's career and how he wrote music geared toward the taste and trends of the time. Since returning stateside from his Army commitment, Harris had experienced commercial success that few jazz musicians had at that time. His arrangement of Ernest Gold's tune "Exodus" (from the movie *Exodus*) was included on his first recording for Vee Jay records and more importantly, was the first ever certified gold jazz recording.[5] Harris's arrangement of "Exodus" made it all way to number 16 on the Billboard Charts.[6] Cedar remembers Harris constantly seeking the "big break."[7] Cedar must have taken notice of Harris's successes during this time. The combination of what Cedar learned from Harris along with Art Blakey's business acumen surely influenced Cedar as he envisioned recordings and groups he would go on to lead. While Cedar wouldn't necessarily seek the big break, he was definitely aware of trends in jazz music and that showed in some of his releases in the late '60s and '70s.

Clifford Jordan

Tenor saxophonist Clifford Jordan and Cedar were friends as far back as their days together in J.J. Johnson's band. The two would play and record together frequently from the mid '60s and '70s in each other's bands as well as on each other's recordings. In addition to *Spellbound* which he recorded with Jordan in 1960, he also recorded *Starting Time* and *Bearcat* with Jordan in 1961 and 1962 while in the Messengers.[8] In 1965, he played on Jordan's album *These Are My Roots*.[9] These records were just the beginning of what the two would create together in the '70s, which would become some of the greatest straight-ahead jazz of that decade.

Milt Jackson

Milt Jackson and Cedar met while Cedar was stationed in Germany. While the two didn't play immediately when Cedar returned to the states, they would perform and record often starting in 1965 with Jackson's album *Milt Jackson at the Museum of Modern Art.* This recording featured Cedar's tune "Turquoise"[10] and is notable because it marks a trend of Cedar compositions showing up on recordings where he is a sideman. Excluding his composing and arranging work with the Messengers, two of Walton's tunes were recorded on albums in which he was not the leader during this period.

Cedar and Clifford Jordan. *Martha Walton collection,
photographer unknown.*

"Turquoise"[11] was previously recorded with Blue Mitchel on the recording *The Cup Bearers* in 1962, and "Mosaic," first recorded with the Messengers, was also recorded with Clifford Jordon in 1961 on the album *Starting Time*. From this point on, it became increasingly more common to see Cedar's originals showing up on sessions where he was a sideman.

Joe Henderson

In 1965, Cedar played on the classic Blue Note album *Mode for Joe*. Cedar contributed two compositions to the recording: "Mode for Joe" and "Black." Joel Harris, for his dissertation *Joe Henderson: A Biographical Study of Life and Career*, interviewed Blue Note record producer Michael Cuscuna. In the interview, Cuscuna shared a story regarding "Mode for Joe" and the tunes that Cedar contributed:

> Joe [Henderson] was the kind of person who could say stuff that could hurt a sensitive person. A person with a sense of humor it might roll off them, but it could hurt somebody. Cedar Walton never forgot that one day, a couple of years after *Mode for Joe*, at Bradley's or Vanguard, one of the clubs, somebody came up to Joe and talked about how great *Mode for Joe* was. Cedar was there. I don't know if they were playing the gig together or if they were just hanging out. Joe said to this guy, "I got the recognition, but he got all the money," pointing to Cedar because Cedar wrote the tune "Mode for Joe." And Cedar was a very sensitive guy. I mean, for twenty years he carried a wound over what Joe said that night. But Joe was just being cavalier and casual and blasé about things. But I don't think Joe sometimes ever realized ... he's like Miles, I don't think he ever realized that the shit he said could affect people as deeply as it did.[12]

Cuscuna's comments reveal that although to most, Cedar had a pleasant and sometimes humorous, lighthearted facade, he was took his work very seriously. To be respected by his peers was something that meant a lot to him.

Trumpeter Lee Morgan also recorded on *Mode for Joe*. Cedar and Morgan would work together on several sessions from 1964-1968. The two first recorded together on two Messengers albums in 1964—*Indestructible* and *Golden Boy*.[13] Cedar recorded *Charisma, The Rajah, Sonic Boom, The Sixth Sense*, and *Caramba!* all from 1966–1967.[14] In addition to Cedar playing on all these recordings, drummer Billy Higgins did as well. The two were starting a musical association that would last their entire lives and be documented on many recordings. Morgan's recording *Charisma* features a Walton original titled "Rainy Night." Walton and Morgan recorded the tune together on the Blakey album *Indestructible* under the title "When Love Is New." While the arrangements for the tune are different on each album, the chordal structure and harmonic rhythm are the same. "Rainy Night" seems to be a Cedar contrafact of "When Love is New." The introduction is reminiscent of the classic Wayne Shorter tune One by One recorded by the Messengers and Cedar.

Cedar!/Prestige Records

The year 1967 marked Cedar's first recording release as a leader. *Cedar!* was released on Prestige and featured saxophonist Junior Cook, bassist Leroy Vinnegar, drummer Billy Higgins, and trumpeter Kenny Dorham who, years earlier, hired Cedar to play on *This Is the Moment* which is Cedar's first recorded work on record.[15] The recording included four Cedar originals: "Turquoise Twice," "Twilight Waltz" (which would later be recorded as "Midnight Waltz,") "Short Stuff," and "Head and Shoulders." Three standards round out the album. Two Ellington tunes, "Take the 'A' Train" and "Come Sunday," were no doubt a nod to the immense respect Cedar had for Ellington, and there was the Gershwin/Weill tune "My Ship." As with all standards Cedar played and recorded, he made them his own. His arrangement of "My Ship" was one that he would play throughout his career. Cedar had an uncanny ability to arrange a tune. He could put his stamp on a tune while still maintaining the melodic integrity the composer had intended and, in some cases, enhancing it. Of Cedar's arranging, jazz pianist Mike LeDonne said,

> He [Cedar] would find these rhythms in the melody and make that the arrangement. It was so organic. It came right from the tune. Something that you might have missed, though. But it was right there in front of you. He was one of those guys that could show the simplicity of how much is there that you're missing. He saw it all. And through him, I know myself and others like myself who idolize Cedar Walton,

we all got into that same thing. Looking for that magic thing that's there already, you just have to find it. And Cedar would find it. And then it would become this fantastic arrangement that not only sounded good but was easy to play. You could throw that arrangement in front of a band that had never played it before and sound like they rehearsed all week for this gig.[16]

In the late '60s, Cedar worked as a sideman for many Prestige recording sessions. The first of which was titled *Chocomotive* led by Houston Person, another friend he met while he was in the Army. Cedar recorded as a sideman on ten recordings from 1967–1972 on records for Pat Martino, Sonny Criss, Eric Kloss, and Charles McPherson, all for Prestige.[17]

From 1967 on, Cedar would regularly release recordings as a leader. He recorded three more records as a leader for Prestige: *Spectrum* (1968), *The Electric Boogaloo Song* (1969), and *Soul* Cycle (recorded in 1969, released in 1970). These records featured a mixture of the straight ahead jazz his listeners were accustomed to as well as tunes that had more of a commercial nature or could be considered in the Soul Jazz vein. Compositions such as "Higgins Holler," "The Electric Boogaloo Song," and "Sundown Express" were all in this vein.[18] Bob Porter, who produced over 200 sessions for Prestige, wrote about Soul Jazz in his book *Soul Jazz*. "In the '50s, soul jazz was, roughly, equal parts black swing and rhythm and blues, with a smattering of gospel and modern jazz influence .... Danceable tempos were an important ingredient: expected and delivered in almost every song."[19] The aforementioned tunes definitely fit into this category. Cedar would also play electric piano on some of these recordings. The tunes that fell into the soul jazz category on these albums are most likely a result of Prestige wanting to market tunes that included popular musical elements to reach a larger audience. Cedar saw Eddie Harris doing a similar thing. While Cedar was not as concerned with making the next big hit, he was aware of trends in music and was willing to adapt. Most importantly, when he chose to record a tune in this vein, his playing and compositional voices were not comprised. Throughout Cedar's recording career, one of his most underrated achievements was the ability to sound like himself in every situation.

Jazz Clubs

Cedar worked regularly in New York when he wasn't touring, and the club scene was an integral part in Cedar's life both for practical reasons such as employment but also in the communal sense. Many musicians have spoken about how Cedar and his contemporaries were known for making the hang and supporting other musicians when they weren't playing themselves. This was part of the culture. It was a community where musicians supported one another as family, and Cedar was regularly on the scene. He frequently played New York City clubs like Slugs', Boomers, Bradley's, and Sweet Basil.

Slugs'

Slugs' got started in the mid-'60s and is infamously known as the club where trumpeter Lee Morgan was shot by his girlfriend, Hellen Moore. Slugs' was on the lower east side, in a rough neighborhood. Initially, Slugs' started out as just a bar. Saxophonist Jackie McLean started a gig there. After that, things took off.[20] As a college student, Michael Cuscuna (who later became a record producer for Blue Note) would frequent the club: "[Slugs'] was the only place you could go and hear a Blue Note record performed live," said Cuscuna.[21] In addition to McLean, many of Cedar's musical collaborators played and hung at the club, including Freddie Hubbard, Kenny Dorham, Wayne Shorter, and Lee Morgan. Jazz pianist George Cables heard Cedar at Slugs': "I used to sit behind and look over his shoulder and watch him play because when he was playing, you could just about hear him think. You could hear him thinking when he was playing because he had a very deliberate way of playing."[22]

Jim Harrison worked as a publicist for Slugs' and Boomers. He formed the Jackie McLean fan club and was also music coordinator for Jazzmobile, a job he held for fifty years. Harrison also promoted concerts with Cedar including a three-piano feature with Barry Harris, Walter Davis Jr., and Cedar. Cedar and Harrison would be friends for life and their paths would cross often. "Cedar was an icon, a pianist extraordinaire. He was a brilliant composer/arranger. I did a lot of concerts with Lee Morgan. Cedar and Billy Higgins and Paul Chambers accompanied him," said Harrison.[23] Cedar worked primarily as a sideman at Slugs'.[24] It was at Boomers where he would begin work as a leader.

Boomers

Boomers opened in 1969. Bob Cooper, a musician and chef, managed the club. "I really loved Jazz,"[25] said Cooper. "I used to play trumpet myself and it was just the music that I loved. I figured that is what I wanted to do, and I knew that the guys that were good. I decided that I was going to do it that way."[26] The club started to receive notoriety when former Messengers' pianist Bobby Timmons, who was a good friend of Cedar's, began playing there. The stage at Boomers was small and could accommodate an upright Steinway. When Cedar spoke about Boomers in interviews throughout his career, there was an endearing tone to his words. In the liner notes of *Live at Boomers, Vol. 1*, which were written in interview format by Gary Giddins, Walton spoke about the purpose of clubs like Boomers and what they meant to artists like himself and Clifford Jordan:

> For more than two years now, this popular Greenwich Village bistro has been unyielding in its presentation of good music. Its management, spearheaded by restaurateurs Bob Cooper and Aubrey Dasusa should be commended for their very together mixture of the best in food, atmosphere, and service.
>
> Cliff and I use these clubs as places where we perform, meet our friends, invite writers and promoters. It's actually a night-time office in a way. Looking to them as a way of making a living is a mistake. You know, this is the only place that's like that. On the world scale, the music is as strong as ever. So I can't really be as bitter about the scene as someone who is trapped here. I just came back from Japan and that reminded me how powerful the music is on a world scale. Compared to here, it's not second class by any stretch of the imagination. It's really a super commodity appreciated all over.[27]

Cedar would befriend Cooper and the two would hang outside of the club. The two followed sports closely. Cedar's son, Rodney Walton, recalls one such occasion:

> Dad loved watching the Knicks. When cable TV first became available, that was a big deal. Before that, if the Knicks were playing at home, you couldn't watch the games on TV. Bob Cooper was one of the first people we knew that had cable. He had a nice apartment.

We were sitting at his place watching the Knicks play on a color TV! We were used to watching on a little nine-inch black and white TV. That was a big treat!

Dad was fascinated with the way Earl Monroe dribbled the ball. Earl had this way of dribbling that was incredible. Dad was always a jokester. He had different nicknames for the players. Phil Jackson was an awkward looking basketball player. Instead of Phil Jackson, he would call him "Spill Jackson." Dad was funny as hell. He always had a good joke for me.[28]

There were some special live recordings that came out of Boomers, and Cedar was at the center of several of them. *A Night at Boomers Vols. 1 & 2* were released in 1973 and featured tenor saxophonist Clifford Jordan, bassist Sam Jones, drummer Louis Hayes, and Cedar.[29] The recordings capture the essence of the club and Cedar and the band play fearlessly as if they forgot they were being recorded. Cedar contributed three original tunes to the session: "Highest Mountain," "Holy Land," and "Bleeker Street Theme." Cedar first recorded "Highest Mountain" with Clifford Jordan on the Jordan album *These Are My Roots* in 1965. The two would record this tune four more times in the coming years. "Holy Land" was first recorded on the Houston Person's album *Blue Odyssey* in 1968. "Holy Land" is a minor blues tune that Walton would play and record regularly throughout his career. The tune varies, however, from the traditional format of head statement, solos, head statement. Cedar wrote solo piano cadenzas for himself that not only start the tune but are sandwiched in between head statements. While these minor changes might seem insignificant, these compositional intricacies gave him additional room for expression and further contributed to make up Cedar's sound both as a pianist and composer. *Boomers* continues with Cedar and the band playing a variety of jazz standards as well as Cedar's arrangement of the Burt Bacharach tune "This Guy's In Love with You."

One of the most important elements with these *Boomers* recordings was the inclusion of blues tunes. The blues was a central part of Cedar and his playing. He would almost always include one blues in his performances or recordings, and it wasn't uncommon for multiple blues to be played in the same set. This was also a regular occurrence for Clifford Jordan, with whom Cedar would play and record with regularly. More than just the typical blues forms that jazz musicians commonly play over, swinging blues-based music is one of the cornerstones within the African esthetic upon which jazz music is built. The blues was much more than music, it was an everyday part of life that has been central in the lives of African Americans for years. Cedar lived this.

There is a very personal quality to these *Boomers* recordings. It starts with the intimate stage and upright piano. The listener can hear the depth of Cedar's touch and the weight in his comping behind Clifford Jordan. Drummer Louis Hayes's cymbals create wash and are the perfect underpinning along with his long-time rhythm section partner bassist Sam Jones. The band plays with swinging abandon and intimacy. In the liner notes of *A Night at Boomers Vol. 2*, Gary Giddins wrote:

> There is a chemistry between certain musicians and the rooms they play. The club ceases to be just a house for the gig and becomes part of a scene of familiarity. The music sounds at home here .... Cedar is a frequent performer at the club and his music seems to define the place, his rich keyboard touch, percussive but not overbearing, and lyric improvisations enhance the cool atmosphere of Boomers. Cedar plays as well at other clubs, in concert halls, and recording studios, but here, for some reason, there is the illusion that he is cooking in a natural habitat.[30]

Drummer Louis Hayes remembers the famous *Boomers* sessions:

> Bobby Timmons was the person who introduced me to Boomers. There was a period where Cedar and myself both played with Freddie Hubbard in a group and then we played at Boomers. Several times. The band on those [*Live at Boomers*] recordings was Cedar, Clifford Jordan, Sam Jones, and myself. We also recorded there twice. We made other appearances together at several other places in the world.
> We [Cedar, Sam, and LH] were friends and it was just something that was natural. When I did that recording date with them at Boomers, I didn't really know the music they were playing because I was traveling at the time with Oscar Peterson. Billy Higgins was the person that really knew the music. I didn't rehearse with them when we recorded. We just went in and did it. We were able to play so naturally because we were friends on that level. We played together and made history.

Cedar and I were friends. Playing with him was very natural. When he wrote something you knew it was a Cedar Walton composition because his mind worked a certain way. I enjoyed his direction and way of thinking. It was modern. It was Cedar. I enjoyed playing the compositions that he wrote because I knew how his mind worked. It was comfortable for me to play his compositions because I liked his approach to this art form.

Cedar was a very important person in this art form. Whatever we call it. I will always treasure it and I'm glad we had the opportunity to be in each other's lives personally and to make history together.[31]

RCA Victor

In 1975, Cedar signed a two-record contract with RCA Victor. The direction of music was fusion. While Cedar had recorded some tunes that did have a commercial vibe, his work for RCA Victor was solely in this vein. During this time many jazz musicians and record companies were chasing this amplified electric sound. Many groups had success in the new style including Miles Davis, Herbie Hancock, and Chick Corea. Cedar followed suit. *Mobius* was released in 1975. The band for this album was much larger than the bands that Cedar was accustomed to playing in. The instrumentation for this 14-piece group included multiple percussionists in addition to drums, bass, guitar, trumpet, trombone, vocals, and tenor and baritone saxophones. Cedar played piano, electric piano, and synthesizers. Drummer Steve Gadd and tenor saxophonist Frank Foster were notable musicians among the group.

In 1976, Cedar recorded *Beyond Mobius*. This recording was the most commercial and mainstream as Cedar's music ever got. The record included tunes such as "Low Rider" and "Canadian Sunset." The instrumentation was expanded from the previous record to include strings and more vocalists. Cedar hired Eddie Harris and Blue Mitchell to be part of the group.

The overall reception of *Mobius and Beyond Mobius* was not as successful as RCA Victor had hoped. In a letter Cedar wrote to his mother, he expressed his disappointment as he learned he would not receive another advance before *Beyond Mobius* as he thought he was promised.[32] Cedar was also aware of criticism from other jazz musicians and critics regarding selling out. Rodney Walton recalls his thoughts of his dad's work at the time:

> Those RCA recordings were during a time when he experimented with some other musical elements. Different feels and beats, but they still had his flavor on it. I never turned my nose up at it. I was like wow, it's just dad playing "Low Rider," and Teddy Pendergrass's "Bad Luck" and stuff like that. We could dance to it. He was experimenting, but he was still himself. There was some mean soul on those records. You could always hear Cedar Walton in the middle of all of that.[33]

In interviews throughout his career, Cedar spoke about making a living as a musician. In fact, once in an interview he said, "I play the piano for money."[34] Cedar's venture into the electronic world of music is probably more accurately viewed as simply taking the work that he was offered at the time.

Cedar's time in the world of fusion was short lived. During the same period, he was under contract with RCA Victor and beginning to tour with a quartet that consisted of Clifford Jordan, Sam Jones, Billy Higgins, and Cedar as the leader. He met a European concert promoter named Wim Wigt who was very interested in promoting Cedar's group as well as recording. Cedar would have to find a way around his contract with RCA Victor.

Chapter 8

Bolivia (1975–1981):
Eastern Rebellion, the Magic Triangle, and European Touring

Cedar's contract with RCA Victor prevented him from recording as a leader for other labels. European concert promoter Wim Wigt approached Cedar to record for his new label Timeless. To skirt the name issue, Cedar came up with the name Eastern Rebellion for the group. In an interview with WBGO radio host Rhonda Hamilton, Cedar explained the name of the group and how it came to be.

RH: Tell me about Eastern Rebellion. This is a band that you founded in the mid-'70s. So it's been around for about 20 years now. Was there a particular concept behind it and does the name relate to that at all? A lot of people wonder if Eastern Rebellion refers to the East Coast or what?

CW: Part of the meaning is referring to the Eastern [East Coast] way of playing bebop. You might say an acoustic traditional approach to playing which is of course my approach. It just so happened that at the time that we had a chance to record this group, I was under contract. The group then consisted of George Coleman on tenor, the late Sam Jones on bass as well as me and Billy. We had an opportunity to record on the brand-new label from Holland named Timeless. We were the first group to record on that label. I was under contract with RCA Victor doing a bit of fusion, which I didn't have any remorse about. It was fun to me, it was like a big electronic game. You could go in there and do

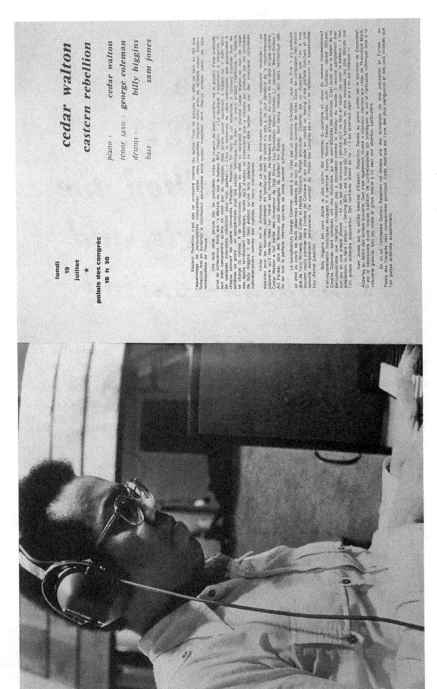

Eastern Rebellion program. *Martha Walton collection, photographer unknown.*

what you wanted to and then go later and piece it together and try to come up with something. I did some of what I considered failure; it just didn't work converting some of Thelonious Monk's and John Coltrane compositions into a so-called quote unquote fusion.

And I couldn't record again [for another label], Rhonda, so we had to get a group name. So I [was] actually rebelling against myself in a way. [laughs] We all lived in the east of the United States and Easter Rebellion [titled *Shake hands with the Devil*, came out] somewhere back in my movie going days. It was a movie that had James Cagney in it with these Irish rebels and they called themselves Easter Rebellion, so I put an "n" on it and it worked out for me. And so it's not that terribly interesting, Rhonda, but that is the story.[1]

The initial formation of the group included Clifford Jordan. This group toured Europe in 1975, but no commercial recordings were made. There are, however, video recordings of the group playing in Europe as well as an interview with Cedar and Jordan.[2]

In a TV interview filmed during this 1975 tour where both Cedar and Clifford Jordan are interviewed, the host doesn't seem to grasp the concept of the group and the sheer masterful stature of Eastern Rebellion, and is more concerned with questions about free jazz and the future of the music rather than focusing on the excellence of the group. Both Cedar and Jordan are professional in their responses, but they both seem bothered about having to field questions about a type of music they don't play. Jordan responds with levity and eventually answers "I don't know much about that,"[3] while Walton's response is the perfect balance of professionalism and truth. "Personally, I haven't had a chance to assimilate any feelings one way or the other about these things, being in the actual profession of earning a living, a livelihood through music."[4] While doing interviews for this book, many musicians made similar comments to the effect of "you either get it or you don't" in terms of Cedar's wit and musicianship. In this case, the host clearly did not.

These types of questions combined with comparisons to newer stylistic developments in jazz were something that Cedar and many of his contemporaries had to endure for most of their professional careers. From the inception of the term jazz, the music has been at least partially (if not more) shaped by critics. For many critics it is easier to simply classify Cedar and many of his peers as hard bop jazz musicians and move on. This type of classification has extended to all styles of jazz and its musicians, as well as all genres of art, for that matter. While style periods and classifications are necessary in any genre of art, it is vitally important not to overlook the stark differences between artists from the same time period. In the case of Cedar in this interview and throughout his life, there were critics who chose not to realize or completely missed that he was a world class pianist with a style completely his own. Instead, they chose to follow a new trend or agenda rather than grasp the greatness that was directly in front of them. Cedar was not one to seek the spotlight, and while he did not receive the type of critical acclaim that others did, he always had the respect from those he played with. The recordings he would go on to make with Eastern Rebellion would be revered and regarded as high art amongst musicians in the know.

In 1975, tenor saxophonist George Coleman replaced Jordan. On December 10, 1975, *Eastern Rebellion* was recorded. The recording included two Cedar originals: "Mode for Joe," which was previously recorded with Joe Henderson, and a new composition, "Bolivia." The album also included "Bittersweet" by Sam Jones, and "5/4 Thing" by George Coleman. John Coltrane's "Naima" rounded out the album.

George Coleman

Cedar and I actually met before 1975. But 1975 was the time that I joined the band Eastern Rebellion. We recorded and went on tour. That's how things began. It was a great experience. I replaced Clifford Jordan the great saxophonist and then I was replaced by Bob Berg. I might have sat in with Cedar's band during that time, Bradley's was the place for guys sitting in and playing and I used to do that quite often, so I'm sure I must have played at least once or twice with him before then. We also played a little at Boomers. That was the place we first started playing together.

Cedar was a very creative pianist. His voicings on the piano were special. He was really magnificent. Cedar had lots of positive things happening in his playing as well as other attributes like his arranging and composing. There were a lot of things that I got from him as I did from all the people I played with including Miles Davis, Max Roach, and of course Lee Morgan. I acquired a lot from each one of these people that I played with, and Cedar was very special, of course. I was in the band with some special people including Billy Higgins and Sam Jones. They were excellent musicians. I enjoyed playing with Eastern Rebellion. Great band. The first Eastern Rebellion recording is one of the all-time great CDs that we did. The first one was really nice. The ones that followed were good, too, with Bob, but the original Eastern Rebellion was the one that really highlighted Cedar's group. That was the one, I think. Others have said the same thing, too, that *that* was the real Eastern Rebellion.

We had some good times out there because of course the supporting cast was always great. Billy and Sam, they were fantastic. Sam was also a great composer. And Billy too. Billy composed some great stuff. Billy had a couple of tunes in the book that we played.

Cedar had his own special way of doing things. We never had any real conflicts. Everything we did was always togetherness. Cedar, myself, Billy, and Sam. We had a great time out there. Cedar was very witty! Yea, he was another one of those guys who was very intelligent, with a sense of humor too. Miles Davis was like that too.

I didn't stay very long with any of the groups I played with. I was with Miles a little over a year. I was with Lee Morgan less than a year. Lionel Hampton, I was with him about a year. I was with Slide Hampton's octet for about year. All the guys I worked with; I didn't stay for more than a year. People have asked me why I didn't stay longer. I don't know, that's just the way things worked out. When it was time to go, it was time to go. I enjoyed playing with all of them and especially Eastern Rebellion. That was one of my favorite bands to work with because there were a lot of creativity and good feelings there. All I had to do was lay back and blend with them, which was quite a remarkable experience. Cedar was something special.

When I was with Eastern Rebellion, we had a couple of rehearsals, nothing long or drawn out. Cedar would write out charts. We had quite a few originals in the book that we played. [Tunes like] "Voices Deep Within Me" and "Bolivia," his famous tune that guys like to play even today. We had another thing called "The Maestro" dedicated to Duke Ellington which is a fantastic tune. I put a couple of things in the book. Sam and Billy had something in the book too. We all had a tune or two in there, but Cedar was the principal composer/arranger for the group.

Cedar and I never really did sit down [and talk about the music]. I would always analyze what he wrote. I was pretty good with his stuff. His tunes weren't too difficult, but you had to concentrate on his music.

It was a little bit involved. I had the good fortune to be a part of his creativity and to play in his band. Everything was good there, man. I don't have any complaints about playing with that band. It was a good band and we enjoyed ourselves out on the road. It was like a brotherly type thing with the four of us there. We had great times.

Throughout all of the bands that I worked with; I was always able to get something from them. [Something] that would probably be invisible to the public or to certain other musicians. I always thought I acquired something great from all of the bands that I worked with and of course Cedar was one of the bands that I enjoyed working with. I was able to learn some things playing in his band. Coming into his band I knew a few things, so there wasn't anything that was too complex for me, but it was interesting because I was able to grasp a lot of the things that Cedar did. His writing was always excellent. His original concepts of music and the original tunes that he wrote were very interesting. And I enjoyed playing his music. Cedar was a special player. A special guy.[5]

George Coleman was a member in Eastern Rebellion for a little over year. Tenor saxophonist Bob Berg replaced Coleman. The group recorded its second album for Timeless titled *Eastern Rebellion 2* in 1977. Berg and the Magic Triangle (the trio of Cedar, Sam Jones and Billy Higgins, named by Clifford Jordan) were joined by trombonist and Cedar's former Messengers bandmate Curtis Fuller. This album featured all Cedar originals, including "Fantasy in D," "The Maestro," "Ojos de Rojo," "Sunday Suite," "Clockwise," and "Firm Roots."[6] With Berg, Cedar and Eastern Rebellion would record several times under the Eastern Rebellion band name and on recordings lead by Sam Jones (*Something in Common*), Billy Higgins (*Soweto, The Soldier, Once More*), as well as with Cedar as the leader.[7] Berg stayed with Cedar and Eastern Rebellion until 1983.[8] The following year, Berg would join Miles Davis. After Berg left the band, Eastern Rebellion did not record again until 1992 with tenor saxophonist Ralph Moore.

In an interview with Rhonda Hamilton on WBGO, Cedar spoke of writing for Eastern Rebellion and the time between saxophonists Bob Berg and Ralph Moore.

Any time you have a pianist like, say, in the tradition of Ellington or Monk composing for saxophones, it's going to be a little harder than, say, if he [Ralph Moore] was writing it. It's piano stuff. You need to have a certain technique that is quite special to grasp it real readily now. Ralph does that. He eats it for breakfast. Anything I might want him to do. Bob Berg before him was like that. George Coleman before him was like that. We considered a lot of horn players, but we couldn't find anybody quite like that, so we remained a trio for a while. There was an interim between Berg and Moore. When Moore came, he not only could fit in there, Rhonda, he had heard us before when he was a student at Berklee and had heard our records before. It's like he could walk in and [do it].[9]

European Touring

According to Todd Barkan, "Cedar was a trooper, he earned his first stripes in the Blakey band. The Blakey band travelled a lot. That of course was his introduction into the European jazz circuit."[10]

Concert promoter Wim Wigt worked as a concert promoter for many years prior to his work with Cedar. Wigt was very enterprising and had a shrewd business sense. Wim and his wife, Ria, worked as a team to promote jazz concerts in Europe for major artists including Johnny Griffin, Monty Alexander, Cedar, and many others. Cedar would work with Wigt from the mid-'70s through the late '90s. During this time period, Cedar would tour Europe frequently. Wigt would also found Timeless Records, a label that Cedar would record with as the leader of his group, Eastern Rebellion, as well as with the Timeless All Stars.[11]

Wim and Ria Wigt

Wim and I were introduced to Cedar around 1975 and were very impressed by his music. We were attracted by his great musicianship and quickly organized a big tour all over Europe in smaller cities and countries where U.S. jazz musicians would not normally tour. From that point on, we worked with Cedar on a yearly basis until a few years before he died.

[During this time] we booked tours for many major jazz artists during the '70s, '80s, and '90s.

Cedar was easy going and very dedicated to each performance. He breathed jazz all the way. No "bullshit." He never tried to act important. Cedar was a role model for many. These are the types of musicians we enjoyed working with.

We are so proud of the many beautiful concerts we presented with Cedar.

Eastern Rebellion Vol. 1 was our first recording on our label Timeless. It was very successful. This album was heard everywhere, and every jazz lover bought and enjoyed it.[12]

Maxine Gordon

Maxine Gordon has spent her life immersed in jazz. She worked as a road manager for Gil Evans, Wim Wigt in Europe, and Italian concert promoter and impresario Alberto Alberti. She worked as Dexter Gordon's manager before eventually marrying Gordon. Maxine Gordon worked with Cedar as a road manager on several of his tours with Wim Wigt. Initially, Cedar didn't see the necessity of a road manager for these tours and thought the position took away from his bottom line. Gordon proved her worth and the two became lifelong friends. Moving on, Cedar would occasionally consult Gordon on business matters throughout his career.

Gordon's work as road manager for Wim Wigt included guiding New York bands around Europe. "They were actually bands from Boomers with Louis Hayes, Junior Cook, Woody Shaw, Ronnie Mathews, and Stafford James,"[13] said Gordon. Cedar started touring on this circuit with Eastern Rebellion which initially consisted of Clifford Jordan, Sam Jones and Billy Higgins. George Coleman replaced Jordan in the group and they recorded shortly thereafter.

European tours under Wigt were intense. They generally consisted of six days of one-nighters with one day off a week. Gordon scheduled all the travel. She carried a book that was four or five inches thick with all the train schedules. This was a big responsibility and a necessity for jazz musicians who were in a foreign country and did not speak the language. Although most musicians grasped the need for a road manager, Cedar did not, at least at first. Maxine Gordon remembers Cedar's initial thoughts:

On the first trip I was studying the train book. We were in the dining car, and Cedar says to the table like I'm not there, "Who's paying her? Who's paying her? Are we paying her? Is this coming out of our money? We don't need her." He tried to act like he was being mean. "She doesn't know what she's doing." And it was like, "We don't need her." And Sam Jones said, "Oh yeah, we do. Shut up." He said to him, "We are always scaring people away that want to help us." And he said, "We're not going to scare her away. We're going to help her learn this." He said, "She actually likes being around jazz musicians. People don't want to be around us. They like the music, but they don't like us once they get to know us. They don't want to be around us." And he told Cedar, "Shut up." And Cedar shut up. He said, "Okay, Holmes. Okay, Holmes.[14] You're right. You're right." And I never forgot that because when Sam Jones spoke, which wasn't often, there was total silence and everyone said, "Okay, sir. Yes, sir."

I always said if I had a career, which I don't know if you call being a road manager a career, it was because of Sam standing up for me. I traveled with that band and heard Cedar play every night. This guy is so great. So great. As I got to know him and follow him, he had this joke where he'd say, "Oh, no. She's here. I have to play Bolivia." If I go someplace where he's playing, I say, "Are you going to play Bolivia?" And he was like, "Okay." So toward the end, if he saw me he'd make this joke about, "I have to play Bolivia to get it out of the way because Maxine is here and she's going to request it."[15]

The European touring schedule Wigt set up was grueling. Six nights of one nighters with one day off for a month or more were draining. On many of these trips there was a great distance in between cities. Frequently, the band would arrive just before it was time to perform with little time to even change clothes before the gig. The music, however, never suffered. The band always seemed to be able to perform at the highest level no matter the circumstances. As Cedar started to tour more as a leader, he understood the importance of keeping his band working. Wigt's ability to schedule long tours did much to cultivate the sound of Eastern Rebellion. With the band working regularly, they were truly a working band with a distinct sound that existed outside of the recording studio.

Drummers Jeff Hamilton and Kenny Washington toured with Monty Alexander and Johnny Griffin, respectively, via tours set up by Wigt. Their accounts help to paint more of a picture of what touring was like with Wigt as the promoter.

Jeff Hamilton

In fairness to Wim, we were a little hard on him because we felt like things should be a little smoother on a tour. If you're going to fly all the way to Europe, and do a month-long tour, there should be heat in the van. You shouldn't have a 14-hour ride, get out of the van and play in a school where 40 people show up. Wim was getting his feet on the ground too. Looking back on that, maybe we were all a little tough on him as far as our complaining. But at the same time, he didn't do much to correct the situation. That being said, in 2018 I would almost prefer to see 20 promoters like Wim Wigt out there right now, than some of the 25 year-old club owners who don't know how to spell Ella Fitzgerald.

Wim cared about the music. He loved the music and did it because he loved it. He wanted to make some money off of it too. And rightly so. The tours were grueling but at the same time, I was 21 years old. And I didn't have a sense of entitlement that I should be riding around in limousines and walking into 2500 seat concert halls and have the drums ready for me to sit down and play. I didn't have those expectations, so I didn't mind banging around in a rented Volkswagen van with just enough room for us and the bass and the drums if we all sat next to each other. I think it got into the music, the closeness of being on the road like that and your day-to-day travel life. It gets into what you do every night. At that time Monty [Alexander] and John [Clayton] and I were doing fifty weeks a year and I think it all contributed to what the outcome of the music was, whether it was a bad experience or a good experience.[16]

Kenny Washington

They were terrible, man. They were terrible. In those days you worked. There was a lot more work out there. Europe was the place to go because it seemed like there were companies and radio sponsoring a lot of jazz. A group could go over there and tour for six weeks.

We would go over there for six weeks and just work and work and work. One nighters. What usually would happen for me is that we'd do two weeks at Ronnie Scott's and that was alright because we were in the same place for a while, but then after that, we would be doing one nighters. The promoter, Wim Wigt, was terrible. All kinds of shit would go wrong all the time. We'd play a gig and head to the next town and the hotel wouldn't have any hotel rooms. Or the hotel rooms would be sad. We would have to wake up at 5 in the morning to leave for the next gig after playing until 1 or 2 in the morning. On a particular day, you might have two planes to catch, maybe three. And when you get to the final destination, nobody would be there to pick you up.

Now you're waiting on these people to pick you up and you'd be lucky if you have a telephone number for them. There were no cell phones. There was always a language barrier. Always a problem. When they finally come and pick you up, you're on their time. They wanted to take you straight to the joint to play without eating or showering. This would happen continuously.

Wim Vigt would book you at all these different places, but the people in these different cities weren't taking care of business either. It wasn't always like that, but you could bet that 50% of the time something would happen.

On one tour I was on a private plane sitting copilot and Johnny Griffin and Ronnie Mathews were sitting in the back. This pilot had the manual of how to fly the plane on one leg and he had the flight plan with a rubber band wrapped around the other leg so it wouldn't fall off. After we landed, the pilot was supposed to come back and get Ray Drummond, but when we landed, the pilot said the plane was unfit to fly back to Oslo. So Ray had to just sit in the airport and wait. He didn't know what was happening. Somehow or another they got word to him and he stayed in a hotel that night and we met up the next day. There was always stuff happening. Those were terrible tours. That's why I can't stand Europe to this day.

Johnny Griffin is the one that helped Wim Wight get into the business of jazz, and he treated Griff like shit. Wim Wight was the only game in town. So all these great musicians like Junior Cook, Bill Hardman, Stan Getz, George Adams, and Don Pullen had to deal with him.

Each day was a different adventure. The hotels were never right, but the thing that bothered and amazed me is that the musicians would get up on the bandstand and play their asses off every night. One of the things about Johnny Griffin and Cedar and all of them is that no matter what happened, when it's time to play, it's time to hit. No one cares about what you had to do to get there. Boom. You played your best. That's what it was like, and Cedar and Billy and either Sam Jones or David Williams, they were there doing the same thing.[17]

Alberto Alberti

Italian Alberto Alberti was an impresario and record producer who was responsible for some of the largest jazz festivals in the world. In the late '50s Alberti and Antonio Foresti founded the Bologna Jazz Festival. The festival hosted many of the most well-known U.S. jazz musicians including Dexter Gordon, Art Blakey, Charles Mingus and Cedar. In 1973, Alberti along with Carlo Pagnotta founded the Umbria Jazz Festival, which hosted artists such as Miles Davis, Ella Fitzgerald, and Sarah Vaughn. Walton was a regular fixture in this festival as well. In the '70s Alberti managed many U.S. artists touring in Europe.[18] Todd Barkan recalls:

> Cedar struck up a profound friendship not only with me but a guy in Italy named Alberto Alberti. He used to joke with me in his inimitable Cedar Walton fashion that he was becoming an honorary Italian citizen. He would say, "just call me Cedartio Waltoni" because he worked so much in Bergamo and Bologna and Palermo and Roma and Ancona and Bari and Milan and Sardinia. He worked in Italy scores of times.[19]

David Williams

> We played in Italy all the time, maybe even four or five times a year. The promoter, Alberto Alberti, had a great passion for the music and he loved us. In Italy we were treated like royalty. [20]

Joe Farnsworth

> Cedar loved Italy. Our friend Alberto Alberti—they called him [Cedar] Generali. He always got a kick out that because there was a bank called the Generali. And so that always made him very excited. He loved dinner time. He loved sitting at the table eating with his bandmates and just laughing. He'd be the same guy with you and me as the President of the United States. There would be no change. Nothing like "well I gotta impress this guy." He was very comfortable in his skin. He loved being around the guys whether you were a musician or just a fan. There was one particular restaurant in Bologna with a waiter there who loved Cedar, but Cedar didn't know he was a musician. He just thought he was an Italian waiter. Cedar would come in and the waiter would say, "Oh Generali!" and he'd have a little reservation sheet and a back table reserved. Cedar was so impressed by that. We had to go there for lunch and dinner just to hear "Oh Generali is here." He loved it![21]

In the mid-'70s, Alberti started a record company, Red Records, which recorded many U.S. Jazz artists including Joe Henderson, Sam Rivers, and Cedar. Cedar recorded six albums as a leader for Alberti and Red Records. Three trio records titled *The Trio* (Vol.1–3), a solo piano album *Blues for Myself*, a duo record with David Williams titled *Duo,* and a quintet record with Curtis Fuller, Bob Berg, David Williams, and Billy Higgins titled *Cedar's Blues.*[22]

Cedar and Alberti were friends and worked together from the '60s until Alberti's death in 2006. Cedar honored his Italian friend with compositions such as "Blues for Alberto," and "Back to Bologna."

The Magic Triangle

Clifford Jordan called the rhythm section of Sam Jones, Billy Higgins, and Cedar the Magic Triangle. In the '70s, Jordan recorded with the Magic Triangle frequently. Starting in 1975, a series of records on the Steeplechase label were released as *Clifford Jordan and the Magic Triangle*. There were three volumes of *Clifford Jordan and The Magic Triangle*, followed by *Firm Roots*, and the *Highest Mountain*, all recorded in 1975.[23] The output of recordings from the group during this time period represents some of the best straight-ahead jazz recorded during this era. Although not marketed as The Magic Triangle, a fan favorite Clifford Jordan album from 1975 is *Night of the Mark VII*. This was a live recording by Jordan and the Magic Triangle in Paris, France, and is an outstanding example of hard swinging blues-based music and the intimate support this unit created here and on so many recordings.

The Magic Triangle played on many albums as part of Eastern Rebellion, as a trio, and to back other artists. In most cases, the trio was not listed as The Magic Triangle on recordings and only given credit as individuals. When listening to the trio play however, it's easy to understand how they got the name. The group recorded the album *Pitt Inn* in 1974 (a favorite Cedar trio album by many) and backed artists including Art Farmer, Jackie McLean, and James Spaulding. They also recorded *Something in Common* for Sam Jones's record date in 1977 which featured trumpeter Blue Mitchell, trombonist Slide Hampton, and tenor saxophonist Bob Berg.[24]

Although not listed as The Magic Triangle, the group's final recordings were a set of three records for the Steeplechase label in 1977. This group was essentially the new formation of Eastern Rebellion with tenor saxophonist Bob Berg replacing George Coleman. The records are titled *First Set*, *Second Set*, and *Third Set*. The band was recorded live at Montmartre in Copenhagen, Denmark. The Magic Triangle was a special rhythm section that left an indelible mark on jazz and continues to influence jazz rhythm section players to this day.

Kenny Barron, Jeff Hamilton, Christian McBride, and Eric Reed remember the Magic Triangle and its impact on the music:

Kenny Barron

That trio was incredible. One time I actually got to play with Billy and Sam together. That was magic. We played at a place called Boomers. I was subbing for Cedar. He was out of town for a week. Playing with the two of them was like driving a Cadillac or Rolls Royce for me. It was exciting. The thing I loved about playing with Billy was his attitude. Jimmy Heath wrote a song about Billy called "Smiling Billy." He just exuberated. There was so much joy there it was infectious. The simplest thing to say is to say that they swung so hard. That's what it was. Sometimes bass players and drummers don't hook up. Billy and Sam definitely hooked up. For me it's all about the drummer's cymbal beat and Billy had that. Sam Jones had such a strong feeling on the bass. Combine that with Billy's sense of time and dancing cymbal beat, you can't get much better than that.[25]

Jeff Hamilton

Knowing Sam Jones' playing, and Billy's before I discovered Cedar, I focused on them a lot when I heard that trio at first. And I think Sam Jones is one of my favorite bass players of all time that I never got to play with. We all play our personalities in jazz. Sam was a gentleman and a character from what I understand. Upstanding, no nonsense, take care of business, sense of humor. All of that rolled into Sam Jones. And I heard that from his playing. I heard strength in his walking, I loved his baselines. I loved him with Oscar Peterson, the way he played with Oscar and his strength with Oscar. Without fighting Oscar, he was just staying at home almost saying, "I need to be here, and you go where you're going to go but I'll be here when you want to come back home," without digging his heels in and being stubborn.[26]

Christian McBride

If you want talk about the Coltrane Quartet or the Miles Band of the sixties or some of the others, Miles, or say the Mingus Band, the unique, really distinctive sounding rhythm sections and combinations of players. I think Billy Higgins's type snare drum and his whole concept of time was so unique and so open as well as being right on the money. I think Cedar was a good complement to that and Sam Jones's big fat bass sound. There was so much space within that band and yet so much going on at the same time. I think that influenced everybody. Cedar's tunes are very specific and playing with that band, you have to go with the flow a lot of the time. Cedar was the sort of player that also kind of wanted people to push little bit, to instigate rather than just coast and follow. He wanted you to lead as a saxophone player, in a way.

I heard that out of Sam, the strength. If there's one word I would say, it would be the strength of Sam Jones. The subtle strength of Sam Jones. And then Billy being able to float over that with his ride cymbal beat and not demand with rim shots or cymbal crashes, where it should go. There was this whole subtlety within the group that was so beautiful that Cedar felt so comfortable playing with that. He had the pillar of strength in Sam, and he had a drummer that could go any direction. And I think that's why they were so compatible.

When you get a trio that good, everybody's contributing to the music. And there's one player that's playing most of the lead part in this act, but it's the whole cast that's making that solo work. And the people who loved playing with that trio, I felt played better with that trio than they did with their own settings that they would choose. That trio would make them play differently. I never looked at it as backing a soloist. I think all great trios are like that. You're all in it together and yes there is a person soloing, but that soloist isn't going to be good without all of the people in the group contributing to that solo.[27]

Cedar and Milt Jackson, 1996. *Martha Walton collection.*

(l to r center) Milt Jackson, Mickey Roker, Cedar, and Ray Brown.
Martha Walton collection.

Eric Reed

The Cedar Walton rhythm section with Sam Jones and Billy Higgins, affectionately known as the Magic Triangle, had supported many saxophone and horn players on a lot of records. As a result, their sound and feeling became infectious. It became the template for rhythm section support. I'm not sure I can put into exact words what they did, but I know whatever it was they were doing, they did it together. They all shared the same pulse. There's this notion or idea that when women are pregnant, they start to feel things the same way in their body. Their hormones all flow the same way. Art is no different. We connect, not just temporally but spiritually, and we don't have to be playing the exact same thing, but the pulse has to be in the same wavelength. When you listen to those handful of records that would have featured Ray Brown and Elvin Jones, they did not have the same approach toward playing time. Ray's beat tended to lean a little forward whereas Elvin's tended to fall a little back, but they still had the same pulse. Cedar and Sam and Billy in particular, were an interesting trio because it was just right. Everything they played together, everything matched. The groove was intense. They had simpatico ideas, too.[28]

Bassist Sam Jones died in 1981. His death was a significant loss to the jazz community. From his work with Horace Silver and Oscar Peterson to the amazing swinging grooves he created with Louis Hayes and Billy Higgins, Sam Jones was irreplaceable.

Chapter 9

The House on Maple Street (1970–1980): *Mary Parrish and Naisha Walton*

In the early '70s, Cedar and Ida divorced. He connected with Mary Parrish. They had a daughter, Naisha who was born in 1975. Naisha began studying piano, other instruments, and art forms at age 3. She regularly traveled with Cedar on gigs in New York, around the United States and abroad. Naisha describes her mother Mary, father Cedar, and what life was like during her childhood.

Naisha Walton

You don't really recognize that living with a world class musician is anything out of the ordinary or special as you're living it, but hindsight is usually 20/20. Looking back, it was a wonderful time. I had a wonderful a childhood. My dad and my mom made sure that I had every opportunity I could have. They were just wonderful people in and of themselves. Mom and Dad came together in the early '70s. I'm not sure exactly how they met, but I have hunch that it was through a mutual friend, Alice Miller, who was very present in the New York jazz scene at that time. What's interesting is that Alice's circle of friends included Cedra, Rodney, and Carl's mom, Ida. They hung out in the same circles of musicians' girlfriends and wives with the purpose of showing support to the musicians and supporting one another. These were friends and other people these women could talk to, hang out with as well as go to clubs and hear people with. My mom was in Brooklyn at that time. Cedar and mom met and had their courting stage in Brooklyn. My dad's tune "House on Maple Street"—that was my mom's house. They did their best to make a good life together.

My mother, Mary Parrish, was a bit of a renaissance woman. She came from the South and moved to New York as a teenager, just like dad. I'm fairly sure they cherished this as something in common. They were first generation New Yorkers just trying to make it. She did some modeling. She was in communications and did some broadcasting as well as DJing. She was also involved in local politics, specifically for the Manhattan borough district. She was also involved with the GOP back then. She attended the Republican National Convention and stayed in Dallas with my dad's parents. This might have been 1975 or 1976. I was a baby, just born. She was involved with Richard Nixon's campaign as well as with a group called the Freedom Republicans which modeled their approach to Republicanism after Abraham Lincoln's. This was apparently the original Republican party that included blacks and whites. Later, she got involved with real estate. She had a property management company throughout the 1990s–2000s called J.M. Parrish Realty in Bed-Stuy.

Once they [Cedar and Mary] got together, they lived in their apartment in lower Manhattan and that's when I came around. This was in 1975. She was a stay-at home mom, and he was out on the road a whole lot. In fact, he was in Germany when I was born. He just kept at it, and she was there supporting and helping me grow up and getting me into schools and things. It was always a fun time when he came home. As a kid it was a great time of joy to hear my dad's whistle and walk while coming down the hallway of our apartment building. I remember thinking "Here comes Dad! Dad's home!" He would have just come from somewhere with stories of where he'd been. I remember the little gifts and trinkets and things from wherever he'd been. Of course, he'd bring t-shirts and posters that he would occasionally frame from whatever festival he was in.

I remember vaguely from my own memory but certainly from what Mom and Dad told me that one day Mom was getting me ready for school. I was still in the single digits, maybe around five or six years old, and she was in the kitchen that morning getting my breakfast together. And there's Dad and Art Blakey sitting there. They'd been up all night and they're still talking shop and just having a good time. Art was definitely one of Dad's mentors. Art turned over and said, looking at Mom and me, "you've got a beautiful family there, Walton." And of course, like I said, at the time that was nothing out of the ordinary.

Our apartment wasn't a hangout, but Dad did have his good friends and colleagues over to the point that it was not out of the ordinary to see them there. Sam Jones would be at the house. Billy [Higgins] of course was at the house all the time. He was one of my favorites. I really grew to love him. He was really great with kids. He'd always be joking, putting the cymbal on his head. I loved him dearly. He was like an uncle to me. This apartment I mentioned in lower Manhattan was actually an apartment that Dad and Clifford Jordan shared before Cliff moved out once he found his wife. That was sort of the bachelor pad before Mom moved in and I came around. It was a nice, large, three-bedroom apartment with a spacious living room out front with a great stereo. We had so many LPs. I just remember music playing all the time. All the time. This was when stereos had those three-foot-high speakers with a huge console with a big, brushed aluminum circular dial. I remember very clearly how it would light up. We'd have all of the other lights in the room off and just the stereo lights on. It was just a beautiful, gorgeous analog sound with beautiful records playing all of the time whether it was his albums or folks he was checking out or preparing to play with. Just music. Music all the time. That's how I grew up.

Sam Jones was the first bass player I heard. That was bass. That was just life. Bob Berg and Eastern Rebellion, that was the sound when I came into the world. Those were the sounds I was hearing in the womb. These guys would be over at the house, or I'd see them on T.V. and say, "Oh, there's Dad, they're looking good, they're playing well." It was that kind of thing for the first eight years of my life. That's when my parents decided to split. My mom moved out and my dad stayed there. For my sake, I would continue to spend time pretty equally with both of them. Spending time with Dad entailed going to the clubs and traveling with him. I remember being a little girl going here and there to the clubs or to rehearsals or to people's houses. He had business to take care of so he would take me along. I would be hanging out with whatever kinds of kids or people were around while he did whatever he needed to do. Whether it was a recording session or an outdoor concert, that would be hanging out with Dad. That's what that meant. I remember my first trip to Paris was going with him on tour. I was twelve. We went to England too on that trip. We didn't do too many overseas things because I was in school. We did go to quite a few places here in the city and in the area. I remember a trip out to Telluride when their jazz festival was pretty new and also to California as well as some time in Chicago. I was his traveling buddy at times. We were very close. It was just fun. I remember a lot of Jazzmobiles—when he played, I'd be up on stage with him sitting behind the rig playing my video game while he was working. I grew up with a lot of wonderful music and wonderful people.

He [Cedar] wasn't the kind of guy to discuss certain things explicitly. They would just be there with him—whatever he was working out. He wouldn't come out and say, "Hey I'm upset." It was a little more subtle. His approach was always to work it out so he could move on and keep on. In terms of discussing his work in other ways, I would be there when he was putting tours together, making calls, sending faxes, or working out the personnel for a recording or tour.

Dad lived and breathed music. He lived and breathed music. Honestly. It was just who he was. Coming into the world, I just thought that's how life was. I didn't really have contact with, for example, Rock and Roll or Rap when they came out. Maybe a little R&B. Dad and Billy respected groups like Earth Wind and Fire. The corporate world and 9–5 jobs weren't in our sphere. Our world was just jazz. Good music. Dad had a deep respect for Classical music too. The way I formed as a person on a human development kind of level was maturing through what I heard. Not just the notes, but everything beyond the notes. That was just living and breathing. The way you could care for a person—for example, if it was known that someone's wife had just passed—someone either in the community or one of the musicians themselves. You could hear a certain care in the music that people were extending to that person. Or if it was somebody's birthday, you could hear a quote come up in someone's solo. It was always so tastefully done, just a suggestion. That made for a community. That's when I started to play for myself. I started to seek out that kind of relationship, that kind of vibe and community in the music.

As far as the specific connection Dad and Billy had, it was just a good connection on many levels for those guys or else they wouldn't have been with each other so long. There are so many other pianists and drummers out there, but their connection was just a natural fit. I grew up thinking this was just music. This was just life for me. What I miss the most is being in a small club and listening to all of the inner conversations that happened within the music between the two of them. For many, many times, I was there for multi-night gigs. I got to see them getting into the music and hearing how it evolved. I could hear, for example, the fun they had that day at lunch. Those kinds of experiences would bubble over into the music. Other things like a conversation at the hotel or just a day apart from each other would affect the music. I loved seeing how the tunes would progress over the course of the week and how the conversation would grow deeper and richer. It was beautiful. I loved it.

Now that I'm a little bit older and because I've had those experiences, I have to come to realize that everyone didn't have the experience I did.

Mary Parrish as DJ. *Naisha Walton collection.*

Naisha Walton graduation, (l to r) Mary Parrish, Naisha, and Cedar.
Naisha Walton collection.

Naisha and Cedar at Ronnie Scott's jazz club, 1995.
Martha Walton collection.

(l to r) Carl Walton, Cedar, and Naisha. *Naisha Walton collection.*

Naisha and Cedar at the Kennedy Center, 2010.
Naisha Walton collection.

Everyone didn't come to music that way. I have to respect that, but also say, there is such a rich heritage that we can tap into and promote and share as musicians. We can't lose that.

Cedar and Mary went separate ways 1983. The next decade would see Cedar moving to Los Angeles. He would continue to record and tour frequently both as leader of Eastern Rebellion, under his own name, and as a sideman.

Chapter 10

Ironclad (1980–2000): *New Friends and the Move to LA*

B assist Sam Jones died in 1981. The Magic Triangle was no more. That trio had played together countless time in a variety of settings. Much of the genius of this group was due to the fluidity and familiarity of the unit. Each trio member was masterful at supporting the music. There was an attitude of selflessness with a focus on making the music swing and supporting each soloist. After Jones's death, Cedar would continue to work with bassists who shared similar ideals with regards to music. Moving forward, he would collaborate with bassists Ron Carter, Buster Williams, and David Williams, who would eventually become a member Eastern Rebellion and tour and record regularly with Cedar until Cedar's death.

David Williams

Sam Jones introduced bassist David Williams to Cedar. According to Williams in an interview with Ethan Iverson, Sam Jones told Cedar, "Whenever I can't do the gig, call him."[1] Cedar and Williams first played together at Boomers in the late '70s and Williams would stop by often after his introduction from Jones. Williams was a natural fit playing with Cedar and Billy Higgins. When Williams started playing with group, he knew most of Cedar's music or at least thought he did. "When I joined the band, I thought I knew all his music," said Williams. "Then I found out I didn't.[2] "Cedar and Billy would just start playing together, ignoring me at first, but I'd have it by the third or fourth chorus."[3] Williams first recorded with Cedar on a live recording, *Reliving the Moment,*[4] at the Keystone Korner in San Francisco which was recorded over a multiple night run at the end of 1977 and the beginning of 1978. From this point on he regularly toured and recorded with Cedar for the rest of Cedar's life. "In that band with Cedar and Billy, we loved each other. Nothing was offensive, it was just three spirits all about the music. We could laugh at ourselves too,"[5] said Williams. During the '80s and '90s, it was common for Cedar to be on tour for two to three months at a time.

Buster Williams

The first recorded meeting of Cedar and Buster Williams was in 1969 on Stanley Turrentine's recording *Another Story.*[6] The two recorded together again in 1972 on tenor saxophonist Dexter Gordon's album *Generation,* that along with Cedar, Gordon, and Williams featured Freddie Hubbard and Billy Higgins.[7] Cedar and Williams collaborated more frequently starting in the '80s. Williams was also part of the Timeless All Stars which was a group that recorded for the Dutch label Timeless under Wim Wigt. The group included Curtis Fuller (trombone), Harold Land (tenor saxophone), Bobby Hutcherson (vibraphone), Cedar, Williams, and Billy Higgins. Cedar would assume much of the arranging duties for this group. In addition to the Timeless All Stars, Cedar and Williams would work together on many recordings backing artists including Houston Person, Junior Cook, Art Farmer, Benny Golson, Milt Jackson, and many others. Buster Williams reflects on his friendship with Cedar:

> Cedar was a great player. He was a very diplomatic guy. He believed in fairness and you could glean that from his conversation and the way he treated you on the bandstand as well as on the road. And he knew how to keep a band working. I was always impressed with the way he handled things. He knew how to put jobs together to really make a good money-making week. He was always writing great music. It was never a bore or the same old thing when you worked with him from one gig to the next.

Cedar played in many kinds of configurations. I really preferred him in trio playing. Because he was great like Ahmad Jamal. Cedar Walton was a master of the trio. Playing with him in the trio setting allowed so much freedom. The kind of chords and his mastery of harmonization was just perfect for me because it always opened up my ears. I could play the notes that I liked. And the notes that I liked would fit what he was doing.

He would call me every now and then and say, "Ok Buster, I am in need of my annual Buster fix" or [laughing] something like that. He had a way. He knew when to comp. When to not comp. He never overplayed. He was always adding to whatever situation he was in. He knew how to build his solo. There was always a starting point, a middle point, and an ending point. And from the start to the ending, wow, you felt like you were really involved in a journey. It was great.

Cedar could have been a stand-up comedian. You know? Without any effort he was funny. He was funny in his retort. He was funny in his delivery. Many things that Cedar would say became standards for us. Every now and then Cedar would call me and say, "Sir Williams, you know he'd go into his British accent. Sir Williams, I'm in need of your expertise. I'm in need of what only you can do." [laughing] So you know the conversation would be a conversation between a British commoner and a British lord. [laughing] I [Buster] was always the commoner and he [Cedar] was always the lord. [laughing]. He was a funny guy. On the bandstand he was a master. Off the bandstand he was a diplomat. He knew how to talk to people, and he never made anyone uncomfortable. He never made me uncomfortable in any way.

Billy and Cedar had a marriage. When Billy died, I really watched Cedar because I knew of their long Siamese kind of connection relationship. I was really concerned with how Cedar was going to take it. Cedar was a realist. I was also with him when his mother died. He loved his mother and was constantly going down to Dallas to visit her. When she was getting older and sickly, he was taking care of her. When she passed away, I saw him take it in such great stride. And the same thing with Billy. Part of living is accepting dying. And I learned from Cedar how to create value in the moment but not get caught up in the moment. How to understand that everything is constantly moving and it's our responsibility to move with this constant state of flux. And with everything there was a sense of humor. He could be very serious. Cedar could be very serious and at times would say something to me that I knew was something for me to store away. This is something in the step ladder of my growth. I knew when to accept what he said as levity and when to accept what he said as a serious learning moment.

At times, Cedar could also be short tempered. One night we had finished working at the Vanguard and Cedar was driving me home with my bass. My wife and I just had our first child and she had called me after work and told me to stop at the store and bring home some toilet paper. I told Cedar, "Cedar we gotta stop at the store, I gotta pick up some toilet paper." At this time, we were somewhere near Bradley's and Cedar didn't say anything. He just drove up to Bradley's and stopped and kept the car running and ran into Bradley's and came out and threw me a roll of toilet paper. [laughing] He said, "Here, here's your toilet paper!" That was Cedar Walton. [laughing]

I can't say, we ever sat and talked about where he was coming from, but you could hear it. He had total respect for all of the giants that went before us. He loved Tommy Flanagan. He loved Hank Jones. He loved Wynton Kelly. He was always listening to Herbie Hancock's development. Cedar was the kind of guy that those who he listened to listened to him. When you hear people coming into their own and you talk to them, they never fail to mention the effect that Cedar Walton had on them. I can't talk enough about the fluency in his playing. I really like players who know how to turn the corner. In other words, how to build on each chorus. How to build momentum. That was Cedar Walton.

This music is built on the mentor-disciple relationship. It has from its inception right on up until now. Anyone who misses that opportunity or doesn't understand that mentor-disciple relationship as being the one essential relationship that one should have to this music if he or she really wants to learn the language correctly so that one can move forward in creating an addition by the fact that they are in this present world and want to play this music. Anyone who misses the opportunity to really accomplish that mission or to fulfill the potential that they have as one who wants to carry on the legacy of this great art form. And if the case is that one really wants to not miss anything, then listening to Cedar Walton's performances and learning how to play Cedar Walton's compositions is essential. I would say to any young musician, not just pianists, don't let Cedar Walton pass you by. Stop. Absorb and learn.

I made quite a few recordings with Cedar, and I'd have a hard time saying which one is my favorite. I hope everyone really delves into his discography and finds gems that exist there.[8]

Ron Carter

Bassist Ron Carter and Cedar had known each other since Cedar came back to New York City after his time in the Army. They first recorded together on Eddie Harris's *The In Sound* in 1965. The two would find themselves in recording sessions backing artists including Milt Jackson, Joe Henderson, Hank Mobley, and many others. Beginning in the '80s, Cedar and Carter began collaborating more regularly, each recording with the other as the leader. In 1981, Carter and Cedar recorded a duo album *Heart & Soul* on the Timeless record label.

In 1983, Cedar and Carter recorded *The All-American Trio* along with drummer Jack DeJohnette. Cedar contributed two originals, "Ironclad" and "Rubberman," to the date. Both Carter and DeJohnette have been part of some of the greatest jazz rhythm sections in the history of the music. Rhythm sections that were at times different than the esthetic that Cedar and the Magic Triangle had created but equally masterful. On this date, as with all of Cedar's trio recordings, he shows his ability to play with anyone and deal with the music at peak level while still sounding like himself. Throughout the recording, Cedar, Carter, and DeJohnette are always serving the music. The trio came together to create an excellent recording where the underpinning for Cedar is slightly different than what listeners are accustomed to when it comes to Cedar. One such example is Ron Carter's tune "A Slight Smile." DeJohnette and Carter shape the straight eighths ballad in a way that prompts Cedar to respond masterfully in the setting, taking what the rhythm section gives while conjuring lyrical sustained lines that are perfect for the moment.

One of the most unassuming aspects of Cedar's trio playing is his ability to seamlessly fit into any group and deftly handle the requirements of a musical situation. In the case of *The All-American Trio*, Cedar, while always sounding like himself, was seemingly sparked by much of DeJohnette's colors and rhythmic interjections and the lack of Carter's walking bass lines traded for melodic responses and pedals in some of the slower tunes. This type of playing was in stark contrast to the 1977 Ray Brown trio recording *Something for Lester,* where Cedar was very much the glue for Brown and drummer Elvin Jones.

For many, the trio work with Cedar, Ron Carter, and Billy Higgins was legendary in the New York jazz scene. The group worked regularly at Sweet Basil. The trio recorded two live albums there titled *St. Thomas* and *My Funny Valentine* from sets on February 15, 1991.[9] The trio also recorded a DVD performance, *Ron Carter & Art Farmer Live at Sweet Basil*, with trumpeter Art Farmer which also included interviews with the band. According to Carter, Cedar would arrive about 10 minutes before the set was to start. It was a quirk that took some getting used to for Carter, and eventually, he did. Cedar was never one to get to any gig too early.[10] When he showed up however, he was ready to play. Ron Carter recalls his experience working with Cedar at Sweet Basil:

Every night we'd play kind of the same library which was fine with me because we knew so many tunes individually. It was nice to go to work knowing that you got these tunes to worry about. [laughs] Not 104 possibilities. It was interesting to me how Cedar would bring in a slightly different arrangement of a song for the night. We'd play "My Funny Valentine," a couple of Cedar's tunes, a couple of blues'. The arrangements, as familiar as they were to the audience, were different enough that Cedar would bring two of them every night. For me it was a challenge "Can I keep up with this guy?" Can I have him not just bring stuff to the arrangement, but is he flexible enough to let me bring my stuff to the arrangement? And one of the fun parts was that he and I would exchange musical comments as to how a tune could also work from this point of view or from that point of view. For me it was a matter of can I meet his challenge every night.

He was living out in Brooklyn, and I was living in Manhattan and going to school at the time. I was already working so my chances of spending quality and quantity time off the bandstand were pretty slim because I was always doing something else. In the course of the night on those gigs we would talk about music and the guys we played with. What's the best key for this tune, stuff like that. During the course of the night when we had three sets and there was a half hour or forty-five minutes between sets depending on the night, I would use this time to poke around his concepts and see how much I could learn from this twenty minutes to half hour or whatever the break time would be between sets to apply to the next set. I was in the classroom all the time.

At the time when he was with us, anyone who played the Cedar Walton songbook would have a difficult time playing something other than what Cedar meant for the tune to sound like. And I appreciated that it put those guys into a different song and different place. They couldn't always play their old tune. When you compared their own songs with Cedar's songs, they generally couldn't hold up to them.

Cedar's reputation was like Tommy Flanagan, a pretty dry humored guy. And if his humor was as dry as Tommy's, I'd need a glass of water to talk to this guy 'cause the air will be dried out by his jokes.

Cedar loved sports. He was a real baseball fan. I think if people knew his love for sports, they would love him for some reason other than writing great tunes and being a wonderful soloist.

The other thing that kind of escaped people's awareness was how good of an accompanist he was. He's kind of like Monk. He'd play part of the melody as part of his accompanying background to wherever the soloist was. I always appreciated and admired his ability to find something in the tune that he could transfer to a background for the soloist. That was an incredible trait and unfortunately, most piano players have kind of overlooked that part of his playing.

We did a duo record, *Heart & Soul*, that everyone has fallen in love with. Especially in Japan. When I go to Japan, someone will almost always come up to me with a Cedar Walton/Ron Carter *Heart & Soul* record and ask me to sign it for them. We did a DVD with Art Farmer that is really precious to me. Art sounds of course as good as Art Farmer ever sounded. And to have Cedar on the bandstand comping behind Art's solos is really meaningful to me.[11]

Moving to Los Angeles

Starting in the mid-'70s Cedar began splitting time living in both LA and New York City. He would continue living bi-coastally until the mid-'80s when he would live primarily in LA for the next 10 years. RCA Victor was based in LA. Cedar began spending more time there fulfilling his record contract that produced *Mobius* and *Beyond Mobius*. Cedar was also constantly operating to set up of work for himself all over the world. In an interview with Richard Schein, Cedar said, "It's not a given that you stay active in the music business. I'm so busy right now, there's no time to play, to relax by myself at the piano. That's why I can't wait to get back to Los Angeles."[12] In LA, Cedar made friends and cultivated relationships that would last a lifetime and were essential to his continued presence as a regularly touring musician in the States. One of the most interesting aspects when researching Cedar's move from NY to LA and back to NY was how many people thought he lived in LA long before he actually moved there. This is in large part to how present Cedar was on whatever music scene he was in. Not only did he perform, but he also attended the gigs of other musicians frequently.

Todd Barkan

One such friendship was with Todd Barkan, club owner of the Keystone Korner in San Francisco. Cedar would play at the club regularly under his own name and as a sideman. He would play on several recordings made from live performances at the Keystone Korner including *Reliving the Moment* and *Charmed Circle*, which were released posthumously, as well as with the Timeless All Stars on *It's Timeless*.[13] Cedar and Barkan would work regularly together until Cedar's death. Barkan owned and operated the Keystone Korner starting in 1972 until its closing in 1983. Following the closure, Barkan continued his life's work in jazz managing Yoshi's in the early '90s followed by producing recordings for nearly all of the major jazz labels. He produced recordings for Cedar on High Note, Venus, and the 32 Records label where he served as the head of the jazz label. Barkan worked as director of Dizzy's Club Coca Cola at Jazz at Lincoln Center from 2001 to 2012. Cedar was booked regularly at Dizzy's and held a two-week residency in the summer most years. Barkan spoke about their lifelong musical association and friendship:

> To go back to the earliest days, we were introduced as so many wonderful things in my life have happened by Rahsaan Roland Kirk. I met Rahsaan at nine years old. Rahsaan introduced me to Cedar when I was in my teens. That would have been in the '60s. I met Cedar in New York.
> My friendship with Cedar really developed in earnest and flowered when he moved to Los Angeles in the early '70s. Our friendship developed when he began working at the Keystone Korner. Cedar become a very important part of the Keystone Korner and the Keystone Korner became a very important part of his life in the mid-'70s. He started to bring his band there and was also part of all-star configurations that I was putting together. In the early '70s, he would bring a quartet in with Billy Higgins, Sam Jones, and George Coleman. Then another band with Billy, David Williams, and Bob Berg.
> I think Cedar had played one engagement at the El Matador in San Francisco, prior to Keystone and then played for me for the next 11 years after I opened in 1972. Working with Cedar during this time afforded us the opportunity to get to know each other. There's a song by James Taylor, "The Secret of Life is Enjoying the Passage of Time."

One of the real important components of my friendship with Cedar and his with me was that we really enjoyed each other's company. That's very, very critical in enduring and productive friendships. Not only did we help each other, I helped by giving him multiple opportunities to play in the Bay Area over the years and then subsequently at Dizzy's at Jazz at Lincoln Center. Aside from that, we just enjoyed working together both on a personal and professional level.

Cedar was old school. He was very much like Lou Donaldson. Cedar Walton created his own booking circuitry and Keystone Korner was part of that circuitry. Thank God, because that formed the real foundations of my relationship with Cedar, which was occasioned a lot by the fact that he was living in Los Angeles. He could route me into his travels in and out of his domicile down there. Cedar did a lot of his own booking and that was part of his rugged individualism as a musician. He shared something very interesting with me. That practice of booking his own gigs really happened a lot per force and necessity because there was no agent.

After he was with Blakey and Jazz Messengers, he just took the bull by the horns and started booking himself. But he also didn't stand on ceremony and took bookings if agents or artists would suggest them. He was open to offers from managers and agents. He just was a very self-reliant individual. As so many things in our music, necessity is the mother of invention. He became his own booking agent both because of his self-reliant nature and the brutal realities of our time and era that he found himself in. Post Blakey, he was into the '60s by then, the ascendant time of Rock and Roll. As a result, he had to rustle up his own gigs because there was no agent or manager offering to handle him either. He made it work on his own and Keystone Korner was a vital part of that development. I was one of the anchors of that period of Cedar's life in terms of his journeys.

One of my most endearing and enduring memories of Cedar Walton is that we talked at least a time or two a week even when we weren't working together. Sometimes every day. Sometimes now when the phones rings, I even think, "Wow, I wish that was Cedar calling." He would call up and say, "Lord Barkan, are you following the contest?" There would be a sporting event, invariably a Yankee game. Or he would call right before a great movie like an Alec Guinness movie or a Richard Burton film. Any film that made glorious use of the English language. Cedar was a grandiloquent speaker in both the language of jazz and in the English language.

Cedar followed the mantra of Duke Ellington, which we never discussed, but I felt he was the living embodiment of what Duke said actually one time in my presence. Duke Ellington said, "I have a secret, I get a 10% commission in joy." Cedar got 10%, he might have even got 15% because he took inordinate joy out of simple things like a turn of phrase or a play on words. Cedar and Curtis Fuller to his ever loving and ever living credit were part of a whole fraternity of wordsmiths and glorious punsters. Their delight in language was part and parcel of their delight in music. They spoke the language of jazz and the Queen's English with equal facility and aplomb and delight. Curtis used to call Cedar "Mein Comp" which is a play on words, obviously, off the book Hitler wrote called *Mein Kampf*. Hitler spelled his "Kampf" and Curtis spelled his "Comp" like I'm comping for you. As in I know how to comp for this guy. There was never a greater comper than Cedar Walton. He was a magnificent comper. Nobody comped better. Kenny Barron, Hank Jones, Cedar Walton. They were the most magnificent compers of all. There were so sensitive, but they never gave up their own identity musically. They gave sublime support while still asserting their own song. Jazz is about seeing your own song in your own way while you touch a few hearts along the way. They comped in synchronization and support of those that they were working with. Cedar had that sublime ability as much as anybody who played our music. He was "Mein Comp, Lord Walton."

He was a keeper of the flame of the language that Lester Young and Lord Buckley started with Lords and Ladies. He maintained that practice and brought it into the modern era of addressing his fellow practitioners and friends with those terms of endearment. To this day, his disciples like Mike LeDonne and Todd Barkan and all his hundreds if not thousands of disciples, we keep that practice going. To me, it came from Dexter and Cedar. They really handed that baton to me. Cedar as much as anybody but Dexter too.

Cedar was very well educated and very well read. He was a great aficionado of film. Especially great English film. He was particular fan of Alec Guinness and Laurence Olivier and the great actors. He was a student of film. He loved a good story and he was a magnificent story teller himself on the piano. It was all of a piece. It was part of what made Cedar Walton a transcendent and iconic figure of our music, unsung hero that he is and was.

Cedar never sought the limelight. The limelight sought him after a time. He was very self-effacing, not that there was anything wrong with it, he just didn't have an ounce of pretense in his being. He was a man of true humility and had a truly giving nature. For a guy who was one of the greatest living jazz pianists of all time, he was remarkably humble. Now I'm sure Martha has other versions of that, 'cause Martha saw the whole spectrum of Lord Walton. But to me, he was a man of infinite wisdom and humility.

As a friend, he did not hesitate to tell me I was full of shit. That's a real friend. A friend doesn't always "yes" you. A true friend will tell you, "Hey Barkan, stop that" or "don't go that way" or "don't let that get you down." He was a true friend in many dimensions of that word. He's one of the best friends I will ever have in my life, and I miss him more every day. He was my "blood and guts buddy." For the rest of my days, I will hear Cedar on the phone saying, "Are you following the contest?" If there was a great film coming up like *Lion in Winter* with Peter O'Toole and Katharine Hepburn he'd say, "Are you ready for the footage?" The "contest" and the "footage." A friendship for the ages.

One of the fondest memories I have of my life and times with Cedar Walton was simply going to a Yankees game with him. It doesn't get better than going to a Yankee game with Cedar Walton. One time I was very lucky. I got Stanley Kay who worked as a publicist for the Yankees and was a great entrepreneur and manager for DIVA, the all-women's jazz orchestra, to get us tickets to go to the George Steinbrenner box at Yankee Stadium. And who did we sit down next to, but Henry Kissinger. Cedar never got over that and neither did I because here we are talking to Henry Kissinger at Yankee Stadium on a bright sunny afternoon up above the ballfield. We're sitting there talking to Henry Kissinger. Yogi Berra wandered into the box at one point. Cedar and I were just in heaven. We looked at each other like "Is this real? Are we actually experiencing this?" We talked about that repeatedly for the rest of Cedar's life.

Cedar's favorite greeting to me when he would call which is also an anecdote for our relationship was "Lord Barkan are you on the phone with Bangkok?" He must have asked me that about 400 times. It was such a delightful way to begin a conversation. I would invariably answer, "No Lord Walton, I just got off the phone with them." [laughs] That's the delight he took in language, and it reflected itself in the music that he played.

There are some sessions with Cedar that stand out to me that he and I talked about quite a bit over the years. One of the earliest ones was actually a record I produced with Cedar called *Highway One*. We were called upon to work on a session with Bobby Hutcherson for Columbia Records. Cedar did some of the arrangements, but he didn't actually play piano. That's when I knew how brilliant of an arranger Cedar was. I watched him use various elements of the orchestra. On that record there are few horn arrangements and string arrangements. Musically, we were able to map out different scenarios for the different songs that Bobby wanted to do on the record. That session was one of the important things that helped develop the strongly collaborative nature of our friendship. Even though he didn't play on that record, that was one of the keystone productions that we did that helped forge a stronger relationship between the two of us.

Among the sessions that we did together, and we did lots of Cedar Walton records, one that really stands out and is a sleeper is called *Mosaic*. Years ago, we did a record of the compositions that were integral in the Art Blakey legacy. Tunes like "Mosaic," "Ugetsu," "That Old Feeling"—that brilliant arrangement by Cedar. We did a trio record of Blakey tunes. That session really stands out to me among all the things I did with Cedar.

Cedar and I were both very proud of and took lasting delight from a couple things we did with Freddy Cole over the years. One record was called *Merry-Go-Round* on Telarc. This is part of the genius of Cedar Walton. And I do think he was a genius. Unmistakable and undeniable. But he was a minimalist genius. Cedar never used more where less would do. He always made the most out of every element that he introduced into a musical expression or arrangement. He could say a whole lot with very little and that's the mark of a true giant and a true genius. The arrangements for *Merry-Go-Round* are based a lot of times on Cedar Walton piano lines that he could come up with for these different compositions.

Another record we did together with Freddy Cole was called *Love Makes the Changes*. On that record we did the Billy Joel tune "Just the Way You Are." Cedar and Freddy would get together for maybe an hour and arrangements for eight or ten songs would be born in that hour. All from them sitting down and talking about different things. Freddy might have an idea and Cedar would incorporate that idea and then elaborate on that idea. Sometimes he'd write little things for the other band members to play.

As great a sense of humor as Cedar had, he also had what I consider to be an anti B.S. protector. He had what I called a shit detector. Cedar was not a backslapper or a crossbody blocker. He could be a very laconic guy. Cedar was not an overstated individual. In fact, quite the opposite, he was quite an understated fellow. That's part of why I loved him so much. His language was not full of hyperbole and false tidings and effusive expression. He was very much to the point. Cedar Walton certainly didn't suffer fools gladly. He could express the greatest warmth and the deepest feeling with a minimum of muss and fuss. He could tell you I love you without saying those words. And that's more powerful than even saying the words. He could share his feelings and his experiences about life with you almost offhandedly. That was an important part of the Cedar Walton's artistic personality and modality as much as it was about him as a person. The person and art were very much intertwined as they are with many great artists. You can't say that with all artists because some artists are totally different as people than they are in the expression of their art whether they are a novelist, or great instrumentalist, or singer. In Cedar's case, they were very congruent. His laconic personality was reflected in his laconic playing. Cedar never overplayed. Never. He was never guilty of playing notes for notes sake. He never sounded like he was getting paid by the note. Everything that Cedar did had a meaning and a purpose and an impact. His ability to say a lot with a little while communicating great warmth without being a gladhander or backslapper. He recoiled from that aspect of modern culture where everything is LOL and OMG. He was diametrically the opposite of that. He was a "Lord Barkan, are you following the contest?" The depth of his expression was enhanced by its minimalist nature, because he made every note and every word count for so much.

Cedar and I were friends for forty years. His friendship with me was real and deep and warm. He just expressed it in an inimitable fashion. Sometimes almost cryptically, but still deeply. I never felt that I had a better friend ever than Cedar. It was a special friendship with a special guy. It was friendship he expressed in his own unique manner. For Cedar, friendship was expressed in the doing. The doing rather than the proclamation of the friendship. In other words, you were a friend because you spent time together and you shared things together. We shared things. We shared in the delight in language. We were able to make verbal puns about nearly everything. We were able to take delight in the language of those things in anything and everything. Cedar is an unsung hero in this music. Every little bit that helps his legacy and his name get out there is extremely important to me and to the music.[14]

Tim Jackson

Tim Jackson was a co-founder of Kuumbwa Jazz in Santa Cruz in 1975. He worked as artistic director for the performance and education center. In 1992 Jackson also assumed the role of artistic director for the Monterey Jazz Festival. Cedar performed at Kuumbwa frequently when in California and Jackson and the Monterey Jazz Festival commissioned him to compose a work for the festival in 1996. Tim Jackson remembers Cedar and their work together over the years:

Sometime in the late '70s, probably 1978 or so, Cedar started playing at Kuumbwa. I think the first group was Higgins on drums, David Williams on bass, and Bob Berg on saxophone. My early memories of him playing at Kuumbwa were with that quartet. I always thought Bob Berg just played Cedar's music really well. In the late '70s early '80s, Cedar would probably play just about every year. Keystone Korner was still around then. Keystone would run Tuesday through Sunday and then we'd do the Monday night here. We would work with Todd Barkan to set that up. We set up a pattern over the years.

Cedar goes back to the early days of Kuumbwa when I was quite young and hadn't worked with too many major artists before. Cedar, Joe Henderson, Bobby Hutcherson, and Phil Woods were the first artists I started working with. Cedar was right in there. I booked him through a very good friend of mine and he was a friend of Cedar's till Cedar's dying day. Lupe DeLeon was his agent. I always booked all the dates with Lupe. It was always a family sort of thing because Lupe and I got into the business at the same time and started our careers together. It was always very comfortable. I loved working with Cedar. He was kind of quiet, not quiet, but I always thought with Cedar there was not a lot of superfluous words coming out of him. When he had something to say, he said it. It wasn't like he was taciturn or anything like that. He was very friendly and open. I would say in certain ways he was a man of few words, but they were always good words. [laughs]

We did a big remodel of Kuumbwa in about 1988 and I remember when we reopened in the new configuration that we had a new piano. Cedar was first piano player to play in the new room and play on the new piano. I think it was his birthday. We had a birthday cake for him that time as well. He also played here with the Timeless All Stars. I remember seeing him in the mid-'80s with that same group at the Monterey Jazz Festival before I started with the festival.

When I started working at Monterey, we did a commission work with Cedar in 1996. We commissioned a piece that he called "Autumn Sketches." It was with David Williams and [Marvin] "Smitty" Smith on drums. He had Ralph Moore on tenor sax, Roy Hargrove on trumpet and Vincent Herring on alto saxophone and a string section from the Oakland East Bay Symphony.

Over the years we followed our paths together. I would see him when I was back in New York. I remember one time I was with my wife at Sweet Basil before it closed. Cedar was at the bar, and it was during a show, and I hadn't had a chance to go over and say "Hi" to him yet, but he had sent us over glasses of champagne. I always found him to be a very thoughtful guy. Cedar was the kind of guy for me that I could ask him questions and I know he would give me an honest answer. You know, "How's our piano doing? Does our piano need any work?" He would tell me. I found him to be an honest and fun guy to be around. I loved to ask him questions because he had such history going back to those early days with Blakey and even before that. He's played with just about everybody. I found him to be an inspiring and very thoughtful guy. I always loved his music. I'm not a piano player but I like that he didn't bowl you over with Oscar Peterson type chops. I always thought his inner voicings, not notes at the top or bottom, but the notes in the middle, were so subtle and perfect. I always thought he could play the mid-range of the piano as well or better than anybody. [laughs] He really approached his music from a composer's point of view. He was such a prolific composer. His quartet music sounded like mini symphonies. Even if you thought "Well, they're just blowing on this tune" there was an arrangement there. In his later years he would often come in with a trio and sometimes he would even play a tune like "Satin Doll," but he would put such a cool arrangement behind it. Cedar just had that way of putting a tag on something or an extra measure at the end of the bridge and you just go "wow that's hip!" I wish I could think of something like that! [laughs]

Sometimes I felt that he would be a little frustrated. I think he wished he was better known than he was. Of all the things he's done, sometimes artists get overlooked in this business and I think that Cedar got overlooked a little bit. And I think he knew that and felt that. It never manifested itself in any way negatively toward me or anything, but a couple of comments here or there. I think there was a little bit of frustration. As I look back as I've been doing this for so long now, I certainly look back to Cedar as being one of the most special people that I've worked with. He was a very humble guy. I just appreciated the way he approached his art and his craft and he really paid attention to detail. Whether it was in the trio setting or when we were doing the expanded pieces with the string sections at Monterey, he was always about the details. He always got the details right.[15]

Jason Olaine

Jason Olaine began working at Yoshi's in Oakland, California, in the early
'90s as an intern and quickly became the booking manager for much of the
decade. He booked Cedar many times during that span and developed a relationship with Cedar.

I met Cedar on my first professional gig in 1993 working at Yoshi's in
Oakland, California, working as an intern there in the publicity department. Before the end of the year, I was booking the club and continued
booking Yoshi's from 1993 to the middle of 1999. That was the old
Yoshi's on Claremont Avenue.

Cedar always booked himself at Yoshi's, he and I just called each
other. We didn't go through any middleman. There were a handful of
artists like that back in that era who self-managed or self-promoted themselves and Cedar was one of them. He had such a signature sound to his
voice that you just knew who it was within the first couple of seconds.
He always had some very funny turns of a phrase and his introductions
[laughs] were always funny and engaging and complimentary too.

Every time I would pick up the phone and it was Cedar, he would
say, "It's the prince of jazz!" or "Mr. Olaine" or "How's the king of
Oakland today?" Every time it was a different salutation. Cedar was
always so humble. [Cedar speaking] "Could I ask you for some work?
Can we make some music in your home?" or something. And then we
would just talk about what we could do to make it work. He's like
"Well how does this sound." Of course, it's with the trio with David and
Billy. Those were the folks he always worked with. Cedar would say,
"What do you think of Milt Jackson?" I said, "I love Milt Jackson." He'd
say, "OK, I'll call him." or "What do you think of Jackie McLean? JO:
"What do you mean? I love Jackie McLean." CW: "OK, call Dolly.
I talked to Jackie, and he said, he'd do it. You just need to call him and
work out the bread." That's how the relationship was.

If I was putting some kind of thing together like an NEA Jazz
Masters all-stars kind of thing, I would call Cedar and say, "Hey Cedar
I'm putting this thing together and I got Bobby Hutcherson and Slide"
and on down the list of people, "I got Jimmy Heath, you want to be
a part of it?" And he's like "Oh my old friends! Of course, Jason."
He never really beat me up for money. He was always very reasonable. Affordable. He's a master of course and deserved to get as much
as he could, but he always made it easy. There were a few other folks
I worked with that are of that era that were self-managed or booked

themselves like Ray Brown or Benny Carter. These guys never broke the bank. They understood that they needed us to stay open as much as we needed them to play. It was a very different mentality than dealing with an agent on the phone where their bottom line is to extract as much money out of a club or festival as they possibly can for their artists as well as themselves. When these guys would call, they didn't have the middleman. They could call and say, "What can you do for me." If they needed a little bit more they'd say, "Ooh it feels a little light." [laughs] It was a very civilized, humane, and a humbling way to work with arguably the greatest musicians of all time.[16]

In 1989, the trio of Cedar, David Williams, and Billy Higgins had one of their performances recorded and broadcasted for a local radio show, *See's Sunday Night Series* on KJAZ-FM. The recording was released in 1995 as *Ironclad: Cedar Walton Trio Live at Yoshi's* and is a favorite '90s trio record of Cedar fans.[17]

Eastern Rebellion

The year 1983 marked the 4th Eastern Rebellion recording. *Eastern Rebellion 4* featured Alfredo "Chocolate" Armenteros (trumpet), Curtis Fuller, Bob Berg, David Williams, and Billy Higgins. This record would include two Walton originals: "I'm Not So Sure" and "Groundwork." After this recording, the band would take a seven-year hiatus before recording again under that name. Cedar would continue to record as a leader in the trio format as well as with other horn players, but none would record under the Eastern Rebellion name again until tenor saxophonist Ralph Moore joined the band. Moore joined the band in 1990 and Eastern Rebellion recorded *Mosaic* at the end of that year.[18]

Initially, the *Mosaic* record date was supposed to be trumpeter Freddie Hubbard's session. Moore had been working in Hubbard's band prior to the record date and he asked Moore to play on the session. Moore describes the session and being asked to join Eastern Rebellion:

We were doing a record with Freddie and Cedar's trio. This was supposed to be a Freddie Hubbard date. I had been working with Freddie at the time so Freddie had me in on it. Freddie had just started to have trouble with his chops and the producer didn't like what Freddie was doing at the session. I thought Freddie was fucking playing his ass off, as usual. He'd miss a note or two here or there, but the content was just incredible. If you knew how that guy was playing at the time it was just beautiful music. Producers can get in the middle of a session and then it's like "There goes the record date." We got one day down, and it was beautiful, but the producer said, "Nah, we think Freddie can do better."

We got there for the next day, it was a two-day session, and the producer says, "Well, we've gotta give Freddie a chance to heal." At this point, he still had the blister on his lip and it hadn't taken full effect yet. I thought he was still playing his ass off, but they sent him home and said, "Since we got the trio and you [Ralph] in the studio here, let's not waste a day." The producer was John Snyder. He's very well-known and did a lot of things on Horizon. We're in the studio and Cedar says, "Well, what can we do?" I'm like, "Shoot, I know a bunch of your tunes, Cedar. You know, I'm a big fan." And he says, "Well, what do you know?" We went to the piano and ran this down, and ran that down and he says, "Shit, we've got a record here." And that was the record.

When the record was done Cedar's like, "We might have to do some gigs; we've gotta band here." When the record came out, true to his word, he called me. We had a couple rehearsals and then we went to Europe. And that was it. I was in the band. That's how that started. Cedar was always working on tunes. I remember that tour in particular. Back in those days, we would do two weeks at Ronnie Scott's. In the afternoons, I'd go over to the club and start practicing 'cause I was always into practicing. And then an hour or two later the trio would show up and we'd start working on tunes. Cedar's like, "I'm working on this thing. Check this out." He'd run it down this way, he'd run it down that way and say, "What do you think? Does it work this way?" We tried putting together another album right away. Once we got back off that tour, we recorded in LA.

Cedar could develop a conception for the band and organize a tune. He had a couple ideas in his head, and we'd get on a gig that night and we'd play it the way we rehearsed it. The next day he'd say, "Yeah, but I didn't like it. Let's try it differently." We'd go back in the club the following afternoon and get it set the way he liked it. One of the tunes that came out of that, I remember, specifically was "Ronnie's Decision." That was great for me. I had some experience at that point, but Cedar's band was incredible. And playing with Billy Higgins, man. Those two had been playing forever; playing with them was like a magic carpet ride.

Billy would just swing like crazy right from the get-go. There was never a warm-up. It was like, "go" and he would be swinging hard, like second, third set swinging already. It was really beautiful. Billy was a beautiful guy. He was my hanging buddy on the road. It was a tight band with David Williams and Cedar, but Billy was just full of stories, and he really pulled me in. He would tell me a bunch of stories when we hung out. He'd say, "What are you doing for lunch? Let's meet." When you get out on the road you've gotta have somebody to hang with. Billy was always so accessible to me that way. The way he used to holler at me when we were on a bandstand when we were playing. He'd be swinging his ass off and he used to grunt, "huh, huh, huh, huh." He would grunt at me and sort of holler at me in between my phrases. In between the time, he was really goading me and pushing me. It was crazy good. I was in my early thirties at that time and like I said, I had some experience with some good people. People like Roy Hanes, Horace Silver, Freddie and different people. But that quartet with Cedar, man. In a year or two, we had fifty or sixty arrangements of Cedar's originals and his arrangements of standard tunes all committed to memory. We'd go into a club and rule. It was fabulous. Back in those days you could still go out and gig. It doesn't seem like it was that long ago, really, but I guess it is now.

One time I was humming this tune, "My Ideal." We were backstage getting ready to go into a concert and Cedar says, "You wanna try that?" We hadn't played it before, and I hadn't played it before with them. Of course, they've played everything. I turn to Cedar and say, "How we gonna do it? Are you gonna set it up?" And Billy Higgins says to me, "Shit, he's gonna set you up in the front row with a table-cloth and a candle." We picked the key and go out there and he does. He set it up like crazy. I could literally just play a whole note and they would swing so hard around it. It was almost like I didn't have to do anything, and I'd be swinging like crazy. Consequently, I had all the space and time in the world to think about what I wanted to say and play and phrase. I could take my time and develop something. I had so much space because it was just swinging so hard. There was never any sort of crowding for the beat and the time. It was so spacious and swinging so hard. And the comping was so beautiful and so thick and lush. I could just take my time and think about what I wanted to say. It was just an incredible experience. I was lucky enough to play with some great piano players and each one of them is unique in their own way and Cedar was definitely a monster.

Freddie [Hubbard] just had absolute confidence in Cedar. He didn't have to worry. That's why Cedar's trio was on the record date that Freddie was doing. At one point in the session, there was a question about some chords on one of the tunes. Freddie said, "Well that's why I got you here. Figure it out and let's do it." I don't think Freddie ever worried about the chords. He could just hear everything. And in fact, I don't think he wanted to know what the chords were.

Cedar never used to like to give me the chords. I'd pester him about them. He liked it better if I didn't know what they were. He'd say, "I like the way you play when you don't know what the chords are." That was crazy to me. I'd continue to pester him and figure them out along the way. When you're playing a lot, pretty soon you figure them out quickly anyway.

Freddie and Cedar's relationship went way back to the Messengers and coming up together in Brooklyn. McCoy as well. I remember I did a tour in Europe with Freddie and McCoy's trio. Freddie was trying to teach McCoy his tune "Dear John." The "Giant Steps" thing with Freddie's head on it with a little introduction. So, Freddie says, "I wrote this new tune." He played it and it was beautiful. I had to learn it because he wanted to do it on that tour so I kinda knew it by then, but McCoy had never played it. Freddie is trying to teach McCoy and of course McCoy knows "Giant Steps." Freddie was trying to teach him to get the pushes on the introduction and McCoy was just distracted and couldn't get it. I watched Freddie go and push McCoy off the piano like, "Get out of the way" in frustration. I remember that moment because I was astonished to see somebody push McCoy off the piano. Picture that!

That for me underscores the type of camaraderie and closeness that they had. It was more than just professional courtesies and respect. These guys went back to starving to death in Brooklyn and practicing together. So he shoved McCoy off the piano and sat down and McCoy got up and never said a word. He just looked right over Freddie's shoulder to see what Freddie was teaching him. Freddie's all arrogant and loud and, "Here it goes," and "It's like this," and just bangs it out on piano and McCoy's like, "Oh, okay," and then McCoy had it. He sat down and there was no sort of "Freddie Hubbard pushed me off the piano." There was never anything like that with those guys. Same thing with Cedar. It was like they were kids. They'd known each other since they were little. To me they were giants, but to themselves they were just pals.

Cedar and David [Williams] used to swap jokes. Every time we got back together, they'd have a fist full of jokes that they would throw back and forth. And Cedar always had jokes on the road. He had a great sense of humor. He also liked to eat. I mean, you wouldn't want to get between Cedar and a plate of food. When it was dinner time, he wanted it to be on.

I have never worked with anybody that was so fair. Not only in terms of sharing the music on the bandstand but after expenses, hotel, flights, and whatever else, Cedar paid everybody the same. Everybody got the same bread. He cut it four ways and I'd never experienced that before. I was thirty-two at the time and I'm an equal part of this band with Billy Higgins, Cedar Walton, and David Williams. Everybody's the same when we got on the bandstand. That was a powerful thing for me. It really made me feel a part of something.

Cedar's sense of fairness was important for me. I still feel that way now. I'd rather be part of a unit more than a leader. These days, everybody's trying to get theirs. The world's changed now. Everybody wants to be a leader. There's no time to be a side man, it seems. And that's a shame because if you get to be a side man in a really great unit, it's an incredible experience. For me, that was important. I wish I could get into another situation like that where there's a unit and we blend well on the road, on and off the bandstand. We were a unit, and we had each other's back, and it was wonderful.

Cedar was very much about how the music was presented. He was very much like Horace in that way, and in fact, when he was writing a tune, his biggest thing sometimes was to ask, "But does it sound like Horace? That's a problem. I don't want it to sound anything like Horace." He and a lot of guys were influenced by Horace. Cedar wanted his pieces to be arranged, a nice introduction, an interlude here or there, something between solos, and a nice tag at the end.

In terms of presenting the band and the music, Cedar would always go major, minor, major, minor, major, minor. Some guys go, "Well I wanna ballad here, we'll start the tune with a nice swinging thing and end up with an up-tempo thing." Cedar's thing was major, minor, major, minor, major, minor. He managed it and wasn't chintzy. Sometimes we'd play eight or nine tunes in a set, which I thought was a lot. But I could just take two or three choruses and get out because I knew I was gonna get a chance to play on the next one. It was good for the house. We weren't beating them to death with a song for ten or fifteen minutes and there's nice variety going on. He'd program some straight 8th things, something in three, some swinging things and a standard or two. He had great originals.

Cedar's band was just like a velvet carpet ride. It was just magical. Beautiful. You knew all the tunes, Cedar made sure you knew the tunes. He had wonderful arrangements with beautiful slick cords and Billy would be under that stuff like crazy. It was an incredible experience. On Cedar's arrangements of "Young and Foolish" or "I've Grown Accustomed to Your Face," oh man, we'd come out of those things and his eyes looked like "Boom." Billy would send me out there with a big rush and start swinging like crazy. And I could just take my time. It was like a jet airplane taking off. All those beautiful tunes and arrangements. And I really felt part of the unit.

Cedar did not like bullshit and would get upset quickly when it came about. He was sensitive in his way, but he was also very gracious. Back in those days you'd show up in Europe somewhere and they would treat you like you were somebody. Now in my recent experiences traveling, things have changed quite a lot. Now it's like, "Take a number" sort of attitude. Cedar had experience from the Messengers, and people in Europe treated him like "The Great Cedar Walton." We'd show up over there and people would put on a dog and pony show for us. There was always a chance to hang and after the set, they'd take us to a restaurant and feed us. We'd hang and tell stories and it was special.

Cedar didn't really have any management. He didn't like that shit. He handled all that stuff himself, which was another reason it was so beautiful. There wasn't anyone getting in the way of the music and him trying to design the presentation of the band. It was all Cedar. Cedar knew how to present the group. When I got in Cedar's band, even though at some times the money was what it was, you knew everybody was getting the same. That made for a beautiful, really connected, trusting, wonderful experience. We'd go to Japan and, after expenses, everybody's making a grand a gig. That's unheard of now!

I loved all my time with Cedar. At the time I left him, Billy got sick. They used to call him smiling Billy Higgins, 'cause he was always grinning and smiling on drums. It was on my last trip in Japan (with that band) when Billy's hepatitis finally caught up with him.

Once Billy would get on the gig and I'd look behind me, he' be grinning like a kid. He couldn't help it once the swing kicked in. It's typical of musicians. Whatever's going on in your life just kind of fades away when you get up on the bandstand and that's a beautiful thing. Art Blakey believed in that so strongly. He always preached about that. "Don't bring none of that bullshit up on the bandstand, I don't care what you're going through. This is sacred up here." And he meant it because those guys went through shit back in those days. And the bandstand was the only place that was theirs. Nothing else was theirs. Freddie and Cedar and those guys came out of Art Blakey's school. One of the really beautiful experiences of my professional life was working with Cedar.

(l to r) Cedar, Ron Carter, and Billy Higgins. *Martha Walton collection.*

(l to r) David Williams, Jackie McLean, Cedar, and Billy Higgins.
Martha Walton collection.

Easter Rebellion program. *Martha Walton collection,
photo by Carlo Pieroni.*

Front: Billy Higgins and Naisha Walton. Back: (l to r) David Williams,
Cedar, and Vincent Herring. *Martha Walton collection.*

Cedar and Ralph Moore, 1994. *Martha Walton collection.*

I think Cedar never really got the respect that he should have gotten. Maybe toward the end he was starting to get a little bit, but when I was out on the road with Cedar it was, it was tough for him.[19]

In addition to *Mosaic*, Moore made several recordings with Cedar in the '90s. He recorded on *In the Kitchen: Eastern Rebellion/Raymond Court, Simple Pleasure, Just One Of Those ... Nights At the Village Vanguard* with Cedar and Eastern Rebellion. These would be the last recordings of Eastern Rebellion.

Chapter 11

Martha's Prize (1990–2013):

Martha Sammaciccia and the Move Back to New York

Martha (Sammaciccia) Walton, a lifelong New Yorker, has long been a beloved figure among jazz musicians and club owners in New York City and abroad. She was at Cedar's side from the the the '90s on.

Martha was born into a family that loved and appreciated music. Martha started piano lessons at the age of 5. Her mother Katie was born in Italy and early on fell in love with the sounds of the Tommy Dorsey orchestra and similar bands of the time. Katie used to write her own lyrics to some of the instrumental tunes. Katie listened to WNEW.AM constantly. "That station only played the singers, standards and big bands. Every Sunday was Sinatra all day!"[1] said Martha. At one point she was offered a contract for her musical talent, but her father "scolded her and told her no," said Martha.[2] "That was the end of that. She was always trying to live vicariously through my musical endeavors."[3]

> When I learned to drive, my girlfriend Rosie and I would go to Jilly's on 52nd Street and 8th Ave. in NYC. Jilly was Frank's bodyguard at one time, and there was always a table in the corner that was reserved for Sinatra. We would wait every weekend hoping Frank and his entourage would stop by.[4]

Cedar and Martha (Sammaciccia) Walton. *Martha Walton collection.*

After high school, Martha wanted to be an archaeologist or a Latin teacher, but her parents were adamantly opposed to the idea and in favor of more practical training. Martha enrolled at the Katherine Gibbs Secretarial School. "It was very exclusive at that time in the early '70s. I graduated and went straight to a law firm,"[5] said Martha. Martha worked as a legal secretary in New York City. Her time in the city would foster her love for jazz and its community.

"I had heard jazz and loved music, but I was a disco queen and I loved rock,"[6] said Martha. Martha's first introduction to live jazz happened on a cold night in Manhattan. "I was walking to meet somebody, and it was so cold. I couldn't go any further,"[7] said Martha. "I went into this little jazz club and these guys were jamming and I just fell in love. Hearing the music live is so much different than a recording. There's a raw quality to the music that is very exciting."[8] That evening, Martha met a few of the musicians and was equally impressed with their musical brilliance and their lack of knowledge on the business end. "They didn't know how to market themselves,"[9] said Martha. "I started volunteering my services to send out press kits, cover letters, and cassettes to help them out."[10] Martha started to become part of the jazz community.

Martha started hanging out at jazz clubs and began meeting more jazz musicians. She recalls the story of her first meeting with Art Blakey:

> I was at Bradley's one night, sitting at the bar, and who walks in with his entourage but Art Blakey. He came right over to me. I had no idea who he was, and he says, "Hey, honey, what's your name? You got a valid passport?" I said to myself, "Who in the hell is this? Who is this little man?" At that time, I was dating a saxophonist, and Art kept saying "Where's your boyfriend? I'll put him in my band. Go talk to him." At the time, everyone wanted to be a Messenger, but not my boyfriend. He told to me to tell Art to go "F" himself. He did not want me talking to him.[11]

Martha certainly made an impression on Blakey that evening. Blakey started to inquire about Martha and found out she went to the same secretarial school his estranged wife had attended. Shortly after their meeting, Art asked Martha to work for him. She was able to go to Blakey's house during the day because she worked nights at a law firm. "I used to sit there and do nothing [laughs] but Art liked having a lot of people around."[12] said Martha. After working for Blakey, Martha started working part-time with another friend who worked PR for Fat Tuesday's typing letters and advertisements for the club.

Martha first met Cedar in 1986. She went to Bradley's with a friend and was introduced to Cedar. "I still had no idea who Cedar was,"[13] said Martha. "When I worked for Art Blakey, he was a big gossip. He would talk about everybody, but he never, ever, ever, mentioned Cedar Walton. I thought he must have really respected him because when he did talk about another musician, it generally wasn't a good story,"[14] said Martha. Cedar and Martha's first meeting was at the bar at Bradley's. Cedar bought Martha a drink and the two struck a chord with their mutual association with Art Blakey. "Working for Art really gave me some street cred in Cedar's eyes,"[15] said Martha. After a while, Cedar invited Martha back to his hotel to learn more about the music business. Martha said, "I told Cedar, 'I don't want to learn that badly, honey!'" [laughs].[16]

That had quite an impact on Cedar. After that meeting, he called Martha regularly to talk about anything and everything from the Yankees or Knicks or to wish her Merry Christmas or Happy New Year. "It never dawned on me that maybe he had some feelings for me,"[17] said Martha. "When he would come into New York, we would always end up getting a bottle of wine and going to his hotel room and just sitting and talking all night."[18] At that time Cedar and Martha would commiserate with each other about their love lives. "We were becoming good friends,"[19] said Martha.

Art Blakey died in 1990 and his memorial was held at the Abyssinian Church in Harlem. At that service, Martha heard Abbey Lincoln sing Cedar's tune "The Maestro." "The whole place was crying their eyes out,"[20] said Martha.

> I had never heard the song in my life, and I kept thinking "Who wrote this?" What a beautiful song! Several years later, Cedar and I had lunch and he had a short meeting with his record company. Afterward, we were walking down Broadway, and he handed me a CD. It was *The Maestro*, featuring Abbey Lincoln! I almost fainted!! "You wrote this song? I've been looking all over the place for this since Art's memorial!!!" The look on his face was priceless, his answer was, "I guess it's fate." I had no idea he was a composer."[21]

Freddy Cole, who was also a friend of both Cedar and Martha, was playing at Bradley's around the time of Art Blakey's memorial service. The two started to talk and Cole let Martha know about Cedar's feelings for her. Freddy told me, "Cedar is so in love with you, he's got it bad!"[22] said Martha. "After that, the next time I saw Cedar, I ran right up to him and gave him the biggest kiss!" [laughs][23] "I sort of hollered at him for not coming out and telling me."[24] Cedar and Martha were a couple moving forward and Martha would start to come to Los Angeles on the weekends. It was during one of Cedar's subsequent trips to New York that Martha learned he still had a girlfriend back in LA. On the fateful trip, Cedar and Martha had planned to go to a play when he got into New York, but Cedar never called her. The next day, Martha ended up going to Sweet Basil (a mutual hangout) and learned that Cedar had been there the night before with his girlfriend. "I was livid!"[25] said Martha.

> Didn't he have a clue that someone's going to call me up and tell me he was there with his girlfriend? He hated conflicts and avoided them at all costs, but only because he was clueless at times. Cedar was very charming and worldly, but he was still the kid from Texas—as hard as he tried, he didn't know how to pull off a good lie. For someone who was addicted to episodes of Sherlock Holmes & Law & Order, you would think he would have learned something about not getting caught! [laughs][26]

Martha broke off their relationship after that incident. In the months to follow, Cedar would call repeatedly, and Martha declined Cedar's calls and invitations to come to his gigs when he was in New York.

After many months of this, the two finally saw each other in public. Cedar and Martha found themselves at Bradley's. Martha tells the story:

> I walked into Bradley's and all my friends immediately let me know that Cedar was there. I didn't care and didn't have any plans to speak with him. After a while of sitting with my friends, I made my way to the bathroom, and of course Cedar's table was along the way. Cedar said, "Hi Martha" and I replied with a very short "hi" as I walked by. When I got back to my seat, he came over to me and said, "Aren't you going to say "hello" to me? What's wrong with you?" I said, "Excuse me? I said, Hello to you." He said, "Who the hell do you think you are, 'Cold' Porter? Don't you know I love you?" Everybody at the bar was burying their faces in their hands and laughing. He got me with that one. [laughs] "Cold' Porter? No one's ever called me that before." How could you be mad at someone who's calling you "Cold' Porter? That was the beginning of it. We were back together for good after that."[27]

Martha would go back from LA to New York. She worked four days in New York and spent the other three in LA. Eventually, this routine got to be too much for her.

> I was in my mid-30s and was tired of being alone all the time. I missed Cedar too much. I was at the prime of my life, and I didn't want to be alone. I told Cedar "I'm tired of missing you!" In saying

that I was trying to get him to move back to New York. I loved him so much. His response was, "Let's get married." I said, "Oh, no. Where did that come from? [laughs] I wasn't giving him an ultimatum, just to move back. When he said, "Let's get married," I almost dropped the phone![28]

In a few years, Cedar moved back to New York and he and Martha were married. On one of Cedar's last trips to New York before moving back permanently, he and Martha decided to go get their marriage license on their day off.

Jazz Pianist Michael Weiss

I remember one morning getting a call from Cedar asking me "What are you doing this afternoon?" I said, "Well I gotta a couple things I gotta do but anything for you. What do you want?" He said "Can you meet us down at the Brooklyn courthouse? Martha and I are getting married, and we'd like you to be the witness." [laughs] So I hightailed it down to the courthouse and little did they realize that there's a 24-hour waiting period. You know, you go, and you register your marriage but there's a 24-hour waiting period before you're allowed to proceed to the next steps. I remember Cedar was sweating bullets. [laughs] I remember he was very nervous. Unfortunately, the following day I wasn't available to be able to go back.[29]

Cedar and Martha were married in June of 1995. As Michael Weiss said, they tried to get married on Monday but had to wait 24 hours. They came back to the courthouse the next day (Tuesday) and were married. That Tuesday, Cedar started a weeklong engagement at Iridium and he and Martha celebrated with an impromptu celebration at the club after gig. "That week, we had a little party after one of his sets. It was fun. Very off the cuff. I never had any plans of getting married. Cedar was just the sweetest, most beautiful man in the world. He was so attentive and very sensitive."[30] said Martha. Cedar's summer touring schedule was very busy. In addition to his own work, he accepted a number of dates for another pianist who was ill. "We literally traveled around the world!"[31] said Martha. "My mother Katie was dying to meet my husband, and she delayed Thanksgiving to coincide with our return to New York."[32]

> I was a little concerned about my mother meeting Cedar because it was a biracial marriage. Even though I was almost 40, I was still a little nervous and I knew I was going to have to tell her eventually. When we finally got together at mom's place, she also invited her sister, my Aunt Florie. Cedar was just wonderful. He played *Name That Tune* with them for hours on a little keyboard in the corner. Isn't that what they call "grooming?" [laughs] After dinner, I went to the kitchen to wash dishes with Aunt Florie and Mom and Cedar got to talking. Cedar was very charming. They talked and talked. The next day Mom called me and went on about how wonderful he was. I was so happy. What a big relief. Then Mom asked where in Italy was Cedar from. I said "Ma, he's from Texas." "No, no, no," she said, "something with a B. He told me he's from Italy." I said, "D as in Dallas, T as in Texas, Ma!" Then I remembered Cedar's relationship with Alberto Alberti in Bologna. Cedar even told Alberto that he was from Bologna. Apparently, Cedar told my mother that his real name was Cedartio Waltoni and he was born in Bologna. What a story! [laughs][33]

Cedar and Katie were like two peas in a pod from then on. Early in Martha and Cedar's marriage, Cedar would call Katie if the two were having problems.

Cedar was traveling regularly and wanted Martha to stop working and join him. Initially, Martha was concerned about money because she had a mortgage and wanted to make sure she could make ends meet. On one trip to Seattle, Cedar and Martha got into a disagreement where Cedar's recourse was to "Call Katie." "He actually called my mother!"[34] said Martha.

> Cedar and my mom were on the phone for about an hour. I could hear him saying "She's not talking to me. She won't explain. If this doesn't change, we're going to have to terminate the marriage." After Cedar and Mom finished, she told him to put me on the phone and told me, "You cut that shit out right now, because he wants to terminate the marriage, and he's wonderful, and you be good to him!" [laughs][35]

Cedar and Martha's quarrels were short lived. The couple loved traveling together and enjoyed the best of what first class accommodations could hold while Cedar was working.

Cedar and Martha's mother, Katie Sammaciccia, 1995.
Martha Walton collection.

(l to r) Cedar, Martha Walton, and Alberto Alberti, 1995.
Martha Walton collection.

Freddy Cole and Martha Walton. *Martha Walton collection.*

Martha Walton, Cedar, and Todd Barkan. *Martha Walton collection.*

Cedar arranging, 1994. *Martha Walton collection.*

Martha was always baffled by Cedar's deft ability to keep his calendar in his head. "That's the type of brain that he had,"[36] said Martha. "He never used a calendar until he started getting older."[37]

Martha recalled one story of Cedar taking the time to show her what he did as a musician.

Cedar was arranging tunes for a recording with Etta James. They put us up in a very nice hotel suite. My mom bought him a little electric keyboard that he would bring on the road and use to compose in his down time. I can still see him playing that keyboard with a pencil in his mouth! [laughs] One day he was playing the tune "The Man I Love." I didn't understand why he needed to do anything with the song because someone already wrote it. The pencil dropped out of his mouth, and he said, "You don't know what I'm doing, do you?" He stopped everything and explained exactly what an arrangement was and what his process was. He showed me some chord symbols and wrote them out then made me play them. It was very sweet. He was very patient, very loving. He was just a wonderful guy.[38]

Later in their marriage, Cedar would tease Martha saying, "I knew that the next woman I would end up with had to be from New York, had to have a job, no children, and she had to love the music." "I guess I fit all the criteria!" [laughs][39] said Martha. Cedar wrote a tune for Martha titled "Martha's Prize." When introducing the tune on gigs, Cedar would say, "This song is dedicated to my wonderful wife, Martha's Prize,[40] and we all know who that is."[41]

Chapter 12

Midnight Waltz: *Reflections and Remembrances*

Many musicians had the opportunity to play and record with Cedar over the course of his career. He created relationships with musicians young and old that lasted a lifetime. Just as Art Blakey did in the Messengers, Cedar mentored younger musicians in much the same way. He was equally respected by his contemporaries.

Roger Boykin

I met Cedar in 1949. He came to the house across the street from me to visit one of my neighbors, Raul Meshack, who introduced me to him. I was nine years old at the time and Cedar was fifteen. His name stuck with me, perhaps because I had never met someone named after a tree. Our neighborhood was called "Queen City" and we lived only three and a half blocks apart. It was one of the best neighborhoods in Dallas for black people at the time.

Cedar and I both had paper routes and we got our papers on the same corner. I didn't see him much after that. I started to keep up with his career in 1955. I became a musician and moved to California to attend San Francisco State College. Cedar was with the Jazztet and they played at the Jazz Workshop. I spoke with him and reminded him of how we met more than 10 years prior, and he remembered. I told him

Freddie Hubbard and Cedar. *Martha Walton collection.*

that I started to play the piano and that I was playing jazz. I told Cedar I was playing piano with Dewey Redman on Sundays and guitar with the Merl Saunders Trio four nights a week. I asked him for a lesson, and he agreed. He was staying with a friend who had a piano. He invited me over. We sat down at the piano, and he was very friendly. I got the homeboy treatment. He showed me some chord voicings that I still use to this day.

I finished college in 1963 and went to New York with Billy Harper. I remember standing out in front of the Five Spot and I was talking with Blue Mitchell, James Clay, and Fathead, and Blue Mitchell asked me for one of my tunes, "Andrea." I gave it to him, and he recorded it that year. Blue Note decided not to put it out then. Years later after Blue Mitchell died, Cedar called me and told me that Blue Note was going to release it. He said "Michael Cuscuna, the producer, is looking all over New York for you." Cedar hooked that up for me. I was able to get one of my tunes on Blue Mitchell's album. Cedar was a good friend to me. During the same time that I was in New York, he recommended me for a gig with a theater group that was rehearsing a play, Black Nativity, that had an upcoming engagement in Europe. They had wanted to hire Cedar but he was with Blakey. It was nice of him to tell the group about me. I auditioned but didn't get the gig.

I moved back to Dallas after that. And Cedar and I would hang anytime he came back. We were friends. He would call and talk about baseball or just drop by when he was in town. I hosted a radio show in Dallas for 22 years. Whenever he put out a new record, he would send it to me. Over the years, we had a lot of opportunities to sit down at the piano together. When I recorded my first album, he critiqued it. I played him some of the tracks before we ever released it.

To other musicians, Cedar was very serious. He was a very intellectual guy and so well read. He was very giving.

When Cedar's mother passed, he came down to do an estate sale as well as sell the house. Cedar gave me his mother's record collection and he gave me a beautiful cashmere overcoat that had been his father's. He was a very generous guy. He was my friend and my piano hero.[1]

Rufus Reid

I was aware of Cedar from recordings long before I had moved to the New York area. Primarily, the album that I began to really latch ahold of was an Eddie Harris recording called *The In Sound*. It was Cedar and Ron Carter and Billy Higgins. This was when I was in the military. I fell in love with that recording, and when I got a chance to play with Eddie Harris, he came to tell me more. When I moved to Chicago, I began to see Cedar come to town occasionally to perform. I never really got the chance to play with him until I came to New York. I got to play in a trio with Billy Higgins and Cedar and the bass played by itself. It was so easy and very exciting. Very articulate. Swinging. It was pretty amazing. I remember as if it was yesterday. That was really, really special. And then of course, to get to play some of his tunes, which I love as well, it was complete. If you got a chance to play his tunes with him, it was really special.

Cedar and Billy had a serious chemistry and they really had it with Sam Jones big time. I would listen to them play a lot. To play with him and Billy, they had many years together. There were just a handful of rhythm sections that were really busy as an entity in themselves. Cedar and Billy were definitely that with Sam Jones on a lot of recordings. Cedar made it easy for everyone to play.

We also played a couple concerts in Portugal, which was much, much later, with Jimmy Cobb, Phil Woods and Lew Soloff. It was like an "all star" situation. I remember on occasion, Phil Woods had Cedar play something. He had to read, and I think he misread a chord change or something, and he [Phil] made some kind of comment, and Cedar put him in his place .... "Don't worry about it. I'll take care of it." Cedar wasn't the guy that you could put anything right in front of him and he could sightread it. He could read it, but he read mostly chord changes, predominately. This was supposed to be a musical setting that was compatible and not to be anything difficult. I remember Phil was trying to make it difficult, but he ended up changing the tune.

Cedar was humorous, very much so, and he always had a voice that was very recognizable. He didn't have to tell you it was him on the phone. He would call me and always say, "Professor Reid."

Cedar and I worked together with J.J. Johnson, when J.J. was basically coming back—sort of a resurgence of his career after being out in California for a long time. J.J. was coming out to rekindle his career as a player, and so he alluded to a lot of the more senior players, particularly Cedar because it was important to him. I remember one of the first times that Cedar and I played with J.J. was in Switzerland. Jimmy Heath and Lewis Nash were on the gig too. That was a lot of fun.

Thinking about Cedar's comping, I guess most people don't even categorize it as such by individual players, but I do. I would listen to him comp and he was one of the few pianists I knew that could comp below middle C. It would be really clear. It was the way he would voice things. It would always be in the right place. He used the whole keyboard. A lot of people use rootless voices in the middle of the piano or comp toward the upper mid of the piano. Cedar basically stayed lower. Punctuation, syncopation, and the rhythm were always strong. If pianists would latch ahold to some of that, they would probably work more. He was always melodic with the way he comped as well. It was never grandiose. It was always just what needs to be there at the moment, and strong. Those are the things that I think get missed by a lot of people.

It was so easy to play with Cedar. Sometimes, you forget how easy it is, until you have to work real hard playing with people. It really hit me hard, how much more fun it was to play when everybody just does what they do as opposed to worrying about [laughing] whether or not you can do it or having to carry someone to make it happen. That's the difference between a lot of the young kids who unfortunately don't get a chance to have that apprenticeship with someone like him.

I think people who really knew him knew that he was very consistent. There wasn't a time that he didn't play well. He never had one of those bad nights. Of course, I'm sure he could tell you he did, but it didn't come across that way.

He was very humorous. He had a punning kind of character. Everybody just loved being around him because he was a lot of fun to be around.

He was seemingly a fun-loving guy, and yet at the same time, if someone got on the back side of him, on the wrong side of him, he wouldn't allow that. He would have a big change, and you didn't mess with that. But you didn't see that often, if at all. I liked him a lot as a man.

Alvin Queen

I met Cedar around 1959–1960 during the Slugs' days when they had J.C. Moses and Dick Berk and Billy Higgins and all of them. That whole thing was a community of musicians. I also saw Cedar with Art Blakey. He was one of the composers who had made Art very popular at that time. He wrote "Mosaic," which was a big feature in Art Blakey's band.

This was a very, very powerful time for jazz music. I was there during the performance of John Coltrane's *Live at Birdland* recording. Elvin had taken me in. And he always told everybody, "That's my son. That's my son." Everybody would get together at Birdland. They would have Gretsch Drum Night down there where they would put me up on the drums. They were having Tony Williams and me play around the same time …. I ended up playing a couple places with Cedar in New York. I got to know Cedar and his playing at Boomers. His band was with Clifford Jordan, Billy Higgins, and Sam Jones. I knew Cedar on and off the bandstand. [laughs]

For several years, I played with Cedar at Ronnie Scott's. We would play three or four weeks there in London with Javon Jackson and David Williams. I also did a tour with that same band all over Germany.

When it came to music, Cedar was unbelievable. He was just one of these genius composers. All of Cedar's music connected with people. Cedar had some beautiful compositions. The way he put all that stuff together was incredible. Playing with him was an honor. It was also a school.

Cedar's stuff was not complicated. It wasn't all written out. A lot of times he used to write an idea on a piece of paper. And he said, "This is an idea. This is how it goes." From there, you were on your own. This was common for a lot of the leaders I worked with. I came up in the era when you had to hear.

Cedar would always take me around to meet the greatest musicians. He was very supportive. When I was on the road with him, we always had dinner at the bar or in the band room. He did things a certain way. He was part of a generation that opened the door for the younger guys if you were paying attention.

When you listen to Cedar and Billy Higgins together, that connection was the same thing that Elvin Jones and John Coltrane had. If you listen to Art Blakey and Cedar, that was one way of saying what he had to do. Billy had a more free way of playing. Cedar gained off of Billy and Billy gained off of Cedar. And for me to be sitting in that chair with Cedar and David, I said, "This is a job boy, Billy did a job here."

Cedar was unbelievable; he was a very honest person. And no matter what the gig paid or how it was, he always made it work. If he wanted to have you, he made it work. He wouldn't say, "Well I can just get this guy. That guy is cheaper." No. Cedar's gonna have what he wanted. That's the way he was. That's what I like about him. 100%, he's straight up and down. He was balanced with the musicians, and he was balanced with the audience. He was a perfect gentleman. He reminds me of Duke Ellington with that voice. I can still hear it.[2]

Brian Lynch

My first experience was hearing the *Live at Boomers* records. Those sides had a great impact on me. Growing up in the '70s listening to the music that was current at the time, there was a lot of music competing for my interest in terms of all the different styles. I started out listening to avant-garde, "electric jazz" and Miles's music.

I loved Woody and Freddie and all the other trumpet players, along with Lee Morgan and other players that were still fairly current. I came across that [*Boomers*] record from a friend of mine who I used to listen to a lot of music with. Between the two of us we would have all the records. And so he had this record and put it on and I was just like, "Wow" with the impact of that music sounding so good. I think the amount of drive in those live performances combined with everyone's playing really stood out along the way as well as the swing that was projected by Cedar. Listening to that record got me off all the avant-garde shit. The fact that this so-called more conventional music could sound so good was a revolution in my mind. It was funny because it didn't have anything to do with trumpet on that record!

I came to know pianist Dave Hazeltine and both of us kind of gravitated toward that style of playing even more. I've always loved pianists and I really want to play like a piano player sometimes. Cedar is just one of the real models for great playing in general. I think it's applicable to any instrument.

I didn't really play a lot with Cedar, certainly not as much as I wanted to. Most of the settings were one-off sort of things, some festivals and so on. I never played in his band, but the impact of his playing and his records was really very strong for me when I was coming up. I think that is something I share with other people that I grew up with or have outstanding relationships with. It seems like they have also had that experience in one way or another.

Another record that was really important to me and still is a very important record to me was Clifford Jordan's *Glass Bead Games*. I always feel like that's one of the secret master records of all time. Secret in that not many people know about it, but it seems like every-body who came across it knows what's happening with that record. It's an amazing record. And I think the intimacy and the immediacy of how it was recorded has a lot to do with it. You can hear the touch and the way the notes are coming out of the piano. There's something about in the way Cedar plays behind a horn player like he does in that record or when he does in Blakey's band or with his own bands, and also the way he phrases.

There's a conversation on I think the back of the *Boomers* record about their position between Cedar and Clifford. They start saying something about the way that he presses the note. There's something very unique in his touch. The weight of the note... It's the same kinda thing I hear in Freddie Hubbard's playing.

It gives you something to remember as you keep going. I still have strong recollections of that kind of weight of playing at something, touch, that when I practice or perform, I'm trying to get to that. It's what some people call a big note or great time. We could get more analytical about it I suppose. But definitely that quality of having attack while being legato at the same time was a big influence on my playing from that point.

It's something about the kind of music he plays and the way that he organized it to get that effect. Again, it's really subtle. His execution reminds me of Oscar Peterson sometimes, but it's looser. It's hipper. It's more flexible.

Thinking about composition, I had a hilarious interchange with Cedar. He was doing a Stanford jazz camp workshop. Now let's say, he wasn't the world's greatest clinician. At the end of the camp, he asked for questions. So I had raised my hand and he said "Brian what do you want?" I said, I always notice that in a lot of your tunes there are

certain things in there that really make me feel like this is your thing.
It's not like you invented that chord but a lot of times in crucial places
in your tunes you use a dominant 13 flat nine chord. Like an E triad on a
G seven." His tune "Clockwise" is a whole chain of them. So, I say that
and he answers, "I don't know what you're talking about." [Laughs].
So, either he just didn't want to say or he wasn't thinking about it in a
real, "oh yeah that's my thing. That's my signature."

Cedar had an amazing sense of humor. He and Curtis Fuller used
to call themselves corn-ographers. Curtis is the one that talks about
corn-ography, but Cedar's quite a practitioner. They'd have all these
puns and jokes. There's always this kind of ironic wise cracking sort of
thing going on.

[For Cedar,] it wasn't about explaining all those things about
music and technique. It was just living life and going through it with
a sense of irony. Being an African American in this country made
it necessary to have a very rich sense of irony at all times. The way
that the players of that generation carried and projected themselves,
humor was very important as a means to deal day to day with a
ridiculous and idiotic general situation, which hasn't changed, by
the way. I'm a big disciple of that old school kind of thinking—
keep some of the stuff at a distance and keep it light. If you got
under the hood, you'd probably find that Cedar or other guys that
I would associate with this kind of attitude, had the same kind of
anxieties and insecurities and issues with performing and creating
that anyone offset that same way would have. That's the way they
worked with it and transformed it.

Music making and performing was very social and very personal
for a musician like Cedar. And that's where all that warmth comes in
that you hear in his playing. Freddie too. Those guys went through
some stuff. There was a real brotherhood. Definitely right behind
you there's a real shared sensibility going on here. It's hard to put
it into words.

Cedar is an important musician and there's something that everyone can get from listening to him. There is something really special
about the essence of music and I've done a lot of thinking about what
a musician like him represents. Not just the piano style, he's an utter
virtuoso, but of a certain kind.

There's something really amazing about a guy like him and how
he functions with the end parameters of his playing. He's got his stuff
set up so he can always play at 99% no matter what. In a way it's
like he makes a decision like, "I'm not gonna be always out on the
ragged edge. Searching." Or "I'm gonna search within my mastery."

Or "Actually I'm gonna enjoy it." He was very clear and very secure in what he could play. There are other players are like that, but they might get a little bit rote or formulaic. Cedar never does. Some people don't get it, but I think a lot of people do. Even people that aren't into that style of playing.[3]

Steve Turre

I met Cedar, when I joined Art Blakey in San Francisco at the Keystone Korner in the Spring of 1973. Woody Shaw was my friend, and he brought me to Art and Art asked me to join the band. Woody was in the band, and Cedar was in the band. I went on to work with both of them. We became friends. It's really all because of Art Blakey. He brought so many people together.

I worked with Cedar on and off a lot, ever since then. There were certain times, if Curtis [Fuller] was available, Cedar might tell me, "Well Steve, Curtis could make this one." I understood that completely. I know a lot of young people in this day and age who'll go, "Well, am I in the band or not? Why don't you use me? I'm here now." For me, I'd be happy to get an opportunity to watch Curtis play all night. Jeez, that's like going to school. I understood that. I knew I didn't play like Curtis. Not at that time, especially. For me, it was no problem. It's like, you get a free lesson.

I love Cedar, and I learned so much from him. Mostly through osmosis. Every once in a while I might ask him a question, because I noticed when he would have a horn part on certain figures, he would play the piano along with the horn part, and he would use certain voices on the piano that would make the two horns sound even bigger. It's interesting to me because Horace Silver did that kind of writing too. I became aware of that. Cedar's compositions were all his own. He had a real style. You could just tell it was a Cedar Walton tune. Even though they were all kind of different, they just had this personality that was identifiable. This is something that's sorely missed in so many of today's young players.

A lot of today's young players are good soloists, but they don't know how to comp. Cedar is from that generation, you know, like Herbie [Hancock], and McCoy [Tyner] ... he's from that generation. All of them are as massive as accompanists as they are as soloists. That makes the band sound that much better. They bring so much to a band. Not just that they can play a dazzling solo, but they make the band strong in so many ways. It's a lost art, in a lot of cases.

I really felt Cedar never got his due recognition. The musicians knew and revered him. He always worked and drew big crowds and everything, but in terms of the media and the press, and just the business in general, they never gave him his real due, as far as I'm concerned. Cedar was very intelligent. Aware of all this shit. He found a way to make it. I just wish he could have been promoted more.

I did those records with Cedar on Columbia—*Soundscapes* and *Animation*. He had some hip stuff on "Precious Mountain," and "Jacob's Ladder," and all those things. I remember playing the music, and even though it had a bluesy, funky, Rhodes feeling, it still had an underlying swing in it—it was still hip. It wasn't corny or mindless. It was hip.

In Buddhism, we have a phrase called, "eshō-funi" and it means many bodies, one mind. Cedar and Billy were two separate bodies, but they were one mind. He and Billy had that. They could move with each other and would play something before the other played it, and yet it wasn't rehearsed. It was spontaneous. It was intuitive. It was magical. My second record as a leader, *Fire and Ice*, was with that rhythm section—Cedar, Buster [Williams], and Billy.

I know the musicians knew Cedar, but people in general didn't know much about him. He had a great sense of humor; it was kind of dry in a way, but it was hilarious. He'd say something that was direct and to the point. Even in conversation, not just when he was being funny. When he was trying to tell you something, he wouldn't beat around the bush. He'd just come straight out with it. Boom. Of course, his humor was hilarious. I remember, for instance one time, I was warming up, and my lips weren't vibrating, so I was playing loud trying to get my sound to open up. We're in the dressing-room and he said, "God Damnit, Turre, quit playing so damn loud, man!" [laughs].

One time, on a Sunday night in the summer, I was late to the gig. It's because all the people were coming back from the beach, coming back to New York at the end of the weekend. I didn't leave early enough, and the traffic was heavier than normal. I just got stuck. I came in about 40 minutes late, and he had already started, and you know, that's a drag, man. I felt bad about it. When I came in and he saw me in the dressing room, I didn't walk out because they were in the middle of a tune. When the tune was over, he said on the mic, "Now we have a trombonist, better late than never. We're going to feature him on a ballad." [laughs] I wasn't warmed up or anything and he put me out there and immediately featured me. That was my punishment. I'm never late, but it happens sometimes.

I learned so much from Cedar. Obviously, it wasn't technical, because I play trombone and he plays the piano. It was conceptual. It's wasn't just the writing thing. Everything he did had that concept. When Cedar would take a solo; the logic, the form, the continuity, it was like instantaneous composition. There was no bullshit in there. Everything he played meant something. He edited his brain as it was coming out. It could have been a composition that you wrote and thought of and edited, then rewrote and made it perfect like you would an orchestral symphony. But it would just come out of him that way, already edited in his mind, and his voice, and his use of tension and release and dynamics. It was not only musical, but so perfect in its compositional completeness. I don't think people understood it, from my perspective as a musician. But they knew something special was going on. They could hear intuitively, the sense of mastery in his brain. Boy, his playing was a motherfucker.

Every once in a while, he'd ask for a little guideline. He'd say, "Why don't you leave a little more space on this or take your time here or go on and hit it?" I don't think he'd have you there unless he intuitively trusted your instincts. Even when I played with the Messengers, we're all coming out of that same school, and there are certain things with that about how you feel the rhythm and how you conceptualize the music. That's one of the great musical universities on the planet and it was such a unique experience to play with Art. Cedar used to talk about Art Blakey all the time, and we all did. Not just laughing and reminiscing about the crazy stuff and the funny stuff, but about the music too.

I have to thank my dear friend Woody Shaw, for introducing me to my dear friend Cedar Walton. And I miss them both tremendously.[4]

Christian McBride

One of the earliest jazz recordings that I fell in love with was a pretty rare recording he [Cedar] did with Charles Davis, Hank Mobley, Sam Jones, and Billy Higgins called *Breakthrough*. It was on the Cobblestone label from the early '70s. I guess it was Hank Mobley's last recording. It was recorded in 1972. There was something about that record, man. The energy is just screaming off that record. I fell in love with that record when I was maybe 11 years old and that was my first introduction to Cedar Walton. Eventually I discovered those great records he made with Art Blakey. Every last single one of those records. I pretty much devoured every note from all those recordings from *Mosaic* all the way through to *Free for All*. What a band of superheroes. And then I discovered all of the *Eastern Rebellion* records. This was all while I was still in high school. I realized that Cedar was one of my favorite composers. I realized all of my favorite songs from a lot of those recordings were Cedar's songs. As much as Wayne Shorter is justifiably a titan in terms of modern jazz composition, I always thought of Cedar Walton being right there next to him.

When I made my first record, I recorded in 1994 and it came out in '95. The song "The Shade of the Cedar Tree," which is at least as far as I know my most well-known song, comes straight from Cedar. You know the whole idea of having a particular theme with some really pretty chord changes that are linear in motion. I think the only thing that separates Wayne and Cedar certainly is not the level of "prolificness" because Cedar has a whole lot of great songs. The harmonic movement of Cedar's songs can be pretty linear in that you might know what's coming but it doesn't matter because it's so utterly gorgeous and it's so catchy. I think that's what I love about Cedar's music. It's very sophisticated, but it's catchy as well. So that melody on "The Shade of the Cedar Tree," that's directly influenced by Cedar. And I think the greatest compliment I ever got was when Cedar asked me for the sheet music to that song. He said "Man, I really like that." I said "Wow!" If no one else in the world liked it but him, I'm cool.

He was great. I remember that I didn't get to play a gig with him for a very long time. But once we started playing gigs together it started happening quite a bit. I think the first gig we ever played together was the CD released for Chesky called *New York Time*. At that time, I was the creative chair for jazz programing with the LA Philharmonic and was in charge of curating all of the shows at Walt Disney Concert Hall and at the Hollywood Bowl. We had a big tribute to Horace Silver, and I asked Cedar to play the Horace Silver chair. He graciously accepted the gig and he played so great that night. Thank God that concert was recorded by NPR, so it's still archived on the internet. But that was such a great night, man. Charles Tolliver played. Benny Maupin and George Coleman, Randy Brecker, Tom Harrell, Joe Lovano, Andy Bey, Dee Dee Bridgewater, Roger Humphries. It was just great to hear Cedar really play the hell out of all of that music, man. His musicianship abilities never waned in his later years. Even after he started to get sick. He was still a great sight-reader, still listened to the entire band and hooked up with the band no matter who was playing. Just a supreme, supreme, musician.

The last time we played together, I believe it was the summer of 2012 when The Nash opened up in Phoenix, Arizona. Lewis Nash's place. And Lewis put together an all-star band with myself, Cedar, Russell Malone, and Houston Person. We played the opening of that place and we had to play a private concert the night before for some of the donors. And you know, it was just great to hang out and play with Cedar. It was awesome.

When we were making that record [*New York Time*] with Jimmy Cobb and Javon, Cedar and I both got towed. The session was actually in a church. And we came out of the church after the session was over and said, "Hey man, where are our cars?" We were like "Uh-oh, I think we might have parked in the wrong zone." And we both got on the phone and realized that we had both gotten towed. And so Javon Jackson had to drive us over to the tow pound over on the West-Side Highway. Especially at that time, the tow pound was so nasty. I mean there were rats running around and a bunch of drunk guys in the little lobby waiting for their cars and stuff. And if they did a breathalyzer test on them, I'm sure they'd get arrested. There Cedar and I are in the middle of the tow pound at midnight on like a Wednesday night or something like that. It was surreal. Who would ever believe the great Cedar Walton and I were here at midnight trying to retrieve our cars from the New York traffic department? He got his car. I didn't get mine because as it turns out, my wife had an unpaid parking ticket that she didn't tell me about. So that's another story. [laughs]

Cedar and Billy Higgins, I thought they were a great comedy team. They had some, you know the little British accent thing. Cedar was a master of puns. Just look at some of his song titles. I remember asking Cedar what "N.P.S." stood for, 'cause that's one of my favorite songs. He said "Oh yea, nipples." [laughs] I said, "Yea that makes sense!" Oh man, Cedar was a master comedian.

I think his abilities as a composer is what separated him from many. He was so prolific as a composer and a band leader. Again, his sound. The fact that he was able to create so much sound out of that instrument and not really tax himself. The way he talked about Art Blakey saying that that is something that every pianist develops. So I started thinking about Mulgrew Miller and Benny Green and James Williams and John Hicks. All these pianists I knew who played with Art Blakey. Cedar had this amazing control when you watched him play. It was very controlled. There was never a lot of excess motion in his body. He got this great, great sound. He swung very, very hard with no matter who was in the rhythm section. And that's just pure musicianship. Being able to do that I think is a great way of not being too idealistic.

It's somewhat OK for a jazz artist to be a little bit of an overthinker and therefore not being able to play with a whole lot of people and somehow justify it. But I hear Cedar playing with Jack DeJohnette, Billy Higgins, Jimmy Cobb, Alvin Queen, Tootie Heath, Roger Humphries, and it always sounds great. Whoever the bandleader is he is just always at a high level.

I think he could have been one of the world's best comedians. I really think he could have had a career as a stand-up comic. Cedar was just, oh God, he was so funny. [laughs] I always wished that I could have been a fly on the wall to see the everyday interactions between him and Freddie Hubbard, Wayne Shorter, and Curtis Fuller, Reggie Workman, and Art Blakey. I mean there must have been a lot laughs in that band. Oh my God there must have been a lot of laughs. I remember being with Wayne Shorter one time and somehow, we saw a picture of Homer Simpson like in magazine or on a billboard or something. And Wayne said, "Hey man, don't that look Cedar?" [laughs] I remember thinking that if Cedar were here right now, they'd probably have a dozens contest and it would be the funniest thing I'd ever heard in my whole life. I wish I could have seen those guys together.[5]

Piero Odorici

I met Cedar for the first time in the early '90s. Alberto Alberti, a great Italian music manager, introduced me to him during a concert of Cedar with his trio. Cedar was an incredible person, very generous, nice, with a great sense of humor and a very big heart. I started to love and study Cedar's music before I met him. I learned a lot of things from him, first of all the importance of human relationships between musicians and the real value of the essentiality in music. This deals with rhythm, melodies and harmony.

He has been like a spiritual and musical father for me. We always kept in touch during long periods in which we didn't play together. We enjoyed going to dinner together and having very long chats about music and our lives. I know his wife Martha very well; she is a wonderful woman and we still keep in touch.

After our first meeting, Cedar returned to Italy with his quartet (Ralph Moore on tenor sax, David Williams Bass and Billy Higgins on drums). I went to the first gig of the tour and at the end of the concert Cedar came close to me and confessed to me that he was really afraid of his driver, because, in his opinion, he drove too fast. So I asked him if he wanted me as a driver and he told me yes! The first tour I did with him was as a driver! During this tour at the end of every gig he invited me on stage to play a couple of tunes as a way to say thanks for driving him and his group everywhere. He was a great piano player but also an incredible composer of modern jazz music.[6]

Terell Stafford

I played with Cedar on a Trumpet Summit tour; basically, it was a tribute to Louis Armstrong and then part-way through they had a bunch of trumpet players playing and that's what the tour was called. We had done some traveling with Cedar in the states and abroad as well.

You know, it's funny, when you play with a great accompanist you never notice. When it's the other way, you always notice. Wherever you went, Cedar was there. That's what I appreciated about him, always swinging and always felt good and always 100% supportive, on and off the bandstand.

He'd always call me Lord Stafford. That was his nickname for me. And I'd always call him Cedaro. He'd say, "Lord Stafford? Would you like to accompany me for an adult beverage?" And we'd talk about life. A lot of these guys played for their work. I would never just sit and pick their brains too often, I would just sit back and let them tell stories. I learned valuable lessons that way. Cedar was always funny and had a great sense of humor, just a beautiful individual.[7]

John Clayton

I first met Cedar through Ray Brown and Milt Jackson. Ray and Milt would reserve their summers to play together. They'd been friends since they were kids in Dizzy Gillespie's band. Milt Jackson would pull away from the Modern Jazz Quartet and Ray would pull away from his studio work and they would just play. They'd do local gigs in Los Angeles, usually a week or two at Shelly's Manne-Hole. They'd play at the Lighthouse. They'd also go up north to San Francisco etc. They'd do at least four to six weeks. In the beginning, they had Monty Alexander. I'm pretty sure that's the way it happened because Monty was with them in 1969 and that's around when they first started doing this. Thereafter, if Monty couldn't make it, they'd get Cedar. In 1970, I was a 16-year-old kid going to hear that band and Monty was with them at first. Soon after, I got to hear Cedar Walton with them and that's when Ray and or Milt introduced me to Cedar. I had heard his name before but I really didn't know how heavy weight he was until after meeting him and starting to research and finding all of the great amazing stuff he'd done with everybody from Blakey on.

Cedar influenced me largely. I would end up transcribing his solos because I loved them so much. He represented what I wanted to sound like as a soloist. I loved his lines and ideas. He can weave in and out of the chord changes in a way that is timely and modern. He also has a bluesy element which I also really relate to. Cedar is one of those piano players that is really kind of the model for me. There's a small handful of musicians that if I could be somebody else, I would like to be them, and Cedar is one of those.

I like his lines, but I loved how in most cases he seemed to build and arch his solos. He'd do that in different ways. It could be with volume, it could be content, it could be the thickness of texture. Again, it wasn't a formula he used all the time. He just naturally took his solos to places that were really interesting for me. In terms of playing with him in the rhythm section, I always felt like he played real jazz. [laughs] It sounds strange, but he never tried to play an impressive solo. He never tried to as we say, "get house." He was totally not about that. He was just 100% jazz. Period. Play it, not trying to get over. I loved that. Milt Jackson was like that too. All the people that I really admire were like that. I tend not to relate to the people who say, "Well let's do this one because the audience really likes it when we do this or do that." They were playing the music because they felt like playing it and sharing it with people. They hoped people would relate to it, but if they didn't, maybe they'll relate to this next one we're going to play for you. Cedar was like that.

I remember he had a great way of keeping it real for himself and not taking himself too seriously. His sense of humor was very dry and full of puns and that was really great, but he laughed at himself too. He'd be playing a solo and in the middle of the line if he played something he didn't like, he would just lift both hands off the piano and he would laugh. He'd just kind of chuckle and then continue playing the solo. I saw that a bunch of times, you know where he'd play something he didn't mean or wasn't satisfied with and just kind of laugh at it and keep going. That was a big lesson for me.

Cedar and I spoke more about his experiences—playing with people and life and things like that, which of course were tied to the music. But he never talked about his harmonic approach or anything like that. He didn't need to. I'm sure if I would have asked, he would have shared it. He might have tried to shrug it off. We were close enough that I could get things from him. He knew how much I loved his music. I arranged for him for different large ensemble situations. It was easy to do because I would just use his content and the flavor of his songs. If it was swingin' and kind of bluesy, then I would have a swingin' and bluesy approach. When I started to write for him, he really started complimenting me. At some point I remember him calling out of the blue. I think he left a message, and the message was that he really admired what I did and loved my musicianship and thought of me as a real maestro. I thought "What?" [laughs] Just out of the blue. It was so touching but also odd because that's the way I felt about him.

The playing situations I had with him were always me coming into whatever group he was involved in. I would ask him specific things like when we played "Bolivia" there's a part of the bass line at the end of the melody just before it goes into the vamp that I wasn't quite sure about. That last bar or two bars. I said "Cedar, is it this note, or this note?" and he said, "Either one." You know, here's the composer of the song and I thought he had a definite idea of what he wanted at that point from the bass player. But nope, he was totally open. Sometimes it was hard to get exact information from him. I'm sure if I was playing the melody incorrectly, he could show me that. But those instances didn't really arise.

Cedar was a very compassionate guy, but it was always hidden by his quiet humble approach. You wouldn't know by hanging around him how much he loved his daughter, for instance. Sure, he loved his daughter, you can imagine that. But the depth of that he wouldn't show obviously. And then it might come out in just some small thing he would say or something he would do. I remember getting a real feeling when Naisha was around how he'd beam, but it wouldn't be an obvious kind of beam. You really had to be around him a lot to see that he was really happy to see her. He had a huge smile. That was always there. The deeper stuff he kept in reserve.

When thinking of my favorite albums with Cedar, the *Reverence and Compassion* record was a really special project. I honestly think about the albums he did with Milt Jackson whether I'm on them or not. Cedar was Milt's favorite piano player. Period. He loved playing with everybody else. Hank Jones, Monty Alexander, McCoy, you name it. He loved playing with them, but Cedar was his favorite. I just loved hearing them together.[8]

Roy Hargrove

I met Cedar when I came to New York. I did a recording with him called *Composer* with Christian McBride and Victor Lewis, Vincent Herring, Ralph Moore. I didn't know he was from Dallas until much later. And then I found out he was from Dallas. His mother actually lived on the same block as my cousin.

He's like a minimalist. You can't really see a lot of motion from what he's playing, but there's a lot of music coming out of it at the same time. It looks like he's right in the middle of the piano, but it's tremendous. There's a lot of swing there. He's coming from the lineage of people like Red Garland. Dallas swing.

Cedar is a very complete musician. We did some duo concerts together. It was like playing with an entire group. I didn't miss the rhythm section at all, 'cause everything was there. All the harmony, all the rhythm, and definitely all the melodicism.

He is definitely one of my favorite composers of all time. Basically just because of the way he uses harmony. It reminds me a lot of my hometown and just the experiences that I had growing up there.

Cedar is definitely one of my great influences, mostly because of the fact that he comes from the same place that I grew up in. There's a lot of blues and a lot of melodic influence there and his harmony, his sense of harmony, that whole bebop thing, it's something that is a big influence on my playing. I'm just glad that I got the opportunity to be able to work with him. It gave me a lot of influence as far as music in my development as an artist.[9]

Terence Blanchard

I always appreciated how intentional Cedar's playing was. Quite often, younger pianists play with a lot of chatter in their left hand. They aren't always connected to and aware of what their left hand is playing. It tends to be very busy and can take away from what they are playing their right hand. Cedar wasn't like that. He was very calm, and his left hand always complemented what he played. He was always in control.

I first recorded with him in 1990 for a record date he led call *As Long as There's Music*. One of the things I remember about playing with Cedar and Billy was the intensity and sound they played with. When we were recording that session, I remember listening to the playback and thinking about the huge sound he and Billy got. A little later I was in the big room where Cedar and Billy were playing, and I was amazed at how focused and intense their sound was while not being dynamically that loud. That stuck with me.[10]

John and Paula Hackett

JH: I knew a drummer that was playing with Milt Jackson in San Francisco, and we went back to Milt's house after the gig, me, Paula, my girlfriend, and the drummer Richie Goldberg, and we're hanging out with Milt. I asked him if he wanted to go out to dinner, and he said, "No, why don't you come back and eat chicken legs with me?" We did, and one of the things he did was he played for us was a recording he made in Japan that had Cedar on it. I remember him telling me that Cedar's the only guy he knows who could play the keyboard and the electric piano and play it well at that time in 1975. So that kind of put Cedar in my ear.

We first went to New York in 1983. Cedar made a CD with Judy Niemack [*Blue Bop*]. She did "Bolivia" and Paula and I wrote the lyrics to it and Cedar liked it! That was a big break for us. It was the first thing we had recorded. We were off and running.

Max [Roach] was putting a record together for a singer Shannon Gibbons, and Shannon wanted lyrics to Cedar's material. Shannon was Max's girlfriend at the time, and she knew my sister Regina, who was a critic in Seattle, and knew that Paula and I were lyricists. She asked us to do a vocal album of Cedar's songs. When we started on this project, one of the things Cedar said to us when we first met him was, he would never ask us to change any lyrics, and we should never ask him to change any music. We went to New York and had demos of "Bolivia," "Night Flight," and "Holy Land." We played "Holy Land" for him, and he jumped out of his chair and said, "I love it."[11]

PH: Cedar, John, and I, and Diane [Witherspoon] had four rehearsals, and we had one with Billy [Higgins] before the recording. Cedar took it very seriously. We had most of the songs. We had to write three of them during the rehearsal time, but Diane was great. Diane was a great singer. And when Cedar met her, we brought Diane to a club in San Francisco, and Cedar said she can get up and do "Bolivia." And after she did, Cedar said, "We have our singer." Cedar loved Diane's singing. The recording took two sessions, three hours each. The first session had to end [early] because they had to go to Japan that day, and Cedar didn't remember where he had put his dry cleaning. So, Billy had to drive around Santa Monica looking for his dry cleaning. [laughs][12]

JH: It was hard to get Cedar to do lead sheets, even to give it to singers, but he was determined in a way to do this stuff. He needed a little bit of a commercial break, which I don't know if he ever got it, but some of the songs that we wrote with him continue to be out there. He got a new audience, in a way.

When we recorded the CD *You May Never Know* in 1991, Cedar had some problems with it. At the rehearsal with Billy [Higgins] the day before, he said, "This may just be a demo," and Billy said, "If it's a demo, it's going to be the greatest damn demo ever made." Billy showed up the day before, and Cedar had rehearsed four or five times with Diane, but they were going to rehearse the day before with the trio and then record the CD, but Cedar didn't hire a bassist for the rehearsal. Billy said, "Where's Dumas?" Tony Dumas was Cedar's West Coast bassist for a long time. And Cedar said, "You know, I couldn't get ahold of him." And Billy was very irritated, which you don't see too much with Higgins. Billy said, "You have his phone number. You have his cell. You have his pager. What was he? Under water, Cedar?" There was no excuse for that.

That evening, Billy was playing at Vine Street Bar and Grill in LA with John Heard on bass. Billy asked John that night to come into the studio the next day and record with us. That was a hard task to do because he didn't know Cedar's material. John ended up playing on some of the tracks and Cedar got Tony Dumas to record some, too. Initially, Cedar used the recording as a demo and gave it to a couple singers. Both Vanessa Rubin and Kevin Mahogany did songs from the demo.[13]

PH: Donald Elfman was the first person we played the demo for. He ran the jazz department at Koch. He jumped on it and put it out in 1999. Cedar was very frustrated by money. He wanted to do more with the songs. He wanted to do the songs with strings, for instance. And we had the trio. He was always frustrated by that. But finally, when he said put it out, we gave it to Donald, and it came out.[14]

JH: We didn't get a lot of money for it, but we got a good presentation.

JH: I was with him when his mother died. He called me and said his mother had passed away, and he had to go do the Drew Jazz Festival in LA with a bunch of younger musicians in his quartet. He asked if I would drive him. Well, if he'd asked me to drive him to Texas, I would have done it at that point. So we drove out there. Cedar composed himself completely the whole time, as if nothing had happened. He was a little quiet in the car and played really well at the festival. After they hit, he was holding court and telling interesting stories and making jokes with the group. As things started to break up, Cedar began speaking to an older musician who was an arranger from LA. I think Cedar had worked with him with some of the commercial stuff. He and this guy were about the same age. As the people began to drift away it was just the three of us there. And all of a sudden, Cedar got real serious and started talking about Ruth. And it was really something to watch the other musician relate to him on that level about his dead mother. It was really touching. Then Cedar began to cry, and he started to really weep. And then he was fine again.

I guess the cliché would be he got it out of his system for a while, but it was really good that he could talk about it. I don't think there were any announcements or anything like that at the festival. He was all business.[15]

Willie Jones

I first became aware of Cedar's playing from Art Blakey and Jazz Messengers, J.J. Johnson's band and the Jazztet recordings. I also had checked out Eastern Rebellion and many of the trio recordings led by Cedar. Whenever Cedar came to LA to play with Billy Higgins and David Williams, I was always right there in the front row.

I met Cedar through Billy Higgins. Billy founded The World Stage in Los Angeles along with poet Kamau Daáood. Billy brought Cedar to his workshop, and he got Cedar to play with us. We were all young students playing his tunes. That was amazing! Four or five years later after doing the workshop, I was still living in LA, and out of nowhere, Cedar called me to play with him. One gig. That was a great experience. I moved to New York a couple years after that and Cedar would call me from time to time to sub for Kenny Washington or Joe Farnsworth. Around 2008/2009, I became Cedar's regular drummer. By that time, I knew his whole songbook and I was ready. Playing with Cedar was one of greatest experiences of my life.[16]

Steve Davis

I first heard Cedar on the J.J. Incorporated records, *JJ Inc.*, on Columbia. I was a high school student in New York and a friend of mine who was a little older than me and also into jazz hipped me to this record; I'd been listening to J.J. some, but I didn't have that one, and that recording just completely galvanized me immediately, and you know

Cedar's on that. I remember in particular, there's a blues called "Fatback." The original version of it is like two or three choruses of just trio out front. And I was always just blown away with Cedar's playing, you know it's just how tasteful, swinging, and how perfect it sounded, and then of course J.J.'s playing too. There was that recording and the *Ugetsu* record by the Messengers. I'd been listening to Curtis Fuller, and Cedar and Curtis did many things together. I remember seeing the Timeless All Stars in person at Sweet Basil. I just fell in love immediately. But I didn't start out with his trio, this prodigious trio catalog; that came later for me. Then I became an absolute devotee to this band.

It wasn't even a conscious thing. I just loved the feeling of those Messengers records. Being a young trombone player, we all owe such a huge debt to Curtis Fuller. His sound is so personal. It was the footprint for us to step into as far as ensemble playing and soloing of course; just the overall concept and sound and approach. And, of course, everybody in that band, Wayne, Freddie, Curtis, and Cedar were such great composers, arrangers, and of course so were Lee Morgan and Bobby Timmons, and then Benny Golson, obviously, before them and so on. That body of work that the Messengers did in that period is just a huge influence on so many jazz musicians, and certainly on me.

I remember seeing Cedar play with the Timeless All Stars in the mid-to-late '80s at Sweet Basil; I saw that group with Harold Land, and Curtis, and Bobby Hutchinson, Buster Williams, and Billy Higgins, many, many times. That was a huge influence on me, and then just going to see Cedar's trio, I was then seeing his trio with Billy Higgins and Ron Carter or with Buster Williams, and of course David Williams, so I was just drawn to his music and pretty much anything he was doing. I wanted to be there, and only dreamt of possibly someday playing with him—that was a far-off dream for a long time.

I met Cedar through Jackie McLean, back when I was playing in Jackie's band in the '90s. And sometimes Cedar would come to hear us. One time he was there, I had written a tune called "I Found You," that we were doing in J-Mac's band at The Vanguard, and I was maybe, 26. And Cedar spoke to me after the set, I was walking back down the hallway back there, and he asked me—he complimented me on the piece, because Jackie had introduced it on the set, and Cedar said, I'll never forget this, he said, "Yo, Davis, how long did it take you to write that piece, "I Found You," all of maybe 20 minutes or so?" And then he flashed that wry grin of his, and I said, "In fact, yeah, it just kind of came out all at once. That was pretty much it." And he said, "I thought so." Obviously, I felt supremely honored and complimented by that, but I also felt like he could just tell. So that was really cool. What a thrill!

It was not too long after that that Eric Alexander had a record date, for the Japanese label; the record was called *Man with a Horn*, and Farnsworth's on it, Dwayne Burno, and Eric. And then for three tracks, he had Jim Rotundi and me join the group. We recorded "I Found You" on Eric's record because Eric knew the story about the tune and my interaction with Cedar and those guys liked the tune. So we had already recently formed One For All, and we had been playing it, more as a Bossa Nova ballad, as opposed to a straight ballad, and Eric wanted to record it and said, "You know, if Lord Walton likes your tune, why don't we do that?" And we did "Midnight Waltz," and one of Eric's originals called "CJGC," which stands for Clifford Jordan George Coleman.

I remember, "I Found You" came out great; they all came out great. With "Midnight Waltz," Cedar brought the parts, and his handwriting, and the absolute flow—he always had something fresh, I noticed. He would rework his pieces slightly, in different ways; he had voiced it for the three of us, and what a thrill. That was the first time I really felt like I'm playing with a band, and to play "Midnight Waltz" with him on Eric's record was amazing. Then a year later we did Joe Farnsworth's session *Beautiful Friendship* back in the late '90s. I think we recorded four of Cedar's arrangements on that one, and Joe had asked me to write an original for that. Eddie Henderson was on the date, I called it "Eddie's Mood." I actually finished writing the tune on the dashboard of bassist Nat Reeves's car on the way to the date. And I remember we heard a playback, and Cedar looked at me and smiled, and he said, "Yeah," he said, "Call and response. A tried-and-true formula." And then he smiled, and I could tell that he thought it was alright.

Joe had asked him to arrange "Lament" as a feature for me which, oh, man, he sure did! I remember at one point, he [Cedar] commented that I should phrase the melody all the way through. I think I broke it up, because I just hadn't taken an ample breath, and he knew it. He said, "You know, Davis, you oughta play that in one breath, if you could." He was so astute; it was just incredible. And it wasn't an insult, it was constructive. He helped me. That was really something.

Cedar called me for a couple other dates a couple years later, around 2000. A Vanessa Rubin record [*Girl Talk*], with Lewis Nash and David Williams, and I think Javon Jackson and myself played some horn parts, took a solo or two. There was one other date with Freddy Cole called *Merry-Go-Round*. Cedar, Eric [Alexander], myself, George Mraz, and the drummer Curtis Boyd. We recorded in one room without any separation. And the way we were seated, I was sitting right at the top of the right hand of Cedar at the piano. I could just look back over my shoulder, and Lord Walton was grinning at me. And I thought, "Wow, this is the place to be right here."

After that, we did play together some, at Smoke, but usually I sat in with his band; or, one night I dropped by Smoke, and he was playing trio with Farnsworth and David Williams, and I'd been working downtown somewhere, and I came in just in time for the third set. And he said, "Would you care to join us, Lord Davis?" And I played the whole set, quartet; we did "Little Sunflower," and a lot of his standard pieces. It was one of the greatest sets I've ever experienced in my life, as far as being on the bandstand. Of course, it didn't get recorded, documented, or anything, but I remember the feeling. It felt so good, and we just had such a good time. I think that was around 2005.

In more recent years, we were friends. He would call me, and I'd call him and just check in, and Martha, of course. I'd love to go see him, and he'd come out and see us once in a while, which always was such a thrill to have him come and hang at a gig. I really had hopes to play with him some more, but, you know, I'll take what I got, gladly.

Cedar was hilarious. I mean, he had a razor-sharp wit, and it always used to knock me out that I'd see .... Here's his number. There it was. And I thought, "Wow, Cedar Walton is calling me." And I didn't necessarily think, "Oh, it's gonna be a gig." I didn't even care about that. I was just so thrilled that Cedar would call. And of course, I would call him too, and we would get into these banters—and the puns were immediate, you had to be on your A-game. You couldn't just speak in a sort of B-flat, stock kind of way. "So, how's it going? So, what have you been up to?" That wasn't gonna cut it. And somehow, he and I really clicked, and I think I made him laugh a few times, and I think he liked that. He certainly had me in stitches all the time. But he also kept you thinking in a sort of acute way; it was just like his playing. What's the most concise, important thing to say right now, or, how to say it. And it didn't make you uncomfortable, it was just—he's a master. He's a keen mind at work, and it was so fun to talk with him.

One day in 2012, I was playing at Dizzy's, in January with Willie Jones III, who had recently joined Cedar's trio after Farnsworth left. So, I'm working with Willie, and it was a tribute to Max Roach. We were making a live record that week. I'm staying in Manhattan at a spot I used to stay at a lot, on the Upper West Side. It's 5 o'clock,

I come back to the pad and think, "Wow, I gotta get dressed for the gig." So, I'm getting ready, scrambling a little, and the phone rings. So, I'm getting ready, and I realize, oh, it's January 17th. I need to call Lord Walton and wish him happy birthday. So, I'm literally putting on my pants, and I'm getting dressed, tying my tie, and my phone lights up, and there it is, Cedar Walton. There's his number, his home number, and I'm thinking, "God, wow."

So, I pick up the phone, and I think I'm gonna be cute with him, you know? I think I have something funny for him. I picked up the phone, I said, "Why Lord Walton, I believe this would be bass-ackwards, as they say, but shouldn't it be me calling you on your birthday?" And there's a pause, a very brief pause, and he says, "Yes, why, Lord Davis, I'm merely employing the age-old tactic of the preemptive strike." I love it. That one makes me laugh every day. [laughs] He really just wanted to ask about the gig, how it was going, "I see you're with Lord Jones," and he was just curious about the band, and just letting me know that he was aware of what we were doing down there. He never did make it that week, but I just love that on his birthday, he called me. And I thought I had something for him, and of course he just— nope. [laughs][17]

Dale Barlow

First of all, my dad's a musician. He was a saxophone player and played some flute and clarinet in those days and was also an arranger. He had a big band. My mom played piano, so I grew up with music around the house. There were all kinds of things, every kind of jazz you can imagine. There were these secondhand record shops when I was a kid. I ended up buying all these records for a dollar each. Anything with a saxophone player or flute player on it, because they're the two horns that I love. I ended up buying all these recordings and one of them was *Glass Bead Games* by Clifford Jordan, which was one of my favorite albums at the time, with Cedar Walton, Billy Higgins, Sam Jones and Bill Lee on bass. Spike Lee's dad on some tracks. Stanley Cowell on piano. I thought the recording was impeccable. It was beautiful. It was just pure poetry.

I transcribed the compositions because in those days that's what you had to do, there was never anything else. So, I wrote them all out and I play piano too, I figured out all of the chords, the changes, and I played quite a lot of them with my band when I was in my teens. After hearing Cedar and that rhythm section, I got hold of the *Eastern*

Rebellion records with George Coleman, and the ones with Bob Berg. I loved them. I compiled quite a bit of a Cedar collection and became a fan of his compositions. I loved the way he wrote, and his songs were so much fun and so playable, too.

Cedar's playing was great and unusual for the time. If you were listening to jazz at that time, there's lots of McCoy Tyner and Herbie Hancock, in terms of piano players. But I thought, "Who was this?" Cedar Walton's just a monster. He's got another angle to his playing rather than just bebop. He's got a really interesting swag on things. And it's all beautiful soul-felt music. I thought it was really deep and rich and just fantastic.

I left for the states when I was pretty young. I was about 20, I'd just finished this jazz course at the Sydney Conservatory, which it was pretty good for what it was at the time. Just a two-year course, anybody who's good could get into it. That sort of opened me up to a whole range of new things. I went to New York, and toured in America with a youth big band. James Morrison and myself were the featured soloists and played at a lot of colleges in the United States. Our group didn't play in New York, and I knew it was the place to be, so I just went there. I ended up separating from the group and I kind of ran away from home. I spent a month in New York and during that time I heard Cedar with George Coleman. It was marvelous and I heard tons and tons of other music, of course. It was summer, jazz was being played all over the city in parks and stuff.

After I finished studying, I moved to New York. I was probably about 20 or 21 and I lived there for three years. I was on the scene and was another young musician from abroad trying to improve his abilities and skills and get to know the scene and learn. I was just there for that, and I loved it. I played lots of gigs with some pretty notable players.

After that I moved to London because my girlfriend at the time was a classical violinist and she got a gig over there and we were incredibly in debt, way back on the rent, hadn't paid the phone bills. It was a total mess, and I didn't know how we're gonna survive and neither did she. Finally, she got this classical gig in London, so I thought, "Well, I haven't got much choice, really, haven't paid the rent for about four months and I haven't been eating for a while and maybe it'd be a good idea."

So, I went to London and it was good. I hooked up with a whole lot of people there and I'd just been doing the thing in New York, so I think I sounded pretty good. In London I started looking around and seeing what was available. Ronnie Scott's was the main place back in those days. That was the only place open late at night. I ended up hanging there every night. I got to know Ronnie really well. Being another saxophone player, we spent a lot of time hanging out together.

He really helped me a lot. He did this interview in *The Guardian*, and it's a glowing review of me playing at the club. Ronnie also called up a whole lot of people and told them about me. One was Cedar Walton, another was Elvin Jones, and another was Victor Feldman.

I ended up playing with all those guys, most notably, Cedar. Ronnie just talked Cedar into letting me sit in. I sat in for a couple of songs and then Cedar got me to sit in on the next set. He said, "Hey, Dale, you mind playing a couple more songs? You know 'Ojos de Rojo'?" And the funny thing was, to be absolutely honest, I had never played any of those songs before, but I'd had them on tape with Bob Berg playing them, Clifford Jordan, Junior Cook and George Coleman, I knew them by ear. I've always had good ears. You can fake it till you make it. I've always been able to pick things up really quickly. I could pretend even if I didn't know it.

I knew the songs by ear. I wasn't exactly sure where the harmonies went and I didn't even know the song forms, I didn't really know what key they were in, because a lot of them move around. When he said, "Do you know 'Firm Roots'" or "do you know 'Ojos de Rojo' or 'Clockwise'?" I could sort of get through them. I knew the melodies. I had no idea what I was doing, but I knew the melodies enough to play them, and Cedar thought I knew all these songs. I mean, I was surprised. You know, when he said, "Oh, man, it's great. You really checked out all of my songs, man!"

We ended up playing things like "Bridge Work" and "Shoulders" and songs that are slightly unusual Cedar songs because I loved his music. I asked myself, "Have I really fooled Cedar? Are you kidding me? How come he thinks I know all these tunes?" I was just faking it; I had no idea really what those songs were about.

I got up there endlessly. The next night Cedar said, "Come down, play some more of my tunes, man." I came down and I played some more of his songs and I felt like I just barely got through by the skin of my teeth. He was happy about that, and he sort of dug it, so I was a bit mystified at first, to be honest. I thought, "Well, gee, maybe you can fool some of the people all of the time and all of the people some of the time." But I was quite surprised that Cedar actually got me in the band. He said, "I got this little tour coming up and we got a record."

At the session he just hit me with a whole lot of songs I'd never played before, and I figured them out by ear and a basic sketch of a chart, and we just played them. We didn't rehearse or anything, we just played the record. That recording was *Bluesville Time* with Billy Higgins, David Williams, and Cedar. After that, we continued doing some gigs around Europe. I just stayed back in the U.K. for a while. Eventually I went back to the States and ended up doing some gigs with him there as well. I played with him sporadically over about probably ten years or more.

Playing with Cedar was a great entry into everything else because the musical fraternity really respects Cedar, and they love his playing and anyone playing with Cedar. It sort of gives you a good leg up. I think that's probably one reason I ended up getting into Art Blakey's Jazz Messengers in 1989—because I'd played with Cedar. He recommended me to Art Blakey. I ended up playing with Art Blakey in the last version of Art Blakey's Jazz Messengers with all the chaps, and that was a lot of fun. Recorded two albums with Art Blakey before he passed away and of course, Cedar was with Art Blakey as well. There's a nice connection there.

I've hung out with Cedar a lot of times; he was an amazing guy, a very different, unusual sort of guy. He was very cultured and refined in so many ways, but he was a real wild man in other ways too. One thing I remember about Cedar is that he had this incredible level of consistency that I've always admired and tried to get. I remember I asked him about it one night. I said, "Cedar, that was incredible, man. It was like, the solo you played was so good I forgot to come in. I was entranced by your solo, just forgot to come in, sorry about that, but you sounded incredible." He said, "Oh, man, you think? That's the worst I've played in for long time, man. I completely mucked everything up. I forgot to go to the bridge, I couldn't remember what the ... you kept telling me I sound good. I sucked, man, I sound terrible." And I'm thinking, "He sounded incredible. What does he mean?" [laughs]

It's a strange thing about music; often it's perception of how you are or maybe the goal posts move. But he had this, even when he was supposedly having a bad night. He sounded just great to me, pretty much the same as he always sounds. A bit more magic one night than the other night, but always consistently great to me. I absolutely loved his playing. In fact, I was there one night playing with him and this Australian guy who's a piano player that I know was there. I introduced him to Cedar and then I walked off and later I said, "Did you have a good chat with Cedar?" He said, "Oh, yeah. Look, I asked him for a lesson. I said, 'Oh, Cedar, can I get a lesson from you?' He said, 'Man, did you hear the way that I played 'Polka Dots and Moonbeams?' I completely mucked the bridge, man. I played all the wrong chords; I couldn't remember the bridge. You don't take lessons from a cat like that.'" He ended up not giving him the lesson because he thought he wasn't good enough to give anyone a lesson.

Cedar was this guy who was an incredibly confident player, but also had a lot of humility. He's always incredibly humble and self-effacing on one level, in a tough kind of way.

Playing with Cedar and Billy was intimidating but really fun and comfortable at the same time. First of all, you know that they know each other really well and they can just operate on a telepathic level and create magic. Basically, I'm invited to the party. I kind of love just being included in the whole thing, but at the same time I had my radar out and I was listening, listening, listening all the time, just trying to get with it and make it all work. And it was because of that hookup, everything was fresh, new and unexpected. You couldn't expect the same thing to happen in the same song from night to night. There were all kinds of things going on. It was magic, beyond magic.

There's a lot of innuendo and subtlety in what they did. Higgins was very much like that with the drums and with music generally. He wouldn't talk about specifics, necessarily. He'd talk about the more esoteric aspects of playing and performing. That's the essence of the music anyway.

I think Cedar was one of those piano players that loved comping, loved harmony and loved accompanying people. It was a really creative thing for him. Monk was like that as a piano player too. I think that's one reason why everybody loves Monk, is his architectural approach to comping or to ideas that continue through the song form while the soloist was playing, that are bigger than the song form. And more interesting than the song form itself is to make it into something that nobody imagined it could be. I think Cedar was one of those. He really had a great mastery of this where he just knew when to play and what to play and when to play it somehow. A lot of that is intuition as well.

Cedar was a master comper. That's the thing with all of the great piano players. Apart from their wonderful soloing, the one thing you really notice as a saxophone player is how they play behind you. You're never playing behind them when they're taking a solo, but they're always playing behind you unless they lay out or something. It's crucial to share the same kind of harmonic, rhythmic language as the person who's accompanying you. I was always aware of that. And that is the mark of a good piano player.

I probably didn't have any right to being up there, but I loved it. It was just an incredible experience and I just loved hanging out with all the cats and having fun and chatting with them. They took me very seriously, but at the same time had fun.[18]

Jeff Hamilton

I knew Cedar's name and I knew that he was a great jazz piano player in my late teens. At that time, I wouldn't be able to identify him on record and I didn't know that much about him or his playing. His name was intriguing to me, so it was easy for me to remember. The first time I really became aware of him was around 1975. I was 21 and on my first tour to Europe with Monty Alexander and John Clayton. And our promoter was Dutch. And he also had the record label that Cedar recorded for. And he gave us a couple of LPs of Cedar's and we visited his home and he played Cedar's music. And that's when I realized, man where have I been on Cedar Walton, I've been sleeping on how great he is. And Monty alongside this promoter Wim Wigt were telling me how great he was, and Monty was telling me also, "Yeah you really need to check out Cedar; he's fantastic."

I picked up some of his records and immediately became a fan. I was self-groomed on Oscar Peterson and those type of piano players who could sound like a big band shout chorus and play great fast lines and two-handed piano. And Cedar was that plus he had a Bud Powell kind of influence that I heard in his right hand. He put both of those things together and that's how I really started to be able to identify Cedar's playing. I also appreciated his sense of humor and his quotes in his music. There's always a Scottish jig or something in there, that he'll throw in out of nowhere, just to kind of raise your eyebrow and go "Okay, yeah, I'm listening ... you don't have to test me, I'm listening."

I heard Cedar live for the first time with Milt Jackson and Billy Higgins and Sam Jones in Europe. And it was just the trio, so Cedar, Sam and Billy. A year or two later we were playing the same festival in Burghausen and I heard a whole set. We had to follow them and "I went holy cow, not only is the trio great but this is Billy Higgins up there too man. What am I going to do after Billy Higgins?"

First of all, I don't smile that much when I play, so already I have two strikes against me. I just remember their trio sounding different than ours and that's when I realized that what they do is great but what we do is our own thing also. And we just go out and do what we do. It was kind of a big event for me, realizing that we don't have to go up and sound like that trio. First of all, we can't, and secondly, we've got our own thing to bring to the music. That was quite a Sunday afternoon that I won't forget.

The next few times I heard Cedar were after I moved to LA in 1978 and he lived there. He would play Catalina's Jazz club quite often with Billy. And when Billy couldn't do it, he'd bring in Tootie Heath. And at that time, it was David Williams on bass. So, I would go in and try to listen as much as I could and he was so shy around me that I didn't get past much more than "Hello, I really enjoyed your playing and I'm a jazz drummer, and I'm playing with Ray Brown." And he'd go "Oh, okay great." And that would be the end of it.

Cedar and I worked together with [Milt] Jackson and that's when he [Cedar] really opened up and boy what a funny guy, man! Very subtle, you really had to pay attention to his inside humor; it would go right by you. One of the memorable events was in Cologne with the WDR big band. John Clayton was the conductor, and it was his project. We did the Milt Jackson project with the WDR, and Cedar was a part of that. John Clayton played bass as well as conducted on some things. We had two weeks together. A week of rehearsing from Monday through Friday, had the weekend off. We rehearsed two more days and then the other three or four days were for concerts and recording. That's when I really got to know him a lot more.

In listening to Cedar play, I wasn't sure where I fit in with Cedar. You know his beat is his own beat. And it was different than Monty or Oscar or Gene Harris. And I'm thinking, "I wonder how I can fit into this?" I had to adjust to Gene Harris also after playing with Monty. And some people might find that strange, but you know, everybody's got their own thing. No matter what genre or style they're in. People like to label swing and piano players in one category but there's a lot of difference in between those cracks of the genre. I was thinking, "Okay I have to open up my time a little more and think of a wider beat for Cedar if I would play with him." Billy [Higgins] would kind of flatten out the swing pattern on the ride cymbal. I was thinking that he loves playing with Billy and that must be what works for him. I used that and kept that in the back of my mind. I'd still play what I play but I kept that in the back of my mind and if I started to tighten up and go for something, I wouldn't. That would help me stay loose and relaxed and kind of lay it in there. Sometimes, Cedar would play around your time. He didn't want to be spot on it like a lot of piano players in that genre. He would kind of lean on it a little and then he'd relax a little. And I don't want to say on top of the beat or behind the beat, I don't mean to imply that. I just mean the phrasing was like a wave. It would kind of come and go within what you were doing. And I really loved that.

It made me have more confidence in where I really believed the time could be and what I could offer to the music. He could go around that where he wanted to go. We never talked about it. I had the same feeling when I played with Hank Jones and Tommy Flanagan. The first time that I played with those gentlemen, I felt like I just wanted to sit and listen to them play the piano. I didn't feel like I could really contribute anything to them. And it's not about them being too busy or playing too much, there was just such beauty in what they did that I thought anything I do might be distracting. I briefly mentioned that to Cedar, and he just started laughing and we didn't even have a discussion about it. He just like, kind of shook his head and laughed. We have recordings of that event that prove that everything worked out okay.

I've never been one to be careful about what to play, but with those three piano players, that really made me think about if what I was offering was worth it. I think that's a tribute to the talent of those three piano players that make you really look at yourself and go, "okay what do I need to play here?"

One of the proudest things that I've been a part of was the Grammy winner of Benny Carter's *Elegy in Blue* CD.[19]

Gianni Valenti

As the owner of Birdland, I remember meeting Cedar in the mid-'80s when he came in to hear the music at the club. He became a frequent visitor who enjoyed coming in to support the other artists. As we became friendlier, Cedar approached me for a gig. It was the start of a beautiful friendship that lasted for nearly 30 years.

When he wasn't on the road or playing at other clubs you could always find him seated at a table or at the bar enjoying the music of other artists. One special quality that Cedar had was his love and support of musicians. He had a special table in the back where he and his wife would always have dinner, enjoy the music and what he taught me most, love life.

Cedar's style of music was a perfect fit for Birdland. Although he was known mainly as an accompanist, his trio was one of the best, which quickly became one of our favorite and most popular bookings. He had a smile that lit up the entire room and we always had a running joke between the two of us whenever he came in. He would lean over, whisper in my ear and say: "Hey, you got a gig for me?" I would always respond, "Let me see what I have available; I'll call Martha and we'll get it in the books."

He and Martha handled all their bookings and management, a very unique setup, which I enjoyed working with over the years.

Extremely funny and smart, you couldn't tell if he was being serious or not. He always kept you on your toes. It was refreshing and inspiring to see an artist at his level being so supportive and encouraging to other musicians. He really was a true gentleman to everyone he came into contact with.

From the first time I heard Cedar Walton play, I realized that I was in the company of a great artist. He was an amazing talent, a consummate professional, fun and easy going, but when he sat at the piano he was in his zone and truly one of the best.

I've had an amazing life and I've been blessed to be in this industry not only for the music but also for the friendships that I've developed with all the artists and guests that I've come to know and appreciate over the years. Cedar will always be one of my high points in life.

I miss him dearly, but fortunately for all of us he left us a great body of music to remember him by. Rest in peace my brother![20]

Joe Farnsworth

I went to school at William Paterson University in 1986. I was going every weekend into New York, and it became quickly apparent that Cedar's trio with Billy Higgins was going to become my direction in life and music. The way he [Cedar] presented himself, the way he carried himself, the way he played and the way he played with Billy [Higgins] influenced me. Rufus Reid (director of the jazz studies program at William Paterson) had Cedar come to William Paterson to play with our group and big band. It the first time we played with him and really met him.

I wasn't listening to any of those records when I was in high school, I was listening to Tony Williams. When I saw Cedar play I knew that's what I wanted to be. That was the way I wanted my conception of music to go. There was no doubt. Especially Billy Higgins, but it was Cedar's thing. I knew then I wanted to be around him and so I would go all the time to hear him at Sweet Basil, Bradley's, and the Vanguard. Everywhere he was, I went. And funny enough, I would sit next to Billy Higgins, but I would always end up talking to Cedar. I talked to Billy Higgins maybe 20 times in my life, but I talked to Cedar like 20 thousand times.

Thinking about Cedar as a person, I'm realizing more and more now just how intelligent he was. His whole being was about the piano and jazz and playing with people. We always talked about that he wasn't one of those people who was a showoff or ego driven. He always wanted to play with guys like Art Blakey. He was always an accompanist. Obviously in a trio he's leading. He was very humble in his playing. He talked about Duke Ellington, Nat "King" Cole, and

Bud Powell. He talked about all these great guys and all the great drummers and all the great players. He played with Freddie Hubbard and John Coltrane. It was always about the people he played with and not about himself. I loved that about him.

Thinking about him as a player. Once again, I realize more now how great he is. Just how great he is dynamically. Presentation. Set lists. It was a real show. The touch he had on the piano. He is deeply rooted in bebop but had the strength to come out of it. It was almost like the strength of McCoy Tyner. That power. Plus, the intellect of playing straight ahead. Amazing! The chords! He'd play "Body and Soul" and get to that bridge, and I couldn't wait for him to hit certain chords. It was really dynamics, that's really what it was. Incredible! He always used to tell me "Slow down Farnsworth, slow down," because I was always so excited. And he would lay and wait. He wouldn't just go for instant excitement. He'd lay for those moments and when you got there you'd be overwhelmed, like "Wow!"

I hung out with Cedar all the time. All the time! After the gig we go places and talk. He was always talking about music. He loved the Yankees, of course. He used to play a lot of tennis back in the day. And he'd talk about his army days. He talked a lot about what it was like in the '50s and '60s. And playing with all those guys like Freddie [Hubbard], Lee Morgan, Art Blakey, of course. And just what it was like to live in that time.

He also knew where his musician friends were playing in the states and abroad, which I found very interesting. It seemed like he was always on the phone setting up gigs. I think he had a few managers but it wasn't like he exploded on the scene like other pianists recognized by the critics. In one way I think he reveled in the fact that he was doing that on his own.

The fact that other musicians weren't setting up their own gigs was something that motivated him. He was the people's champion; it was like a ground swell. He was accessible. And he was accessible in Germany, Italy, everywhere. You could sit and have dinner with him. He wasn't always staying in a 5-star hotel or making 50 million dollars, but he was always accessible. Guys like me could approach him and have a few drinks with him or he would invite you to dinner and you could sit and listen. He was a true New York guy in the same way Barry Harris or George Coleman are. Guys that live in New York City that come to see your gigs. Back in the '50s and '60s all those guys lived in New York, and they'd all hang out at gigs. That didn't really happen in the '90s because all those guys were gone. Cedar was one of the last men standing. You would play a gig and Cedar Walton would show up. Unlike some of those guys where you don't see them unless you're on a big gig. What he [Cedar] was doing in New York, he was doing all around the world. After a gig he wasn't getting whisked off by a limo. He'd drive you home, stop and get a hamburger and talk. Here he is talking about Duke Ellington yet we're sitting there! And this was before I was even playing with him. He was giving me that time. He was very giving. He would always talk about that. There were people who gave to him. Important lessons. He's giving back freely what was giving to him. I love that about him. I was no superstar, but he would sit there and give his time to me.

Cedar listened to a lot of other people's music. He was very on top of what other people were doing. He went to check out other people. I liked how he would never sit up front and act like "Cedar Walton's here" or try to sit in. He was always in the back away from the spotlight to just listen. He was very in tune to what was happening. He respected others. If he heard someone sounding great, he loved it. He wasn't like "oh I'm better than this guy" or anything egotistical. It was back in the day where those guys loved each other, and they loved hearing great players.

I think his [Cedar's] whole day was geared to the performance. He didn't just go to the performance on a whim and play. His whole day was planned around that gig at night and what he was going to do and how he was going to present himself. And carefully thinking about his setlist and what the listener was going to think. He practiced a lot. He was always moving forward. Always moving forward.

One time, I introduced him [Cedar] to an alto player. I said, "Hey Cedar this is my friend so and so, a great alto player" and he got a little offended and said "Great? Duke Ellington was great, I wish I was great. And this guy's great?" [Joe] "I said no [laughing] he pretty good, he's ok." So now every time I hear someone say, "oh man this guy is great" I say, Duke Ellington is great!

I remember Cedar told me something he learned from Charlie Parker. I must have written him an email that said "Yea ok, I'm good for that gig" or something like that. And he called me up and said, "Young Farnsworth, one must always exchange pleasantries before business." That was a lot to learn. I needed to write: "Hey Mr. Walton" or "Hey Cedar how are you today? How's everything? How's your wife?" Exchange pleasantries and then you talk about business. I liked that about him.

I liked the fact that he seemed like he had eyes coming out of the side of his head. We would go somewhere and he's talking and he could see you but he's looking straight ahead. We were walking off the bandstand in Chicago once and then he says, "Listen Farnsworth, slow down." It's like he slipped in a massive life lesson without having to pull my shoulder or tug my coat and look at me. It was just like, bam. The impact was tremendous. He did that all the time.

Cedar might be one of those guys like a great painter that after they're gone people realize just how great he was. 'Cause you don't see that anymore. A guy that presents himself that well, that intelligently, with those tunes. No one is playing each other's tunes anymore; like they used to play. Like you might play a Coltrane tune back then. But now people are starting to play Cedar Walton tunes. And that's a huge thing.

He created such an umbrella of greatness that people flocked to him to be around him and sit next to him. He was jazz royalty. And it made you feel like you were at the happening, you were there. You're in New York city sitting next to Cedar Walton, you're listening to him, and you felt like you kind of arrived. I think it made me feel like I was riding his coattails. When he died, it left such an exposure to myself, and I think I was like "Damn I need to step up. I need to fill a little bit of the shoes he had as far as presenting myself, the way you dress, the way you speak on the mic, the way you play, the way you approach it. The way Cedar sat at the piano was powerful. There were no extracurricular movements. There was a massive smile on his face. But it wasn't corny. It wasn't jiving. It wasn't cheesing. It was the real deal. A lot of people fed off it. And now with him gone I think a lot of people are thinking, "wow." Jazz is getting so far removed from that greatness, I think a lot of people that knew him [Cedar] are stepping up to fill in the hole that he left.

Cedar never showed emotions like "I deserve better" because he was so tough. But I do remember when Billy Higgins died, he [Cedar] must have had a hundred pieces of mail from around the world that people had written to him about what he and Billy meant to them. We were flying business class to Israel and he was opening these letters and someone sent Cedar a *DownBeat* with an article about Billy's death. The only two people they mentioned were Pat Metheny and Ornette Coleman. And he [Cedar] just chucked the *DownBeat* and that was a little glimpse that he showed me. It was just a natural reaction. But damn, that Billy Higgins played with him for damn near thirty-five years and they couldn't even mention Cedar's name? That's something. Isn't it? A guy that great. That got to him. I don't think he was ever in the *DownBeat* polls. That didn't get to him.

Here's another thing he says. "Why do you think they call him smiling Billy Higgins? 'Cause he's playing with me!" I thought that was funny [laughs]. Yea, I understand because I played with him, and I wish I could have smiled more. I was always so nervous, like "Damn I'm playing with Cedar Walton. My Gosh!" Sitting in Billy Higgins's chair. Whoo!

I remember Arthur Taylor told me once that he felt bad for me that I never got to meet Philly Joe Jones as a human being and got a chance to hang out with him. Forget hearing him live. I feel the same way about Cedar. A lot of these guys now are playing Cedar Walton tunes. But they have no idea about the human being behind it. And what he brought as a human. Obviously, it was his music, but when you meet the man, the music just opens up. There's something that you just can't get unless you've met him.

Beautiful Friendship is a perfect example of what I'm talking about. That record didn't pay that much. Cedar was doing the session for me as a favor. A lot of those greats would need $20,000 to do a record date. For that record date, Cedar wrote every single sextet arrangement for it. He went to Jersey to get the lead sheets copied out. About three hours before the date, he calls me at 5 in the morning. I pick up the phone and say, "Farnsworth" and Cedar says, "I don't think I can make the date; I'm just thinking about how much I'm getting paid and I'm physically getting sick." And I'm like "Sorry about that, man." He'd already written all the stuff out and we'd rehearsed. I said, "I don't know what to do about it." We talked a little more and he came around. That was interesting. He must have known that he wasn't getting paid much. There must have been that little conflict in there. That dude should have been getting $20,000 everywhere he stepped foot. He's that good. But once again he was accessible for guys like me and other guys.[21]

Jed Eisenman

I started working at the Vanguard in 1981 washing glasses, and at that point in time, the founder of the club, Max Gordon, was pretty old and he was getting a little tired of the programming aspect of it and running out of ideas to apply. So as soon as he found out that I had some talent myself, in a very unorthodox maneuver, he just invited me into his counsel, and it was beyond unlikely, really. But it was fairly shortly on that he took some faith in the idea that I got what the Vanguard was about and that I had some knowledge or was learning stuff about the music and that I could help him. And so he took me under his wing and it was not official or anything like that.

I kept washing glasses at the same time. It was not that kind of promotion. It's not like anybody else was doing it anyway without making the whole thing too belabored. This is the early '80s. Max died in May of 1989. And a few years before that Lorraine Gordon, his wife, had come in to also try to help him, not as much with the booking, more with the general management of the club, which is not to say that she didn't offer him a lot of booking advice, but he was much more resistant, at least initially, to her advice than he was to mine. So 1989, he dies, she's there. And she and I start doing it together at that point. And interestingly, her influence grows at that point because we both figure out that each of us had something to bring to the other one's perspective.

Lorraine was a very difficult person in general, but we developed, at first in uneasy truths and then after that, a not uneasy alliance and we figured out how to work together on the whole thing. The bookings of the Vanguard, the whole '90s, and the 2000s up to about a little after 2010 were very much a combination of me and her. I'd be giving you the wrong story to suggest that Max died and then I just took over and that was it. It's not true. She and I did it together for almost 25 years. Just thinking back on it blows my mind, but we did. And then she got very old and not as firm as she had been, and so at that point, her daughter Deborah Gordon, who now owns the Village Vanguard, started collaborating with me and that's the way we've been doing it since then. Lorraine died in 2018, but since about 2013 or so, it's been me and Deborah doing it together. And everybody brings their own thing to it. Deborah is not anywhere near as much of an activist presence in the whole affair as Lorraine has been. But I would be remiss not to both give her credit and also indicate that it is a collaborative process.

When I met Cedar, I was just washing glasses at the Vanguard, pretty young. The first time I think I met him, he probably was playing with Milt Jackson. Milt's primo rhythm section at the time would've been Cedar, Bob Cranshaw, and Mickey Roker. That group showed up at the Vanguard pretty shortly after I started. And it was weird, guys of that stature had no reason to pay any attention to me, but they did. It was the strangest combination I knew of; them being nice to me was special and I had no reason to expect that [laughs]. And Cedar in particular was, he was so erudite. And the first time I used the not oft-used word in his presence correctly, [laughs] I went up a notch or two. He had the greatest sense of humor. We hit it off pretty quickly. In spite of the fact that he was Cedar, and I was nobody. He was a strange combination of incredibly open to an unlikely friend of that nature, and at the same time, very elitist and very unlikely to make friends with just anybody of any stripe. I was always very honored that he liked me and it was not so much later that I was in the position of being either de facto or actual artistic programmer at the Vanguard and thereby choosing the date or dates that he would be playing there. And I certainly did come up with Cedar's Christmas residency, and it was so special for quite some time, over a decade.

The pianists in particular were always very keen to pay homage to Cedar. When he would play, you'd know you'd see Kenny Barron and George Cables and Ronnie Mathews and Harold Mabern, beyond reliably. Cedar very quietly slipped into that position. When Bradley's was still open there were all these giants that you could go see there, as well as Cedar, like Hank Jones and Jimmy Rowles. Cedar was great, but he didn't really get to be the Cedar of later until some time had passed, and some people have passed on, and it's always that way. So right now, for example, Kenny Barron occupies that spot that Cedar did. But Cedar was a quiet and almost reluctant king of the scene. He loved the attention, and he appreciated all the honorifics and all that.

When I worked with Cedar, we did it directly. I never worked with an agent in all the time that I knew him. Like I said, he would call me and I'd be delighted even if it was business. He was not difficult to deal with. Most people that are tricky to deal with are the ones that don't trust you or that don't trust the place or some combination of the two things where the money is in question. He wasn't like that at all. He found the Vanguard, at least inasmuch as I could tell, a great place to work, I think he was very proud of how long he worked there, and his association with the place. And then particularly of that Christmas gig. It was a big deal.

Cedar had the greatest sense of humor. I would call him "Lord Walton" and he would call me "Lord Eisenman." He loved to call Todd Barkan, "Lord Barkan," which always particularly made me laugh [laughs]. Cedar wore his primacy lightly and he was very self-effacing as well. He had a very high opinion of himself, but he certainly was not ever beyond taking advantage of the innate humor in puncturing one's own self-importance. To me, he was endlessly delightful. And one of the things I really miss almost as much as hearing him play was when I would have the rare honor of him calling me on the telephone. It wasn't even that rare, but it was an honor. I was just so excited because I knew I was going to laugh. [laughs] He was one of the most urbane people I ever knew, certainly. And in jazz, there have been many very funny musicians that I have also had the honor to know, but Cedar was first and unequal, certainly.

Vincent Herring

I grew up listening to Cedar play piano on recordings as almost anyone playing jazz coming along these days would. I first became aware of him with the Jazz Messengers. And then, enjoying his playing, I sought out his own projects and discovered more about him that way. The first time I met him was in Switzerland. I was there with Horace Silver at a jazz festival, and he was there with Nat Adderley and J.J. Johnson. That was my first time meeting him on the bandstand. Nat saw me there and asked me to come up and play. I came up and played with Cedar and Cedar asked me for my telephone number and sure enough he called me for a gig some short time later.

Playing with Cedar was a long, long learning process and of course a maturity process as a musician. It was just a great experience. I teach at a couple universities. One being William Paterson and the other being Manhattan School of Music, and the type of experiences and learning I got working with Cedar, you can't duplicate that. That's not something you can create in an academic environment.

As a bandleader, Cedar allowed you to be yourself. He wanted you to be yourself. If he chose to have you there, he wanted you to be yourself and to bring what your musical personality had naturally and let what was special about you shine. It wasn't like he was a drill sergeant or anything like that.

Cedar's sense of humor was legendary. It was constantly going. Either you caught it, or you didn't. That was a big part of his personality and who he was. Most of the time it was a very sophisticated subtle humor, but definitely a part of his personality.

Cedar was a big Yankees fan. I never had a chance to go to a game with him, but he was always into the stats of Yankees. Other sports? Mildly. Almost socially. Just enough to know what was going on. But the Yankees he was into. He wore a Yankees cap often. I remember being on gigs and during the break he would ask to check the Yankees score because I was able to do so on my smartphone.

He was an honest musician. There was nothing really hidden about him and his life. What you see, what you hear, is what you get. He was a person that was very knowledgeable but still down to earth. And regardless of how great he was he didn't allow that to separate himself from the people in his band. It was separate, but you never felt it. He was just one of the guys. It always felt like that around him.

Cedar was one of the premier composers in jazz. He wrote some iconic songs, and we deal with them every day. [laughs] We really do! Being able to have the experience of playing with the composer for a long period of time, I learned some subtleties and things. Like a few melodies that people play he was particular about. "Fantasy in D" which is also "Ugetsu"—you know the way Freddie [Hubbard] played the melody on the record with Art Blakey and the Jazz Messengers. Everyone knows and loves that recording. Cedar's like "that melody is wrong!" [laughs] So I was playing it like that, and he corrected me to play it right. Wow! You know things like that. Or the way I played "Bolivia." He would say to me "I love that you play it right every time." Some people take liberties with some of the rhythms and that's not what he envisioned when he composed it. I learned a lot hearing him play on those songs. He had the ability to make it feel and sound simple when it was not.

I'm elated to have had the chance to be in Cedar's life and elated I had the chance to make music with him and learn music from him and be in the mix. I hold it as one of my career highlights.[22]

Kenny Washington

One of the reasons why I got to play with Cedar was because of Billy Higgins. I would see Cedar and Billy and David Williams. I saw Sam Jones with them too, a few times. But for the most part, we were going on those long, awful tours with Wim Wigt.

I was playing with Johnny Griffin. We would either be playing on the same bill with them, or they would be in town. Or I would see Billy with Cedar and maybe Clifford Jordan, Bob Berg, or Steve Grossman. I used to see Cedar quite a bit. Billy Higgins of course is one of my idols. And he and I got pretty tight. I had filled in for Billy when he would have a gig with somebody else and there was a conflict. That's how I started playing with Cedar. When Billy unfortunately got sick, I became the drummer in that group. Unfillable shoes, man. I loved that trio.

Of course, I had all the records he'd [Billy Higgins] made with Lee Morgan and all these great recordings of the sixties. And even though I like those records, I was more at that time a Philly Joe Jones fanatic. I was into him a little bit more than Billy Higgins. And it wasn't until I saw Billy Higgins, who I first saw with Tete Montoliu. And then later on of course I saw him with Cedar. When I saw him live playing with Cedar, that's when I went back home and listened to all those records. It made all the sense in the world. It took me having to see him live for the first time, and then I got it. I really got it.

From that point on I became a Billy Higgins fanatic. I am really into the music. I'm a jazz historian and I collect records and all this kind of stuff. I had all the records, man. Not only did I have the records, but anytime that they were in New York City, I would go down to see them. That's what the real guys did. At that time, I wasn't thinking about ever taking Billy Higgins's place with Cedar. It never entered my mind. I never thought about it.

But the reason why I was down there is because they sounded so good together, whether it was with David Williams or with Ron Carter. People like myself, and Peter Washington, Benny Green, and Lewis Nash. We would go down just to hear these guys because we wanted to be just like that.

They just played so great, all the time. Guys now-a-days go to clubs hawking somebody else's gig thinking they're gonna get the gig. We never thought about it. None of us. If you ask any one of us that same question or if you mention it to any of them, I'll bet you ten to one they would all say the same thing. These were the masters, and we were there to learn and dig the music. And if we were lucky, we'd get to hang out and talk with them. That's what it was all about.

Cedar and Billy had something very special. That's why when I replaced Billy, I felt weird for so long. I knew I could never do that. I could never in a million years do that. Finally, Cedar told me, and I can hear him now. "Oh, Lord Washington, you're doing fine. Don't worry about it. You're Kenny Washington." Billy, Sam, and Cedar, they had something very, very, very special.

Billy started playing again in New York City after a kidney operation. He was doing a gig maybe with Ornette Coleman, or somebody like that. And Cedar was working down at Sweet Basil. David Williams and I were on the gig. We heard that Billy was in town. We were sitting there during the break and who walks in but Billy Higgins. Billy walks in the club, "Hey, man!" Oh man, it was great. Billy sat down at that first table with all of us and got something to eat. We were all sitting there talking. When it came time to play the last set, Cedar says, "Mr. Higgins, would you like to play some?" And he said, "Well yeah, sure." Billy Higgins looks at me and he says, "Well man, can I bless it?" I said, "Man have you lost your mind? This is your gig, man! Of course, you can play!"

They start and I'm telling you, man, the magic was there from the first note. Billy didn't bring any sticks or nothing. He came empty handed. He took my sticks, and he didn't adjust any component of my drums and those cats just started playing. The communication between Cedar and Billy was like, "Hey man, so how have you been?" "Oh, I've been alright, man." He says, "Well yeah, you certainly sound good." "Well look man, let's play this." You could hear that in the way they played together. It was magic. And Billy hadn't been playing that much because he had to lay off for a while. I went right to the door of Sweet Basil. And at that time, they had that extension in the doorway that went out onto the street. And you know Seventh Avenue South, it's always noisy, and people are going back and forth. Billy Higgins hit that floor tom-tom. That tom-tom said boom! I mean, he had not lost his sound at all, man. I mean, he hadn't been playing in weeks. That was really something to behold. So of course, he played one number, and then he played two numbers. There was no way in the world I was getting back up on that bandstand. No way!

He played the rest of the set. That was a beautiful night. It just so happened Billy hung out with all of us, and I remember Tony Reedus and Billy Drummond and all these drummers just happened to come to Sweet Basil that night. And we all hung out. Not one of us knew that Billy Higgins was gonna come down and play. But all these drummers came down and it was just a great night.

Between Billy's cymbal beat and what Cedar was playing, Cedar's rhythm, it totally and always meshed together. I mean it was just perfect. Anytime, anywhere. Perfect. When I played with Cedar, the thing that got me, the thing that really knocked me out about Cedar was he played what I call concentrated piano. His lines were so slick, musical, rhythmically and harmonically hip. And if you'd watch him, he would look like, "Oh, it's all in a day's work. No big deal." The rhythms and the harmony felt like I was in a musical rainstorm, but it's good! The feeling, I mean all this music, it's just like you get caught in the rain. All these notes are just hitting you. You're saying, "Yeah, man. Take another chorus. Take another, fella." It'd just go on and on and on. It was just so heavy, and so deep. Sometimes it would be hard to pay attention to what you're doing. He knew what to play behind you.

I made a record with Milt Jackson called *The Harem*. Cedar was on the record, and so in the beginning of the session the producer wanted Cedar and Bags to do a duet performance, and they said, "Okay, yeah. We'll do it at the end of the day." We finished the session and I'm packing up the drums and everything. Cedar and Bags had their hats and coats on. They were on their way out, and the producer said, "Hey, you all were supposed to do that duet for me." And they looked at each other and didn't say anything. They took their hats and coats off and just sat down. They said what they were going to play, and they set up and started to tape. It was just one take. It was perfect.

Those two, they knew each other. The duet was out of time. It was just the two of them, but the chances that Cedar was taking accompanying Bags, it was like he might get ahead of Bags in one part, but they knew exactly what they were doing, and their hook up was perfect. One take and they got right up, put their hats and coats on, and they were gone. I never will forget that.

Cedar talked to me a lot about Kenny Dorham. He loved Kenny Dorham. He would talk about Art Tatum, Duke Ellington, and he would talk about Hank Jones and Tommy Flanagan, too. You could hear that in his playing. Another person that he was greatly musically affected by was Horace Silver. In fact, compositionally, you can hear where Cedar was coming from. Cedar had a knack for writing these compositions that anybody could get into, whether it be the butcher, baker, or candlestick maker. You didn't have to be a musician. He wrote singable tunes. Very musical tunes that even people that weren't into jazz were into.

If you heard these tunes, you just liked it. It's the kind of thing that you can put on at a party and have it in the background and I'm telling you, I've done it myself. There'd be somebody who's not really a jazz person say, "Wow, who's that?" That's Cedar Walton! They're intrigued by Cedar's music because it's very listenable, it's easy to get into, but then at the same time as a musician you can see where it's complex. It's not as simple as you might think it is.

Horace used to write pieces like that. Listenable, singable, you could whistle them, and they were easy to get into. People friendly. Then at the same time if you really get into them musically, there's a lot there. That's why Cedar's tunes are still played. Anybody that likes music and has even half an ear can get into it and like it. He had it all covered.

Cedar was a funny guy. Just silly. There was one guy that came out to our gigs and happened to have a lot of kids. Cedar started calling him "Semen, first class." [laughs] This cat was silly. He was also rough at the wheel. Driving with him, he'd scare you to death. Sometimes he could drive like Mr. Magoo. I'm telling you! Me and David [Williams], we were in the car one time, looking at each other like, "Oh, man, we gonna die." [laughs]

There was so much beauty in his music. Heart. The human quality of his music. When you heard his compositions, they reflected his attitude, and the way he was. He was always nice to be around, too. Like I said, funny cat.[23]

Larry Clothier

I met Cedar in San Francisco at the Jazz Workshop. He was with Blakey then. We started to have more regular interactions in New York in the '70s. One of our strong connections was through Bradley's.

Around 1976 a whole lot of stuff started kicking off. Cedar was living in LA for a period of time there in the mid-to-late '70s. He was out there and doing a lot of studio stuff and a lot of record production. Walter Booker and I had a recording studio uptown on 87th Street and Amsterdam [New York City] called Boogie Woogie Sound. Initially we had an upright piano in the studio. A good one with a good sound that we were able to get. Cedar had a Yamaha grand piano in LA that he wasn't using a lot and he offered to loan the piano to us.

We shipped it back from LA to us in New York and we had it in the studio for a number of years. We did a bunch of projects up there with him. All through this time I had a lot of association with Cedar and his favorite drummer Billy Higgins, who was in and out of the studio there with us a lot. And we did a recording project up there which was Billy Higgins's first record under his name.[24]

Cedar was Milt Jackson's favorite piano player. And I remember when Milt and I were talking, years before they dissolved the MJQ the first time. His goal was to have his own band with Cedar, Mickey Roker and Sam Jones. He had that in his mind for years. We used to talk about that a lot. That was in the early '70s when it looked like there was gonna be a change. Milt loved Ray Brown, but Ray was so busy doing so many different things that I don't think that was a solid hope for Jackson. Ray was such a hard-working LA studio musician. He was on everything.

I had Cedar involved in one of my favorite tours of all time. I was able to put a tour together in 1986 with Carmen McRae. The touring band included Cedar on piano, Ray Brown on bass, Mickey Roker on drums. Ah, it was ridiculous. We were all over Europe, we made all those European festivals in the summer. Just laughed all the way through. All those guys are nuts. We had a great time. Cedar had an incredible sense of humor, but so did Ray Brown and Mickey Roker, who was one of the funniest people on earth. And Carmen was hilarious too, but in a very sedated, curmudgeon way.

It was not long after that that I met Roy Hargrove when he was still a high school student in Texas. Cedar was from Texas. I was doing a whole lot of things with this performing arts center in Fort Worth, Caravan of Dreams. I had Cedar and the guys down there a number of times, and other guys like Walter Booker and Billy Higgins and Mickey Roker. Cedar and Roy were able to hook up down there when Roy was still in high school. Subsequently, Cedar took an interest in Roy. When Roy got to New York, there was a lot of interaction there. That was 1987. Cedar got a hold of him. Roy's first gig at the Village Vanguard was with Cedar. Then a whole lot of things took place after that. They did some incredible duo concerts in San Francisco as well as at Jazz at Lincoln Center, and abroad. Just astounding stuff.

Cedar was extremely intelligent. Some of his antics and everything, the way he carried himself, that fact escaped a lot of people. He had his approach well figured out in his own mind.

Cedar, behind the piano, was able to create an incredible sound. Both of his arms seldom ever moved from right in front of him. He played for the most part right in the middle of the piano with an occasional reach up to the right or reach down to the left. It always stunned me just watching him, his hands were always in the middle of the piano, but you heard all the sounds. Cedar was just a stunning musician and composer. Just amazing.[25]

Javon Jackson

I first met Cedar in Denver. One night I went to see him at a place called the Oxford Hotel. He used to do some isolated performances there. Later that night I was playing at a place called El Chapultepec. Cedar was very good friends with Freddy Rodriguez [who played there regularly] from his time in Denver as a college student. Cedar came and he didn't play, but he listened to me play and he listened to the music. I got a chance to speak with him that night about a couple of things.

The first time I actually worked with Cedar was when I reached out to him. I put a group together that was a Messengers tribute group. The concert was at the Mount Vernon Country Club. I also did some things in California with Cedar as well as Freddie Hubbard.

From then on, Cedar would contact me yearly and I would go over with him and play at Ronnie Scott's. We did it every year for several years, as well as some other tours and other isolated concerts out in California.

Cedar didn't have big heavy rehearsals, but he liked to get together and talk things over at a sound check. He liked to make sure everyone knew the songs and knew the arrangements. He also didn't have a problem with people making mistakes. He wasn't a guy who needed everything to be perfect. But he did want everyone to know the roadmaps. And he was specific about the way certain things had to be. Very organized.

And a couple different times, he said, "I don't know if you can hear that, Brother Jackson, but we're playing the ending this way." I think there was a rhythm I played differently, and I said, "Well,

I was actually trying to do something different." [Cedar] "Yeah, but I want you to do what everybody else is doing. It sounds like you're not with us." He was specific on some things. It made everyone sound like we were a unit.

Cedar loved if you could play the chords. He wanted to play the chords and I had no problem with that cause I wanted to play the chords too. Cedar's playing was so strong, but never to the point where he would challenge you. He was not a person that liked to attack you or go at you. If he didn't feel you could do what he would do, he might make a comment or two. But he'd just as soon not use you anymore and not call you again.

I was a guy that would always ask him questions. I'd ask him about recording sessions, or I'd ask him "Hey, when did you first meet Coltrane?" Or "Did you ever play with Sonny Rollins?" "What were your thoughts on Kenny Dorham?" I've been in his car many times. There were only two musicians, pianists, that I ever heard him listening to, only two. Art Tatum and Ahmad Jamal. Those are the only two musicians that I ever heard him playing in his car. When I would go out to California and ride with him, Art Tatum was playing all the time. And then, when he had his car here in New York, there was an Ahmad Jamal CD that had just come out and he was listening to it all the time.

With me, we discussed music. I talked to him about Charlie Parker. He played with Charlie Parker in Denver. In fact, Bird came and sat in with him when he was in Denver. Cedar once told me that he sat in with Duke Ellington's big band. I used to talk to him about a record that he did that I love with Ray Brown and Elvin Jones.[26] We discussed that.

I even asked him one time about chords. And he wrote out a C blues with his progressions. With his chords. With his voicings. I used to talk to him about musicians and music all the time. He also loved talking about the Yankees.

Cedar was a great accompanist, and it was a lesson to watch him. Cedar played those incredible long lines, and they made such great sense. They were so soulful. He swings like crazy. He had everything. He was sophisticated but soulful. He could really play the blues. He didn't always wanna stretch out or push the tension too much harmonically. He always made it feel good and was a consummate professional. That guy was a giant. It's just an honor to be around him.

If you check out his compositions, his songs have a built-in arrangement. It sounds like you're a band when you play one of his songs.

I always joked with him, there's only one time I saw him silly on stage and I happened to be there. I was out there with Elvin Jones. We were playing the Hollywood Bowl. And it was hosted during those years by Bill Cosby. Bill would always put a group together. And this particular group was called the World of Cosby. It was Nat Adderley, David Sanchez, Reggie Workman, Billy Drummond, Cedar, and a guy that played the bagpipes named Rufus Harley. They played "Moanin," they played "Work Song." And Rufus wore a kilt and the whole thing. It was kind of a crazy configuration of people. And I used to joke with Cedar 'cause he was laughing just uncontrollably onstage. He was laughing because this guy on the bagpipes was trying to play the blues. It was comical. I always used to remind him about that. He loved it.

When recording with Elvin Jones you get one take. Two takes tops. They don't mess around. There's no need to go redo what you did. That's what you did at that moment. We can live with that. They never felt like they had to improve on anything. There's no need to try to go back and improve it. That's the real old school way. Cedar was very much like that too. One or two takes, boom. As long as the arrangements were fine and everybody did their best, he could move on.

I remember toward the end of Cedar's life he was playing trio at the Vanguard. I went on the second night of his run, and he didn't look like Cedar. He didn't look good. He called me the next morning, and said "Man, I really wish you'd come on down and play. I need some help, can you come on down and finish the week?" I finished the week with him and have been playing the club since then. I play there annually with Cedar's band, and we play Cedar's music. Because to me, that's the spirit of keeping his music alive. And my appreciation for my friend giving me that opportunity to be in the club. I played those four nights with him at the Vanguard and those were the last four nights I ever played with him.

Cedar didn't take himself that seriously. He didn't have a huge ego. He didn't complain. When he came in the room, he didn't like to draw a lot of attention. He was a real private guy. But when you got with him one-on-one, he was hilarious.[27]

George Fludas

The first time I met Cedar, I talked to him real briefly. He was sitting in the back at the Jazz Showcase. I was with some friends, and we were just hanging around in awe of the musicians. Just young guys trying to eavesdrop on their conversation. Somehow, we got into it. Cedar was very outgoing. If people were in earshot, he was basically talking to them. He was holding court, and I remember him saying something right at that time about the sacrifices that jazz musicians have made for the music in terms of the lifestyle and how difficult it was. I think this is because we were all hanging around hoping for some words of wisdom to drop, like what advice do you have for a young upcoming musician kind of thing. In the mood at that moment, he just brought that up. He just said, "Man, you know, a lot of cats have really sacrificed a lot." He said, "I sacrificed a lot, having a stable family, for this music." That stuck with me. I remember I was probably about 19 at that time.

It hit me like, wow, yeah, this is what I'm thinking about getting into, and I got to consider that it might not be the most conducive to the typical nuclear-family-type situation. That wasn't the first time I saw him play, though. The first time I saw him play was at Rick's Café, that's a defunct club in Chicago. That was with Milt Jackson, Ray Brown and Mickey Roker. That was the first time I saw him play. That was in 1985.

I never imagined I'd get to play with him. That came later. It was because there was a tour promoter in Spain by the name of Jordi Sunol, and he brought me over to play some gigs. I played with Benny Green for him shortly before that, and he remembered me. I guess he liked how I played, and he was putting together a tour with Cedar. He told Cedar about me, and Cedar said, "Sounds good, sure. If you say, he can play, I'm sure he can play." The first time I played with Cedar was overseas in Spain. Then I did a couple tours with him. I also played with him with Phil Woods. We did some quartet stuff with Phil.

I started to gradually work with him a little bit after about 2003. That's when I sort of reconnected with him again. He always remembered who I was, and he would give me a shout if he came to Chicago. He was always real communicative that way. He would just call and say, "Hey, Lord Fludas. Coming to Chicago. Hope we get to see you this time around. Hope you can make it by the club. We would be graced by your presence." He'd get in touch, and I'd go hear him with Billy Higgins. That was always one of the highlights, to get to see him and Higgins together.

I called Cedar and Billy's connection "Hand in Glove." Speaking of his tune, I said "Cedar, you must've written that for you and Billy, because that's how that works." He said, "Nah, yeah, yeah, maybe I did." The relationship that they had was so special. It was so special because it's like they shared the same vocabulary on different instruments in some ways. There's this rhythmic kind of thematic way that Cedar often develops. When he's playing a solo, he's comping for himself or setting up, I don't want to call them shout choruses, but he's got a very arranger's kind of sensibility when he's soloing. He'll shape a chorus by playing a rhythmic figure and maybe repeating it or developing the motif of that figure, and Higgins was always right on him with it. It seemed to be the same kind of language or dialect of the language that Cedar and Billy had.

I remember thinking the first few times I played with Cedar, I was nervous because he's a giant. Then there's also that added pressure to play in a way that is coherent with his style, which is referencing Billy, but then I don't want to be aping Billy or like I'm just mimicking what he would play. I found that I would often feel like, ah, the perfect thing to play here is what Higgins plays. I'd rely on a lot of those licks or the kind of phrasing or that language or vocabulary of Billy's. I just remembered thinking the first few times I played, "Man, what am I doing here? This is where Billy's supposed to be, not me." I felt like I was driving Billy's car or something, like this isn't my property; this is his property. But Cedar was always really generous and cool about it. He wasn't the kind of band leader that when you played with him, he wanted you to know who the main guy is. He never asked anything like "Did you check out the record?" or said, "This is how the arrangement goes and just listen to that." Cedar never did any of that. It was always like he assumed that you knew the shit because that's why you were there, and you basically know his tunes and his arrangements. Of course, I had the utmost respect for him and his music, so I would come as prepared as possible, but there are always little slight variations, or there were tunes that I'd never played before.

He was very extemporaneous. He might just start playing a tune. He'd call a tune and just say the name of the tune. It's a tune that I know maybe by name and maybe I've heard on a record once or twice or something, but it wasn't something that I had really down like his arrangement of "Off Minor," for example, or just other tunes that are a little bit more iconic. He'd go into something. I remember one time he went into "Groundwork," and that tune's got a lot of hits. There's a lot going on, and it's kind of "Firm Roots"-like, but there's a little more to it. He'd use it as a drum feature for Billy sometimes. Cedar's like, "You ever play 'Groundwork'?" He's saying it across the stage, and we're on stage. I go, "Uh, no. I'm not too cool on that." He's like, "Oh, you'll hear it, you'll be fine." Then we started playing it, and man, I was just stepping on every little landmine because I really didn't know it that well.

By the end of the tune and then the end of the set—I think it might've been the last tune we played of the set—I just felt battered, just like I just got run over. We come off the stage, and I'm just feeling that feeling when you know it wasn't happening. I said, "Oh man, Cedar, I'm sorry, man." I said, "I know I was stepping on all the cracks on that one." He goes, "Ah, no, man. That was wonderful." He goes, "Hey, look, perfection has no place in my music."

Not only did he not make me feel bad by going, "Yeah, man. Well, check that one out," he didn't take that line at all. He basically made me feel better about the fact that he wants it to sound fresh and that's how you learn. He was accepting of that. Of course, if you keep doing that and you fuck it up every time you play it, then you're just not going to get the gig again. It was cool because in a way because it was like a little confidence booster. I've never forgotten that, either.

A lot of guys aren't like that when it comes to their music. I worked with Ray Brown for a couple years, and Ray was very different from Cedar in that respect. You made one mistake, and Ray was on your ass. There were a lot of arrangements, and Ray wanted it to be clean and tight. If you slipped up, you were going to get a look, or you might hear, "Uh, what was that? Hey!" I never got that from Cedar at all.

Cedar found it enjoyable when things got a little bit slippery, but you know, it was like it was exciting or something. That's his personality, too, when you hung with him. I always felt like he was just open to what you had to contribute.

Now that I'm a little older, I can relate to that with younger guys. The aim isn't to cross every "t" and dot every "i" all the time. You got to stumble a little bit in order to really discover the music. I don't recall ever getting charts from Cedar. I don't recall setting up and there being a music stand and him handing me music. That's fine. Everybody has their different strokes, but that wasn't his way at all.

The same with Tommy Flanagan. I played with Tommy a pretty good amount around that time in the late '90s, too. Tommy had a lot of arrangements. Actually, I tended to play with piano players who seemed to have a lot of arrangements and no music. I played with Barry a little bit. I played with Hank Jones. Hank had music, though. Hank would often have charts, but a lot of things he didn't have charts for, too. He just said, "Well, you know, listen to this record, and we're going to be doing some of this music." Of course, I'd listen to the CD.

With Cedar, he never really showed up with a book or anything. Matter of fact, I think he might've had music more for the bass player than the drummer. I seem to remember certain bass players would have—not David [Williams], because David knew everything—but he had music for Jon Weber and Tony Dumas when they played.

Every great musician who's contributed to the art form has such a unique and distinctive personality and voice. Cedar really had that. I think not just in terms of his compositions, which are completely his music. It's like Benny Golson. It's got a very distinctive stamp harmonically and melodically too, and there's always the blues; there's always soulfulness in it.

One of the key things with Cedar for me is that his language is so hip and contemporary or modern at that time, but it always is rooted in the blues. His feel, it's always got that slick, hip kind of attitude that's inherent in it. Also, then rhythmically, there's something about his way of playing the time, his eighth notes are so percussive. Where Barry is a little bit, I mean, all those guys have great percussive touch and attack, but there's a little bit more legato feeling with Barry or Tommy Flanagan.

Cedar's is so fun to play with as a drummer because you could just really lock into it. Whereas there's other pianists that I've played with who are great, it's almost like the function is more to keep things locked in a way that certain piano players like. They don't like a whole lot of interaction, where I feel like Cedar liked it. He liked you to get in there and play off of what he was playing. He's kind of an amalgamation of the language of Bud Powell and Horace Silver. There's a lot of guys who aren't necessarily that. Cedar is that to me. I really feel and hear a lot of Bud, and I hear a lot of Horace in his playing. Then again, that's that soulful kind of funky touch, that taste that's so prevalent in Horace's music and I think in Cedar's, too. What's so magnificent about him is he's such a distinctive voice as a soloist and as a composer.

I feel like a lot of the defining characteristics of Cedar's tunes are very drum or rhythm oriented even though he's a complex composer harmonically. Some of that shit is very complex, but it always has that blues feeling, the reference to the blues, and it always has that percussive drummer-like feeling. I don't know if that's just who he was and how he heard it or if some of that came from being a Messenger and playing with Blakey. Maybe that was instilled in him. Because to me, he sounds like the kind of pianist who does, whereas a guy like Tommy Flanagan, not as much to me.

I love Tommy. Playing with Tommy and playing with Cedar and Hank, that's the triumvirate. That's the three kings for me. Hank and Tommy are a little more similar to each other, but Cedar, it's just a dream come true, really. That's what I think about his compositions. There's certain rhythmic clichés, which he favored or liked, like Bremond's Blues. The music he wrote had so much pop to it. It's like when a drummer plays. You can hear Higgins, so it's a perfect symbiotic relationship between him and Billy.

Cedar was a really funny guy. He was a great wit. He was a great storyteller, and he loved to have fun. He always had a grin on his face. At the very end, he got salty and impatient with people, and he was kind of irritable. It was because he was sick. It was a side that I hadn't seen before, and even David had a talk with him when we were in Japan in the hotel. After a gig, Cedar snapped at him in the van. We were waiting to get driven back to the hotel. We were at the venue, and Cedar was sitting in the front seat. David and I were in the back of this van. David asked one of those simple questions like, what time are we getting picked up tomorrow or whatever it was and Cedar snapped at him. He said something like, "Goddamn, motherfucker, you must be deaf. I told you."

That's how he was reacting to people a lot of the time at that time, and that was within that last year or eight months when he was declining. That was hard to see because I wasn't used to seeing that, but I knew what it was like when you deal with a family member or someone who's elderly and then they get ill. He was just impatient, and easily frustrated and kind of irritable. That was May the year before he passed away, and he died in August. He was still funny on that trip in Japan too; it was kind of like he was two people.

I would usually play with him at the Jazz Showcase from the early 2000s every year. It seemed like if he came to the Showcase, I was the drummer. There might've been one time where Farnsworth was with him or Kenny Washington, but most of the time I played the Jazz Showcase with him. Then I would do a lot of gigs just here and there all over the place.

One time before a gig, Cedar comes down. He comes through the revolving doors, and he's dressed for the gig. He looks sharp and everything, but he's got scissors in his hands. He says, "Look here, Fludas." He said, "Do me a favor, man, and just trim up some of these hairs on my neck." I was like, "Uh." Weber looks at me, and I said, "Aw man," I said, "Cedar, you sure you don't want Weber to do it?" Jon's looking at me. He kind of makes a face, and he goes, "No, no, man. You're the one with the surgeon's hands. You've got those drummer hands," Cedar said, "I trust you. I trust you with these scissors." I had to stand there and clean up his kitchen, as they call it, trim the hair on his neck. [laughs]

I actually played the last gig with him in the States. We played at the Vanguard in July. When he was sick, it was a little different story because he had an edge. I remember he was too tired to go back to the kitchen at the Vanguard and spend the break in the kitchen, so he was sitting right next to where the drums were set up. He was spending the break there, and of course all these people came. Well-wishers are coming up to say "hello," and it was obvious that he was sick. He had a cane. I remember this Japanese guy was shaking his hand, with adulation.

He comes up, and he's just like shaking his hand. Cedar goes, "Oh, thank you, man." Cedar's sitting down. The guy is hovering over him. He goes, "I saw you in 1963 with Art Blakey in the Yamaha Center in Tokyo." He's all excited telling him about how he was there. Cedar goes, "Oh, beautiful, man. Yeah, thank you, thank you." The guy is still shaking his hand, and there's a little bit of a language barrier. Finally, Cedar just goes, "You can let go of my hand now, mother fucker." The guy just kept smiling like he didn't know. It's just those kind of little moments to me are just really funny. Classic Cedar, but he had a grin on his face. Generally, he was a pretty happy-go-lucky kind of guy.

Cedar called me one time right after Freddie Hubbard died. It was the day Freddie died, and I didn't know Freddie Hubbard. I'd seen him play and been around him, but he didn't know who I was. Of course, Cedar and Freddie were close friends. I thought it was interesting because he called me, and a lot of times when Cedar called me, he would call to talk and ask how's the family and stuff like that; he was more than just the elder band leader and I was a young guy that he would hire sometimes. It's not like we were super close, but on the other hand, he liked to stay in touch and communicate with me, which I thought was really nice, because not a lot of other guys do.

Usually, when it's an older cat that I was working for like that, if they call you, it's about a date. It's pretty much business, but Cedar, and Monty's [Alexander] like this too, they'd call to stay in touch. I was surprised because he said, "Yeah, Lord Fludas, Hub's left us," and he started talking. I said, "Yeah, I saw that. Man, wow, that's very sad." I don't know, what do you say to Cedar Walton about the loss of Freddie Hubbard; you know what I mean?

I think he just wanted to talk to somebody, and maybe he did call a lot of other people that day, colleagues or people that he's worked with like David [Williams] or Ron Carter. I was flattered. He just wanted to talk about his friend, so he started talking about Freddie a little bit. We had a 15-minute conversation and that was it. He asked how my family was doing, and then he said, "All right. Well, take care." It wasn't a business call at all.[28]

William H Walton

Cedar was the only cousin that I never saw at any of the family gatherings growing up. We'd gather for Thanksgivings and at other times. He was never there but he was always mentioned, and that made him kind of mystical to me. Who's this other cousin? The age difference and profession explains it but I knew and met other older cousins growing up; I only knew Cedar from pictures. There was always music around my house. My mother played piano and played in church and my sister listened to R&B and Soul music and my brothers listened to jazz. All my siblings played instruments and it just seemed like it was my turn at some point, and I chose to play drums.

At first, I never really had thoughts of becoming a musician. I just loved listening to music. But as I began to play, that love of music just blossomed for myself and my interest in my musician cousin grew as well. Who's this cousin that's a musician? At some point, my dad and his brother [C.A.], I guess, talked about my interest in music and next thing I know, [laughs] my dad put me on a bus and sent me up to Dallas by myself. My uncle Cedar picked me up and took me to my first jazz concert. I do remember I saw Thelonious Monk, Dionne Warwick and a few other people. That was so cool. It was not unusual for the extended family to show this kind of love.

Growing up in central Texas, it wasn't the same as being in a larger city. We didn't have as many opportunities to hear music of a higher caliber. My brother played saxophone and he went to the University of North Texas. He was an art major, but he very much wanted to play music and much to everybody's surprise, he just up and left college. He and one of his buddies moved east toward New York. Years later, he told me that he did that to be in the atmosphere of his cousin Cedar and Coltrane. This was in the mid-to-late '60s. Around this time they were having a lot of social unrest. There were riots up in New Jersey. At some point my dad and I went up to check on him. While I was there, my brother Charles took me into the city to hear my cousin. The trip to and from was a whole different adventure in itself.

We went to some club in the village, and I'm assuming at this point it was Boomers. Cedar did take the time to acknowledge us and spent time with us at the table. That made me feel really, really nice, that he didn't shun us in any kind of way.

That night, the music was really great, but my senses were on over-
load. [laughs] Being this kid from central Texas, being in New York for
the first time, all of the sights and smells and sounds and music were
just overwhelming.

The next time I recall seeing him, I was in pharmacy school in
Houston in the mid-'70s. I'm not sure why he was in town, maybe for
a gig, but he made time to go see his aunt Erma and me. That made me
feel good in a way that I don't know if I can explain. At that point I had
a little bit more time to realize just how much of a great professional he
was. I felt like, "Wow. He came to see me!" I was still going back home
and playing in some local bands throughout this time.

After I got licensed, a friend told me about a job in Dallas. And
I ended up moving there and because the family was pretty close, my
dad and uncles were my role models and heroes. It was natural for me
to go see my uncle Homer in Fort Worth and my uncle Cedar. In fact,
my uncle Cedar had told me once I graduated and got a license, that
he would assist me in establishing my own pharmacy. Unfortunately,
by that time he had had a stroke. His memory was not the same.
It would not have happened anyway, even if he wanted to, because it
had become the age of the chain stores.

Aunt Ruth did bring him by the place I was working. They actually lived fairly close to where I worked. She would bring him by,
he'd say, "Well, who's that young man?" And she'd explain to him
who, "Oh yes." At that time, I began to visit their house quite often
and Cedar would book gigs just so he could come home and visit his
parents. I began to see him much more regularly. And that's when
we established a relationship of our own. When he was booked in
town, I showed up. They used to have a series that the museum of arts
did every year called "Jazz Under the Stars." They had the budget
to actually bring in an entire band. Cedar could use his regular guys
from the coast. I got a chance to meet some monsters musically.
I remember the first time I met Billy Higgins. He walked up to me,
and he knew my name! The fact that he did that was big, twofold.
I played drums, but it also meant that Cedar had talked to him about
me. The musicians I met by being close to him was just monstrous to
me. Other times when a local promoter would bring him to town, he
would supplement the band with some local musicians such as Roger
Boykin or Marchel Ivery.

Marchel Ivery was getting ready to record his debut album and
Cedar being the guy he is, liked helping other talented young musicians. He played with Marchel on the project and also came down and
played at his release party. I remember one of the tunes on the CD was

"Giant Steps." And that's when I first found out that Cedar was on the original recording of *Giant Steps*.

After the show, their cars had been towed, [laughs] and they knew that they'd done what they weren't supposed to do, but that didn't matter to them guys. Cedar volunteered me to take them over to the lot and that was perfectly fine, but the dilemma to me was, what do you play on the radio or on your CD player when these guys are in the car with you? I wonder sometimes what he'd be thinking about some of the stuff I might put on. I tried to choose something applicable because my interests were still a mix of the music my sister and brothers had played.

I was highly influenced by fusion and actually wanted Cedar to dwell a little bit further into that. He did some stuff that was really, really nice in Mobius, and Beyond Mobius, and Animation. I was listening to Herbie Hancock and George Duke and Chick Corea, Weather Report and Miles's new stuff and they had this whole other fan base they tapped into. I thought it was only a matter of just a bit of different synth voicings, stronger electric bass and horn arrangements at a higher octave for the most part. I always wanted him to get the acclaim and have the arena type audiences that other fusion musicians had. I think he very well could have done it if he really wanted. Of course, I would never ever, ever, ever tell him that. [laughs]

Starting with artists like Cannonball Adderley I discovered new jazz artists over time that entered rotation on my turn table and anytime I mentioned somebody to him, oh man, Cedar always had a story about them, whether he had brushed shoulders with him or played with them. That was always amazing to me. I remember telling him, man, I really love this Brazilian chick and her husband, Flora Purim and Airto. Cedar said, "Oh yeah, he came in and sat in with us and he really couldn't speak English at that time. So, to tell us his name, he pointed to his eye, his ear, and his toe." [laughs] I loved hearing that stuff.

Cedar had a sense of humor, which I guess was not for everybody. It's funny, but it takes some intellectual capacity to understand it and not be offended. Cedar told me once, he said that back in slavery time, there were some aliens that came down to earth and they were black and they were really offended by the fact that these people had black people in bondage and in servitude, whereas they could have just wiped them out. When they questioned them as to why they could be treated in such a way, the plantation owners said they could not survive without their free labor. The aliens say, "Look, we're going to give you all of the technology to get this work done, but you got to let these people go." And they realized they really didn't have much choice. So, they accepted the offer and the aliens left and sure enough, the technology worked.

The aliens came back years later. And the former slave owners were just sad and distraught, and aliens really couldn't understand. The aliens said, "Oh, did the machines not work, what's wrong with you guys?" And the plantation owners said, "Yeah, everything's working with the machines." So, they ask what could be causing them such despair and they responded, "We miss the singing." [laughs] It's that kind of humor that is not for everybody.

I listened to a lot of music and keyboardists and gosh, I liked them all. They were all different, from Keith Jarrett, to Ramsey Lewis, to Joe Sample, to Horace Silver, to Joe Zawinul, to George Duke, Chick Corea and on and on. And I guess the one thing they all had when listening to them, was I liked them because they moved me. There was a good feeling that you get when you hear music that you like. I felt that same thing when hearing my cousin.

The difference was, I never separated that from the fact that it was my cousin Billy that was wowing me, that I'd hear something and go, "Wow," but it was with the added distinction of, "That's cousin Billy," and I guess that was the main distinction. I remember his dad said one time that he didn't know how his fingers moved so fast and he was just as great as any keyboardist I ever heard, technically, but he was my cousin. I just never could separate that one aspect of it, I guess, that was most important to me for some reason, that I was listening to great music that I love from so many different musicians, but this particular music was coming from somebody I learned to love as family.

To me, it was the wow factor. The music was just f-ing great. But the fact that my cousin Billy was there with all of these guys and he was a leader of the band or on equal footing was incredible. The thing I loved about a lot of his compositions is that he would come up with stuff that you could remember and recognize. "Bolivia" being, I guess the main example of that. As soon as that bass line hits, you know what it is. "Fantasy in D" is another one. The other thing is his particular touch and way of playing was recognizable. Until more recently with some guys who have studied him intricately, the only person I mistakenly thought was Cedar was Bud Powell.

When I got to Dallas and began to make a little bit more money, I bought some keyboards and stuff. I did not read music, but I wanted a way to show other musicians what I was hearing in my head. When I grew up, there was a piano in the house. I was always tickling around

Cedar and Bobby Hutcherson, 1996. *Martha Walton collection.*

Cedar and Vincent Herring, 1995. *Martha Walton collection.*

Cedar and Javon Jackson, 1995. *Martha Walton collection.*

Cedar and John Clayton, 1995. *Martha Walton collection.*

(l to r) Jackie McLean, Cedar, Kenny Barron, and Ben Riley, 1997.
Martha Walton collection.

(l to r) Ralph Moore, Billy Drummond, Michael Weiss, Jon Weber, and
Johnny Griffin. *Martha Walton collection.*

Phil Woods, Cedar, and Martha Walton. *Martha Walton collection.*

(l to r) David Williams, Gina Harris, Billy Higgins, Cedar, and Benjamin
Higgins, 1994. *Martha Walton collection.*

(l to r) Cedar, Ray Drummond, Ben Riley, and Kenny Barron, 1995. *Martha Walton collection.*

(l to r) Billy Higgins, unknown, and Cedar. *Martha Walton collection.*

Cedar and Roy Hargrove, 1995. *Martha Walton collection.*

(l to r) Billy Higgins, Cedar, Milt Jackson, Ron Carter, and George Coleman. *Martha Walton collection.*

Cedar and Freddie Hubbard. *Martha Walton collection.*

on it. So I wasn't that intimidated by the keys. I was right there at the dawn of all of the electric and computer stuff, going on. I would send Cedar a tape every now and then, not expecting to get any feedback, because it was just completely different than straight head jazz. He never really said anything and I just blew it off. One of the last times I talked with him, he questioned me about that. He said, "Well, why did you stop giving me that stuff?" I explained to him about life and my daughter being in school and into track and field, he said, "Man, you shouldn't stop." And I can't tell you how powerful that is for me right now.

Anytime that I'd be around other jazz lovers or musicians and mentioned my name, they'd say, "You know Cedar Walton?" And I'd say, he's my cousin, and they would start telling me how much they liked his music and about his stature in the jazz world.

That was exciting for me to see him credited in movies like *She's Gotta Have It* and *'Round Midnight*. Another exciting thing for me was getting to meet or hang out with people like Abbey Lincoln. Growing up, she was in an age of few black movie stars. She was it. And I'm sitting at a table across from her. Are you kidding me? My cousin gave me that opportunity. Meeting some of my other heroes like Eddie Harris and others.

It really bugged me that he wasn't more loved in Texas. Not that there were not people who loved him in Texas and in Dallas, but the love and the admiration for him around the world was much more than in his own hometown. I never understood it.

To this day, one of my favorite albums is that very first one, Cedar! The one that has the wood background and just his name. And when I told Cedar that he said, "Really? Really? All of the stuff I put out, that's your favorite?" [laughs] But it is one of my favorites. After all these years, I still say that hearing Cedar live is leaps and bounds above any recording I've heard. I don't know what it is, but for me as a listener, I've never heard that type of power and energy on most recordings that you feel hearing him play live.

Cedar told me once, "Cousin, I'm a performer. I'm not trying to be a star. I'm a performer." I said, "Okay, man." I wanted him to be out there more like some of these other cats. He was amazing. He was magical. He was everything that everybody says he was. All I know is I miss him so much but feel so grateful he left us such a great legacy.[29]

Chapter 13

Voices Deep Within: *The Pianists*

C edar was an integral part of the New York jazz scene. He would frequently hang at clubs on his nights off listening to friends and younger musicians play. His playing influenced generations of pianists. Here is a collection of interviews from jazz pianists who were his contemporaries, as well as younger pianists.

Harold Mabern

I was listening to the radio one day. And it was a record playing by J.J. Johnson, the title was "Red Cross." I heard the piano, and I was very impressed, but I was more impressed with his name because I had never heard a name like the name Cedar for a person. I knew about a cedar chest and stuff like that, but they said Cedar Walton and I said that sounds like a different kinda name rather than Willie Smith or Bobby Jones.

After I got on the scene we met and start hanging out. Cedar, myself, Ronnie Mathews, and Bobby Timmons. We were like the younger cats then; this was way before Herbie Hancock and Kenny Barron and all of those guys. We were like the youngsters on the scene. 'Course we were a lot younger than guys like Barry Harris, Tommy Flanagan, and Elmo Hope who had been around a while. We'd hang out and

100 Gold Fingers: kneeling (l to r) Bob Cranshaw and Alan Dawson;
standing (l to r) Harold Mabern, Lynne Arriale, Ray Bryant, Junior
Mance, Hank Jones, Monty Alexander, Roger Kellaway, Kenny Barron,
Tommy Flanagan, and Cedar, 1990. *Martha Walton collection,
photographer unknown.*

listen to each other. In 1961, I was staying on West 73rd Street playing
with Lionel Hampton. Getting ready to go to Wildwood, New Jersey.
And Cedar was playing with the Jazztet at Birdland. He was getting
ready to leave the Jazztet to join Art Blakey's group. That's the way
things were then, if you could play a little bit and you're hired out, you
could get a gig or a record deal. Of all the people, he called me up and
said, "Brother Mabern, I'm playin' down at Birdland with Golson and
his guys, you might wanna come through and sit in." So, I came on
down and sat in. I was just compin' because Cedar and I always talked
about that we both loved to comp. If you play piano and you can't
comp, you lose it all. Comping is a special kind of art quality. It's not
just putting your hands on the piano. I was playing and Benny Golson
was looking at me smiling. When we finished the gig, Art [Farmer]
said to me, "Yeah, man, so I liked what I heard; if I hear something
I'll let you know."

What I didn't know that night was that somebody was already
tapped to replace Cedar. The very next morning, I got a call about 8 am

and it was Art Farmer, saying, "Hey, Benny and I talked it over and we want you to join the band." I thought I was dreaming. I found out later that the pianist who was supposed to get the gig was Kenny Barron. He's gone on to do bigger and better things. But I got the gig because I had a little bit more experience, and I knew how to comp. That was the biggest thing Cedar did for me. When I got the gig, I went by his house, and he showed me a lot of the music.

This was October 1961. The Jazztet went from New York to The Howard Theater in Washington, D.C., Pittsburgh, Atlanta, Georgia, and then to Chicago. That's where I met my late wife. I always said Cedar made all that possible. I really owe all of that to him. For the rest of his life, we were very close friends. We always supported each other.

The 100 Gold Fingers productions started with me. In 1989, I went to Japan with Joe Newman. At first, the promoter who brought Joe over was very standoffish with me. I didn't think much of it and just played the gig. We played the first night and then went to this famous spot in Tokyo called Body and Soul. I sat in and played "My Favorite Things." I'd been playing that for a long time because McCoy wasn't really playing it. The next day as we were flying to Sapporo, the same promoter approached me about bringing over ten piano players for something called 100 Great Fingers of Jazz—100 Gold Fingers. He asked me who I liked and eight of those ten guys were recommended by yours truly.

That's how that got started. I recommended Kenny Barron, Tommy Flanagan, Cedar Walton, Monty Alexander. I recommended James Williams and Geoff Keezer—but it was a long time before they became a part of it. I also recommended Lynne Arriale. She made the first tour. Cedar and I hung out a lot on that, too.

Cedar Walton's very revered by all the musicians. I didn't know a musician that didn't love and appreciate Cedar Walton; he had that kind of thing about him. He wasn't one of those guys whose chest stuck out. As a matter of fact, quite the opposite. He was laid back with a quiet sense of humor, always whistling.

He had a great sense of humor. Kind of quiet, almost like Tommy Flanagan. Tommy had a dry sense of humor. Cedar was like that. He would say, something, and if you didn't pick up on it, that was on you. That's the way Miles [Davis] was. Miles didn't like to explain a lot of stuff. John William Coltrane was quiet. That's the thing that makes this music so great, because you got different kinds of personalities. Cedar Walton was very special. I'll always cherish the friendship that I had with him.[1]

Kenny Barron

I met Cedar in Philadelphia. I had just graduated from high school, and he came through Philly with J.J. Johnson. They were working at the Venango Ballroom. I was in a band playing opposite them, their warmup group. J.J. had a great band that included Tootie Heath, whom I already knew, Clifford Jordan, Nat Adderley, and Cedar. I've known Cedar since that time. Eventually when I moved to New York I ended up living around the corner from him in Brooklyn.

He was very funny. He had a very droll sense of humor. He said some things that made you stop and think. [laughs] And he was very quick, too. Before he passed away, he used to work two weeks in December at the Vanguard, and I would go there without fail to hear him play. I loved his writing and his playing. He was fun. His group with Billy Higgins, that was really fun.

We spent the most time together on the 100 Gold Fingers tours. I did 10 of those tours and Cedar might have done eight or nine. These tours were three or four weeks at a time. We really got a chance to hang out late at night and go to other clubs and play and listen to other musicians. That's when I really got to know him. We played together once or twice on those tours. For me he was very easy to play with. About a year before he passed away, we did a duo concert in Savannah. I enjoyed playing with him. Our styles were pretty compatible.

Many of his songs have become classics. I just always loved his writing. It's logical and the songs propel themselves. They have an instant groove. And to hear Cedar comp, the thing he did with Eddie Harris, "Freedom Jazz Dance," that's classic Cedar.

Cedar was a consummate musician. Whatever the situation called for, he could do it. He could comp, he could swing, he could solo, groove. All of the above. He was a great all-around musician in addition to being a fantastic soloist.[2]

Monty Alexander

Cedar is one of those people from a circle of people in the world playing jazz that goes back to the '60s. When I first came to New York, Cedar was one of the people I met in this circle. I met him through Milt Jackson who I also played a lot of jobs with.

In the late '60s and early '70s Cedar and myself were two of Milt's choices for piano players. I was flattered that Milt asked me to play with him on occasion. I think Cedar was more active with Milt.

I went to Europe for the first time in '74 or '75. Cedar and I both toured using the same booking agent [Wim Wigt] in Holland. We would often see each other crossing in some airport. We always had funny interactions and laughed a lot about the sad transportation that was provided when we had to travel around in a funky little red Volkswagen bus. I will never forget it.

He was one of the guys with the driest sense of humor I have ever known. He'd have these little quips and anecdotes, or he'd tell you something and you'd fall off the chair laughing your head off. He liked to talk as if he were British. He used to play at Ronnie Scott's in London, as I would. I remember he loved the British [vernacular]. "Lord Alexander" and all that stuff.

I'm a guy who hears tone. I hear sound on the piano when a guy is playing. One of the things I happened to observe without thinking about it is how does the piano sound when a guy is playing it. Not just about playing lines or the style, but the tone you get out of the instrument. Cedar had his own sound. In two bars you knew it was him.

He was no nonsense. He wasn't looking for any flowers. He'd just get right to the cut. He was right there with what he was doing with his music and it's no nonsense. He'd sit there and do that certain Cedar thing. He had his own style. It wasn't like some other people like me who like to adorn and embellish. He was a master of getting to the point. He had this thing about him. The humor was there when you heard him play. It was almost connected with his character. Cedar loved how Bud Powell played. He was a Duke Ellington disciple. That voice. If you listen to Charlie Parker talk. You hardly ever heard Bird speak. But when he spoke it was like the same voice as Cedar's.

All his compositions were so specific. So marvelous. And when you put them in the hands of other musicians like Milt Jackson who liked to play some of those songs, they were wonderful. Cedar was a treasure and a one in million musician.[3]

Freddy Cole

I first met Cedar in Chicago when he was playing with Art Blakey. He was very masterful. He and Hank Jones didn't play any bad notes. We didn't work together for quite a while. I did a couple of CDs with him, and I was a guest on one of his CDs. We hung out all the time. He and I would go to dinner and go around and listen to the cats. He was a beautiful man. He had a beautiful family and kids. He was a great guy.

That's what he did, he accompanied you. A lot of people go all over the place when they're supposed to be accompanying someone and that can throw you off. Cedar knew exactly what to do and what to play and that was the thing with him. I like everything he did, and he took his time to do whatever it is that he did. There never was and there never will be another Cedar Walton.[4]

Eric Reed

You can't talk about jazz or New York City and not talk about Cedar Walton. His presence and his influence were consistently flowing through the scene. There are a handful of musicians that, when you think of them, you think of jazz in New York City. When you think of Detroit musicians, you think of people like Barry Harris. Barry Harris was crucial to the Detroit scene. When you think of the Los Angeles local scene, you think of someone like Shelly Manne, and Buddy Collette, and Curtis Counts. These musicians were crucial to the development and the sound of each scene. With New York City you think Cedar Walton. Earlier people like Bud Powell, Randy Weston, and Thelonious Monk were musicians who were such an intricate woven part of the fabric that it manifests itself in almost every room in the city.

Cedar has always been a very laid-back individual, but he was no pushover. He had a very witty and droll sense of humor. Sometimes, it would go over your head but then a couple of days later, it would hit you like a sledgehammer because you finally got what he was saying. It's like "aw man, he got me." It was never direct. The intent and the feeling was direct, but the words themselves were always much more subtle, even though the intent was like a bullseye. His playing matched his personality in that way. You really had to be listening because Cedar was so slick and so clever, if you weren't paying attention, you were going to miss a lot. Not because it was overly complex, but because it was so deceptively simple. There was nothing simple about his playing. He had all of these inside things and all of these references that he'd make. His writing was a reflection of his playing. You can hear his influences. You can hear the influence of Ahmad Jamal, Bud Powell, and Horace Silver, but he was still distinctively and uniquely Cedar.

Everything comes from something else. Nothing physical exists apart from something else that was created before. We continue to progress in this music by constantly listening and checking each other out. Cedar had such great respect for other musicians. He and Billy Higgins were like brothers. It was really something to watch Cedar with his peers because everyone respected him. Cedar was one of the most respected musicians on the scene and Cedar wasn't a flashy player. He wasn't overly technical. There's a term that we have called "getting house." Musicians who do this do a lot of things like moving around a lot, jumping up and down, waving their hands, and shaking their feet. Cedar wasn't any of that and you could tell that he was comfortable and content knowing and being who he was. He was never the guy that people always talked about and pointed to. He was the guy that's like, "Listen, this is what I do. This is my lane," and musicians respect him because of that. That carried him and created his legacy, and his legacy is hefty and rich.

Cedar was so melodic. Take something like "Hindsight." Very clear, very distinctive, or something like "Groundwork." It sort of reminds me of Richard Rogers. Richard Rogers essentially explained his writing by saying he simply played the scale. He played a C major scale. If you think of something like "Have You Met Miss Jones," or "Blue Room." You don't really have to go too far away from basics in music to be creative. Cedar Walton's "Fantasy in D," everything rhymes a certain kind of way. His music wasn't just melodic. It was also lyrical without actual lyrics. Something like "Turquoise Twice" I think is certainly a bit more complex harmonically, but the melody is lyrical.

Cedar was never trying to be someone who was writing these overly profound and arcane and abstract types of things. Cedar believed in the melody. Oftentimes the songs would not have a typical kind of melody, but they would be vehicles for the drummer. So "Groundwork" in particular is a vehicle for Billy Higgins. "Plexus" is more of a vehicle for Freddie Hubbard and also for Philly Joe. He would write these compositions much in the vein of Herbie Nichols. He would write these compositions that oftentimes wouldn't be manifested through a clear melody. Sometimes, it was just a riff like "Shaky Jake," which is a vehicle for Art Blakey's shuffle. It's a very simple melody but it really shows off Art Blakey's ability to be able to orchestrate without actually conducting the band.

The influence of Horace Silver was always there, but it was still uniquely Cedar. It was a very strange way that he did that, and that he was able to be himself totally. But that Horace Silver connection was so strong and so funky, it was really something. I think "Mosaic" may have been the first tune of Cedar's that was ever put on record. That melody develops the kind of way in something like "Turquoise

Twice" or "Hindsight" or even something like "Firm Roots." There are the songs that he wrote that were vehicles for the ensemble and then there were songs that were songs outright in terms of the melody structure with the chords and the rhythms.

When Cedar Walton talked about some of the earliest records that he enjoyed, he always mentioned a tenor saxophone solo by Gene Ammons on a tune called "More Moon," which was based on "How High the Moon." To hear him talk about that, he said, "That got me Reed." He always called me "Lord Reed," He loved Gene Ammons. Ahmad Jamal would always reference "Contrasts" by Erroll Garner, and he would light up. To hear these brilliant, genius, creative, innovative, diligent, amazing musicians talk about what influenced them, man, there's nothing like it. Imagine being able to talk Picasso having checked out Rembrandt and Chagall. It's something to see where a genius comes from. That's heavy.

I met Cedar in the mid-to-late '80s. He was living in Los Angeles at that time. I was able to see him play around town quite a bit with his own groups. At that time, he was working a lot with Ron Carter and Billy Higgins. He was also playing with Milt Jackson and Ray Brown, so I got to see him quite a bit and he was just so hip and so cool to me. When I would play some place, he'd come out. I often play with my eyes closed. At some point in one of my sets, Cedar had one of the servers put a note on the piano, around the harp, around the pegs. I looked up and I saw this note and it was on a napkin. I opened it up and it said, "finger removal," [laughs] and I'm like what the hell is this? Who, what? Finger removal?

I got off stage and I'm looking around the house thinking that somebody's after me and Cedar's in the corner snickering and he said, "You know, Lord Reed, you're playing entirely too much piano up there. I'm going to have to call my cousin from the old country and get some finger removal." I still have this napkin somewhere in my memoirs, in my scrapbook some place. That was always his thing. With these musicians, there was always a healthy competition but always undergirded with love and respect. They would make these little jokes with double entendres and things like that. That was validation for me, to get something like that from Cedar Walton. Ultimately on the scene, as musicians, as players, as creators, as students, we long for that validation from our peers and from our elders because they're the ones we came up listening to. What they say goes. It counts for a great deal, and it matters.

He had an amazing sense of humor. He was funny as hell, but not mean-spirited. Cedar was never mean. He could be a little edgy. He could be a little, "oh that kind of stung Cede," but he wasn't mean.

And if he was saying something that stung, then it was totally appropriate. I just had such respect for him, not just as a musician, but as someone who represented such a large part of what jazz and the New York scene was about.

You can't get away from Cedar. His influence is quite apparent, and people are still playing his compositions. He's one of these guys whose sound piano players have copied and whose songs are constantly played. They're still being played at jam sessions. Cedar could play a whole week of sets of just his music and never repeat himself. He wrote constantly, I think that's also something that helped to establish his place on the scene.

I mentioned Picasso before; he and Chagall were contemporaries, but who knows really who got what from whom because we weren't there. We can only assume that their paths crossed because of the timing, because of what was going on. And of course, Picasso had all of these periods. He had the blue period, he had the African period, he had cubism and all of that. Then of course everything that came before him, El Greco etc. Cedar being on the scene at the same time as Thelonious Monk, Horace Silver, Duke Ellington, Bud Powell, he was there. Sometimes being there is the only opportunity that you need. You don't really have to do too much when there's that much information on the scene except show up. Just being in the right place at the right time, which in New York in the '60s wasn't hard to do because every jazz club you went to was the right place to go.

The artists that had the influence on the music in Cedar's generation all carried the same common denominators. They all went toward a common goal, and it seems to me that those denominators are becoming smaller and smaller today. It's not something as simple as "you don't check out enough Bud Powell." It's not that simple. It's more along the lines of we've got no base from the grassroots of this music. We're getting away from the foundations of this music. You can mess with structures aesthetically, the shape of things, but you can't mess with the foundation. You cannot play this music genuinely and convincingly without the African element. You just can't take it out. You can't take the feeling of it out. You can't take a solid groove out of it and then still call yourself someone who's playing this music in your heart and soul. You can be playing something else, but once you start messing with the foundation, it becomes something different. No structure, no shape exists without a bottom. There's no building in the world that doesn't have a bottom. If it doesn't have a bottom, you can't go inside it.

You can look at the works of Frank Gehry, and there are all these different kinds of shapes and it's at an angle. It's got that slant, but the floor is solid. The floor is there. You're not getting away from a foundation. In this music, the foundation is African based. It comes out of the African American experience. It comes out of the African American church. Obviously, there are European influences because that's where we get our harmonies from, but there's still an intrinsic vocabulary within African American culture that comes from those Negro spirituals. You have the melodic dissonances that are inside of the vocabulary of the African American culture. From the minute you begin to try and extract or take those things away, you start going into some other place and I'm not saying that's good or bad, but you can't go to some other place and still want to call it this. You have to deal with the foundation of this music and the foundation is cradled in African American culture. I'm not necessarily saying you've got to call it black music. The label and what we call it is only going to distort the issue of what it actually is, which is something that's not really definable by a word, but you know it when you hear it.

There is a difference between Art Blakey and Peter Erskine. Don't get me wrong, Peter Erskine is a phenomenal drummer, but Art Blakey is the cradle of civilization in this music. People like to come in, rape the foundation and the culture and the soil of all the precious metals and elements, and then leave the culture dry. This is where you get blood diamonds. They want to go to the Middle East and get the oil and then leave the civilization and the culture. You can't just come inside of here and plunder our goods. You can't just come in here and just take what we have. Desmond Tutu told a story. He was talking about the religious missionaries that came into Africa. He said they came in with Bibles and they came to our land, and we had the land, and they had the Bibles. They taught us to pray. They said close your eyes, bow your head. And when we opened our eyes, we had the Bibles, and they had the land. It's deeper than it being a race thing. It's a humanity thing, respect for humanity.

Cedar Walton played with any musician who he thought could play and he didn't care if it was black, white, Chinese, or whatever. He had Bob Berg in the band, Dale Barlow from Australia, Piero Odorici from Italy, Joe Farnsworth. We can all sit here and say, color doesn't matter. It's not about color. African Americans aren't the ones who are making it about color. We embrace everybody. This is intrinsically and conceptually "our music," but the music is for everyone. It came from the African American culture, but it is shared with and for everyone.

When you listen to musicians like Pepper Adams and Victor Feldman and Bill Stewart, Geoff Keezer, Benny Green, Ben Wolfe, Peter Martin, they get it and they unapologetically own up to the notion that yes, this music is intrinsically African American. They know where it comes from. David Hazeltine, Mike LeDonne, Eric Alexander; these guys, when you hear them, they're not trying to run from swinging. They're not trying to run from that soulful element that makes this music what it is, and those guys also recognize the greatness and the importance and influence of Cedar Walton. Cedar Walton used a lot of those guys. They played Cedar Walton's music and Cedar represents the essence of what this music is. Harmonically, he took some chances. He checked out Chopin and Beethoven. He dug all of that as well, but that part of the structure, the foundation is deeper.

I put together a group to perform Cedar's music at Dizzy's and Cedar came to see me play. That couldn't have made my week any better because he came twice. He came once with Martha and then once with Martha and Bill Charlap and Renee Rosnes. He stayed for both sets and he was just beaming. I'm not bragging, but I think he just appreciated that somebody would honor him in that way. I know Cedar knew who he was. Of course, he knew his importance, but Cedar wasn't full of ego. He was a very humble man, but like I said, he also knew his place. He knew where he stood, he knew who he was to the scene, and he was revered. He was revered and venerable. He's one of the very subtle icons in the music. He didn't have an overly aggressive personality and his music would not slap you in the face like, "look at these chances he took," and this kind of experimental stuff. His music wasn't the kind of stuff that writers wrote about because they simply didn't know. It was too subtle and too slick. It wasn't that it was so complex that it went over their heads. It was so subtle and so clever that it went over their heads. They totally missed it.[5]

Michael Weiss

I first became aware of Cedar on records in college. Probably records with him and Jazz Messengers. One record that made a big impact was the Dexter recording *Generation* with Dexter, Freddie, and Cedar, Buster Williams and Billy Higgins. That made an impact. In fact, I was in school at Indiana University, and in what would have been my third year of school, I was offered the opportunity to write a book on jazz piano through styles and analysis and transcriptions and stuff that would be published by *DownBeat*. I took a year off and I was just transcribing. Not that I wouldn't have been doing it anyway, but I was transcribing hundreds of piano solos and I think his [Cedar's] solo on "Milestones" was one of the first things I did.

I was probably 20, so I was already immersed in Cedar's style and really getting into it. From that point forward I was listening to him a lot on recordings.

When I finished school in 1981, I went back to my hometown Dallas for a couple of months before I spent the summer in Europe. Coincidentally, Cedar was performing at a little club in Dallas. He was probably home visiting his mom and so I met him there. And then when I went to Europe, I heard him like two or three times over the course of the next month. I heard him at the North Sea Festival, I think with Buster and Billy playing behind different people. And then I heard him in Paris on a double bill with McCoy. So I heard him three times all in the span of six weeks or so and I went by to say "hello" each time [laughs]. It was kind of like "Man, are you following me or something?" But it had just happened that way. A couple of months later I moved to New York. I heard Cedar all the time in New York playing. Even when I was visiting New York, I heard him in all kinds of settings. Unfortunately, I was little too late to hear him at Boomers. I really wish I could have heard that group. I heard Sam Jones's group, but I never heard Sam and Cedar play together. In the early '80s Cedar was working a lot with Ron Carter in duos and trio with Billy.

I became friends with him pretty early on and talked to him quite a lot. He would have me sit in on his gigs at Bradley's a little before I started to work there. I started to work there in 1988 or 1989 and I had my own trios and quartets in there for a few years. I don't think I ever took a lesson from him. I don't think we had any type of student-teacher relationship. But the more he got to know me and hear me around town and when I started to work with a lot of his contemporaries, he had a chance to hear me play in a professional context. I played opposite of him on a couple of occasions with Johnny Griffin. We were on a double bill at the Blue Note. He was with Bags, sort of an all-star group and we played opposite of him there. I think there were other occasions where we were on the same bill with various bands.

All of the great jazz musicians that have such a personal style are so immediately recognizable and equally as individuals as people. Their music and the way they play, their musical style is a great window into their personality and identity, but personally as well, and that's what's great about being in New York and getting to know these people as people and to have friendships. The personal relationship I've cultivated with people like Cedar. Pianists like Hank Jones, Barry Harris, Walter Davis, Tommy Flanagan. These are people I knew well. And horn players, Jackie McLean and the list goes on. Being part of the New York jazz community is a very, very special kind of thing.

It's a privilege in a lot of ways. Being able to develop these friendships and interact on a personal level influence you as well. Not only of the highest professional standards that they embody, but the whole aspect of identity and individualism and personality as you ultimately want it to come through in your own playing. You want to be you. All these players are products of their influences. I know from my own development and my own professional experience and career, there comes a point that you start to realize who you are. When you're young you're studying and you're dealing with your influences and you're trying to get to the core. The very essence of those players who are influencing you the most add some depth in your playing. Any student of jazz who just skims the surface will never have any depth to their own playing. It's only when you study. Only when you listen on such a detailed, concentrated, macro, micro level to the players that you want to emulate the most can you develop an identity within yourself. Just being around, not only playing with great players on the bandstand. Even being around other great players on that level of individualism and style. It inspires you to get to your core to bring out your story. Knowing these people on a personal level also contributes to that because they were all such great individuals.

Cedar had a pretty wicked sense of humor but was very serious in how he delivered his art. No bullshit. I played with a lot of great musicians and as silly as they could be, Johnny Griffin was the silliest of them all. When you got on that bandstand it was not bullshit. It was as serious as your life. Once that set starts and that tempo gets counted off or once we hit that first note of the set, it's fasten your seatbelts and put on your thinking cap and give it your best and concentrate as hard as you can. And be as much in the present with as much determination and seriousness of purpose as you possibly can. When I listen to someone like Cedar play, the concentration is unparalleled. He's one of those guys when you hear him play and you watch him play, he's 100 percent in the moment in the creative process. He's not distracted. His power of concentration is just a joy to behold. No distractions whatsoever. And that's very influential to be around people like that. His execution is so clean. The way he has this seamless continuity in his phrasing. It's funny, whenever I'm on a gig and I feel like my mind is not 100 percent in the moment, like I'm feeling a little distracted or needing effort to push away distractions, I think of Cedar, and I put my head down close to the keys and I stare at the keys. [laughs] I lower my head so I can't see anything in front of me except the keys to try and bear down. And the person that I conjure up in my mind to help me do that is Cedar. It's not only concentration, it's a physical thing, too. You know his hand position, he had great piano technique. Very great to watch. Economical. No extraneous motion, which is very important to me. I divide pianists—I call them pianists or piano players. The pianists for me are the ones that look good when they play the piano. No extraneous motion, good sound production, good hand position, good fingering. In other words, there are no physical impediments due to a lack of technique that are preventing them from getting exactly what they want out of the piano. There is nothing self-defeating in there whatsoever. They look right. I used to love watching Cedar play like that because of his tone and his touch. You look, you watch him play. How does he get that sound? His wrists are always low, and he has strong fingers. Whenever he grabs a voicing in the left hand, like a wide chord, he's got that kind of claw. You see the strength in his fingers. It's the kind of physical position that he sets on the keys. Sometimes I conjure up that image in my mind when I'm playing, you know, to give me that little added inspiration to focus. Whenever I feel like I lack of focus, that's what I think about.

All the pianists that I mentioned have such distinctive styles. What's interesting let's say with Barry [Harris] and Walter Davis, they're Bud Powell 100 percent. And Bird. Barry got a lot of things from Bird that he didn't get from Bud. Tommy [Flanagan] too, although he has other influences at play. But their style is so distinct that the influences they had, they molded into their own style in such a way that their influences are obscured. Their style is so strong. Their identity is so strong, just like Cedar. Who are Cedar's influences? Who does he talk about? He'll mention Ahmad Jamal, he'll mention Ellington, and probably of course Bud Powell. But those influences are thoroughly obscured. You can hardly point to anything you would hear Cedar play that says "Ah, there you go, that's Ahmad right there or that's Horace Silver or that's Bud." It's not there, you can't find it! His influences are totally obscured because he has his own way of putting stuff together, the way he tells his story, the way he uses the language. It's so distinctive and personal. It's really something. It's amazing. He's one of the great stylists of modern jazz. And at the same time, it's kind of hard to put your finger on it. There's no such thing as a Cedar Walton lick, but there are certain things that he does. It's more a matter of organization or ideas and that type of seamless continuity of going from one thing to the other in his very kind of clever seamless way. I mean, you can imitate Cedar. I know there are two piano players that are more influenced by him than anything else and they play in a way that's like Cedar to the Nth degree. But again, it's not any one lick or one chord. It's a matter of organization.

If you had to make a multiple choice and say, "go down the list of piano players and pick one. Emotional or intellectual?" If you had to make a terrible generalization, you know, does this player seem like they are coming more from the intellectual side or the emotional side, I would put Cedar in the intellectual side, because he never plays with an emotional abandon. It's like he keeps his emotions in check, which is not to say that it's cold and heartless. I wouldn't go in the opposite direction. But there are a lot of players like that. Cedar's clever. That's more from where he's coming from. I think Barry is more on the emotional side. He's more lyrical. In other words, his blues runs deeper. It's more direct. With Cedar, the blues is sort of more of a device. Not that it's not honest. Not that it's glib. It's just different. Everybody is free to do what they want. This is how I relate Cedar among his contemporaries.

He and Martha several years ago moved several blocks away from where I live so as we became neighbors, we became a lot closer personally and socially and hung out quite a while.

Cedar was kind of a last-minute guy when it came to preparing for record dates. So, I was his go-to guy to either write out parts or even make some arranging suggestions when he had to have some music ready for a record date. I wrote out a lot of music for Cedar over the years, probably the last of his several record dates, I would guess. At least once or twice a year or more, I'd have to bust ass over a weekend to write out a bunch of parts for a record date. And he was very generous as far as that goes. I welcomed the work. Being in the Messengers, he had a great arranger's sensibility. It came right out of his own style of playing. You know, the way he played and the way he composed. The organization, bass lines, fleshing things out beyond just the song itself.

I learned a lot of Cedar's tunes. It influenced me but it also solid-ified the other influences. In terms of composing for small group, I mean Horace Silver was my first influence in terms of organization and arranging for small group, utilizing the piano in a lead role and going way beyond just the song. Not accepting just a song, you've got an introduction, an ending, a coda, an interlude, backgrounds, solo sendoffs, written bass lines, and ostinatos. All these things that help to give a song more personality and allow you to express your-self through your composition and arranging. Cedar did that in the same kinds of ways that Horace was doing. And with the Messengers, of course.

Cedar was very generous. He liked old movies. A lot of guys of his generation [did]. I know Jackie McLean and A.T. [Arthur Taylor] and

Walter Davis, guys like that. They knew their classics. They knew their movies. I remember, I think Cedar told me the actor Van Johnson was a favorite of his. Cedar could go into a character at the drop of a hat with certain witticisms or quotes. Those guys had such a great wry sense of humor. Clifford Jordan is another one. Very good natured and smart. It was a smart kind of humor. You had to be on your toes. There were a lot of cultural references. Which shows you that these guys were attuned to a lot of things going on beyond just music.

Cedar was a big Yankee fan. He and Martha loved to go to Yankee games a lot. In fact, he was buried with a Yankee cap on. [laughs] At the wake he had a Yankee cap on. [laughs]

In the last several years of his life, I enjoyed a very fruitful and nice relation with Cedar and Martha. I think they came over for dinner and we've been to their place several times. We went out to dinner a lot. We saw a good amount of each other socially. Cedar liked to drive. He kept a car despite the difficulties. He had a lot near his apartment, so we rode back to Brooklyn dozens and dozens of times late at night after a gig or whatever.

What was funny is that he only listened to himself in the car. Very rarely would the radio be on. He might have (W)BGO on, but almost inevitably whatever his newest record he had, that's what was on in the car. [laughs] That's something I found interesting. A lot of us just can't stand to hear ourselves. I mean the last thing I would want to listen to is myself. [laughs] You go through that painful process of picking takes. I want to get the best out of what I did. I'm listening on a very detailed level as painful as it may be. And then it's over with. There might be a few things that I'm happy about, how it went down, and a lot of things I'm very unhappy with and you just have to move on. With Cedar, it didn't bother him. He liked to listen to his own recordings all the time. [laughs] I thought that was very funny.

I have some great answering machine messages saved from various people. Jackie [McLean], Lou Donaldson, and different people. Cedar. He left some great ones. I've got some real gems. He says "Michael, just returned from India. I'm back in town and just wanted to check in with the genius of Park Slope." [laughs] "Lord Weiss, this is your neighbor." [laughs] A very wry sense of humor.

That has made living in New York so great. So many of those guys of their generation are gone now. All the other younger players in town, they don't know anything about that. They have no idea of the climate of New York in the '80s and the '90s, for that matter. Because those were the guys who set the standard. If you're new to town and want to establish yourself and get your career off the ground and get experience, you had to go through them. That was the standard of excellence. The players that were playing in major clubs, they were the ones who held court. And you had to aspire to be on their level and get your seal of approval, your recognition, your credibility had to come through them. So many players, the biggest names, the lesser names were all here. Like John Hicks, Ronnie Mathews, Junior Cook, Bill Hardman, Harold Vick, Tommy Turrentine. All these kinds of guys. They're here on the scene. It's a very, very different world now as far as jazz goes. But all that's to say that Cedar was a very strong presence in the jazz scene in New York. And played here a lot. He performed here quite a lot. You know, I think Pat Metheny lives in New York, but you never see him. The "Cedars" of New York, not only did they play a lot in New York, but they would hang out and come out and hear each other play. He'd come to my gigs. I remember playing at Bradley's sometimes with my own trio and looking out my field of view from the piano from left to right was a who's who of the jazz community. Cedar, Tommy Flanagan, Cecil Taylor, Art Blakey, Dorothy Donegan, Clifford Jordan, Kenny Barron, Gary Bartz, George Coleman. Right down the line. And they're all listening and checking out what you're doing. That doesn't exist anymore. [laughs] And now I feel particularly fortunate to have come up in New York during that time when all those giants were still around holding court.[6]

Renee Rosnes

Cedar Walton was the kind of person who made you feel good just being in his presence. He had a brilliant mind, he was unpretentious, and he was very funny. It has often been expressed that he was a musician's musician, and history will also show he was one of the most swinging, original and influential pianists of all time. Like the man himself, his music was full of personality. His playing had an earthiness, and a bell-like clarity that was unmistakably his. Even on his initial recordings as a sideman, Cedar had already cultivated a complete language and approach all his own.

The same could be said of his arranging. Whether it was a song by Strayhorn, Monk, Arlen, or Bacharach, Cedar instinctively put his signature on it with a few skillful twists of the harmony and rhythm. Suddenly, the piece became "Cedarized," and the arrangement was often one that would stick in your mind. An early example would be his arrangement of "That Old Feeling," from Art Blakey and the Jazz Messengers' 1962 recording, *Three Blind Mice*. As a composer, he also had an enormous melodic gift. Out of over one hundred compositions, pieces such as "Firm Roots," "Bolivia," "Holy Land" and" "Ugetsu" will forever remain classics of the jazz canon.

I first heard Cedar in a Vancouver club in 1984 with Milt Jackson, Ray Brown and Mickey Roker. It was also the first time I ever heard that kind of buoyant swing in a live setting. Cedar's comping was just as consummate as his soloing, and I listened in awe. Hearing him live added another dimension to his greatness. He had an amazing level of focus. My friend, Wyatt "Bull" Ruther (bassist with Erroll Garner for several years) introduced me to him that night, and we became friends. After I relocated to New York, I never missed an opportunity to hear Cedar play in any context. I recall hearing his trio with Ron Carter and Billy Higgins at Sweet Basil. All three giants clearly had a deep human and musical connection, and it was fascinating to hear them bounce ideas off each other. I remember watching Higgins ride the cymbal with his eyes sparkling. I also enjoyed hearing Cedar's trio—live or on their numerous recordings—with the magnificent bassist David Williams, who was recommended to Cedar by none other than Sam Jones himself. Whenever or wherever I heard the master play, I'd always leave the concert feeling elevated and inspired.

In 2003, I toured Japan as part of a group of ten pianists performing solo, duo and trio. On the evening of May 26th, shortly before our show in Sendai, a powerful earthquake jolted and rocked the theater, registering 7.0 on the Richter scale. It was rather terrifying and many of the concertgoers abruptly left the theater. Backstage we were all a little rattled, but the concert was scheduled to go on. Cedar was the opener. He walked on stage, sat down on the bench and began a rendition of "My Heart Stood Still." With the first notes of the melody, the tension lifted.

Cedar once said of his meeting with Duke Ellington, "that's an experience that just stays alive in your system." That's how I always felt listening to Cedar play.[7]

David Hazeltine

I started transcribing Cedar solos when I was about 15. It was right on the heels of Dexter Gordon. I was listening to different jazz recordings because I was taking jazz lessons from this blind organist in Milwaukee, Will Green. He was just showing me exactly what to play. Shortly after that, I started trying to figure out what guys were playing. Dexter Gordon was kind of an automatic thing just because it was so clear and so slow. It made sense to me. It sounded really logical. And I remember learning to play several Dexter Gordon solos. I don't know how it was that I heard my first Cedar Walton thing, but that propelled me into piano transcriptions. I had never been into that before. I went right from Dexter Gordon to Cedar Walton, and I learned several solos of his. I remember my first jazz gigs in Milwaukee, at the age of 16, playing with Brian Lynch and those guys. I would recall some of these tunes I had learned from Cedar solos, and I would just play his solos on them. They just felt so good. It was like "Yeah, this is what people are supposed to play." That was my thing, I just grabbed on to Cedar. I didn't know what a wise choice that was at the time. I didn't know about all the other hip aspects in his playing. All I knew was I could figure out what the notes were, and it sure sounded good to me.

In retrospect, when I think about it, what attracted me to his playing was his swing. His heavy swing. I don't think there are five seconds of Cedar anyone can play where he's not swinging. It's just his swing, his feeling of swing, and his precision in swinging. When you think of jazz guys you think, "Oh it's swing. It should be loosey goosey blah blah blah." Cedar was loosey goosey, but it had a preciseness to it that was always very clear. That's the next thing, his clarity of melodic rhythms was so outstanding. There was no ambiguity. It was very clear what he was trying to play, and it made it clear for a student like me, at that young age, to try to emulate.

For piano, touch is everything. Given that you know some vocabulary, given that you know how to play, the touch is everything. With Cedar, the touch of his harmony is so perfect with the moving voices and everything that's going on there. Whether he's going to play solo or with a trio, he brings out the melody in his deep voicings. He brings out the most important notes, with the moving harmony, and the melody. His touch when he's improvising in eighth notes, or even in sixteenth notes, essentially hits exactly the right notes. There's no question about how it's swinging and what the feeling of each line is. It's just so obvious. He's so clear at what he's trying to do that he makes it obvious to me how he wants to be accompanied.

The first time I met Cedar was in 1981. I'd been transcribing his solos for years. I knew all about him. He was my idol. That was my guy. And Brian Lynch and I were playing at the Star Cafe on 23rd, just off of 7th Avenue. We were playing with this former drummer of Horace Silver's named Harold White. It was a funky little bar. There was a guy walking around with a pistol. It was just weird. It was an out scene.

One night, we were all there. It was me, Brian, Harold White, and Ed Howard was playing bass. The band was usually Junior Cook and Curtis Fuller with Brian. It was a great thrill to play with those guys. These guys started to come through there because they knew about the joint. Cedar was living in LA and Billy Higgins was too. Billy would come through there only because he would stay with Chris Anderson, this blind pianist that lived in a home for the blind just up the block on 23rd street. Right before 6th Avenue.

Higgins would come in with an armful of groceries, put them down on a bench and get up and play the drums. There were three times where I played with Higgins, and I was 21 years old. It was amazing.

One night, Cedar came in. That was the first time I met Cedar. He was in town doing something. He came in there with an entourage, but the only thing I cared about was "Wow, that's Cedar right there!" He was listening for a while, then he went into this backroom, and we took a break. The band went into this backroom, and he called me "Keys." That was our first meeting. Our next meeting was maybe six months later when I saw him at the Star and Garter with Billy Higgins and Buster Williams. I recorded the whole thing! He never knew that I did that. [laughs] Not too long after that I moved back to Milwaukee, and I started to only see him at the Jazz Showcase in Chicago. I would go down there and see him. We had some conversations there. There was one night where I took him to an after-hours thing in Milwaukee and we had some fun. And then we drove him down to Chicago for his next gig.

When I came back to New York in 1992, Cedar had moved back there. We began a sort of a relationship. Brian Lynch had a gig at Bradley's one night and I played, and Cedar came and sat at the bar. I was so beside myself and freaked out. Cedar was sitting right there at the bar! He could see my hands. When I got off, he said, "Hazeltine, I didn't see any Czerny." [laughs] That was the real beginning of our rapport.

Whenever I was with him, I was just focused on his mood because he's my hero. I'm with Cedar Walton. Shit. To me, he's like Mozart. If you could hang with Mozart for a second, wouldn't you just like shut the fuck up and think, "What do you have to say today, Mozart?" There were a few times where we came together, and everything was in the right place, and he was ready to talk. One time was on 43rd Street. There was a bar called Mr. Biggs. I had just been dropped off there right in front of this place, and I had to get a taxi home. As I was standing there looking at the joint, I saw Cedar. He'd just been visiting someone up in Manhattan Plaza.

I was like, "Cedar, oh my God I can't believe you're here." And he says, "Yeah man, you wanna come in and have a drink?" So, we went in and had a drink and we talked. It just so happened that I was getting ready to write some string arrangements for a singer and I knew that he had done that before. I just said, "Hey man, can you tell me anything I should be aware of in string writing? I've never done it before." And he did. He just started talking about string writing.

I think he would probably never admit this, but he prided himself on writing and arranging. I've seen some of his charts. He did it the old-fashioned way. There was no computer.

I've been involved in the music for over 40 years and have studied the greats. Cedar is such an icon, I guess maybe not an icon, because he's so unknown, so disregarded, so taken for granted. I don't know why that is. There are a lot of people that feel the same way. Freddie Hubbard told me that in the early days after the Messengers, that CTI and those labels wanted him to use Herbie Hancock because he was "The hit." Freddie said, "My man was Cedar Walton and I kept insisting on him."

When I think of Cedar as an accompanist, the first thing that comes to mind is the intricacy of his voicings. It's so clear that his voicings are very intricate when you listen to him, especially playing solo. But even in a band, trio, or as an accompanist, his voicings are very clear, intricate, and full of harmony. I don't mean that from one chord to the next, but I mean within each chord he had a flow. Or within each modality he had a flow of harmony that was unprecedented. He could just manipulate harmony in a very precise way.

Herbie did that with Miles, but it was much looser. It was so abstract. Cedar did it in a very formal and less abstract way and it's just gorgeous to listen to and then to figure out. It's very rewarding. Secondly and maybe even more importantly was the precision of his rhythm. He had rhythms in mind. I think that's what hooked him up with Billy Higgins so precisely. Cedar comped with a very particular rhythmic motivation. No matter what the chord is he is playing, it's very precise and rhythmic. He's accompanying in a way that moves the music forward and is very hip, rhythmically.

Billy was the only drummer I ever heard that was on top of every phrase Cedar played in his right hand. Part of that has a lot to do with Cedar being so clear and so bebop-like with his phrasing. There are very few Cedar solos that you can't sing, just like you would sing a Hank Mobley solo. They're singable. They're very memorable in the way that they're created, both rhythmically and melodically.

Billy was one of the only drummers who were all the way on top of all that, probably because he spent so much time with Cedar. It's almost as if he knew what he was going to play. And he probably did. It's that weird intuition. Like, "I know what he's about to play. And I've experienced that before and he does that with me." But it's on an even higher level. With Cedar, you can listen to any of the great records with those guys and you'll hear the phrasing of Cedar's right-hand lines. Billy is right there putting the accents where they need to be with the words of the right hand. But then also, accommodating the bass drum and snare drum hits with his left hand, too. The way Cedar plays with his left hand when he was playing a solo, that's all in there. It's one of the great drummer-pianist combinations throughout history. Elvin Jones and McCoy Tyner, for example. That's another one. They're doing it and it's great and it's moving forward and all of that, but you're not going to hear the precision that you hear when Billy Higgins is playing with Cedar. It's almost as if it's one guy playing.

Add Sam Jones to that. They always talk about Sam having the extra notes. Man, he could hit at just the right place and combined with Cedar's left hand and Higgins's comping with his left hand made something special. It's funny because the drummer's left hand is like the piano player's left hand, (considering the drummer is right-handed). Those things go together and they're not necessarily duplicating each other. They're just coordinated. It's not like Higgins is playing exactly what Cedar is playing, but it's complementary to what Cedar's playing. That's where the whole thing of comping comes in. Comping doesn't mean duplication and doing exactly what the other person is doing, but rather complementing it. There are so many examples in just about everything you can listen to.

There's a video on YouTube of the Timeless All Stars. That was one of the great theater groups that I saw him with in the '80s. The group with Curtis Fuller, Harold Land, Bobby Hutcherson, Billy Higgins, and Buster Williams and Cedar. Cedar wrote most of the arrangements. They did a great arrangement of the theme from Annie. "Tomorrow." Cedar just arranged the shit out of that. The concert is in 1985 in Hamburg and it's the first time they play the blues [on that concert]. When Cedar plays his solo, it's so clear what Higgins and Cedar are doing together. It's uncanny, telepathy, whatever you want to call it. They're in there together. It's unbelievable. That was a connection. And I got a chance to hear that live many times in my life. I'm so happy that I did. Those were some of the best nights of my life.

The Timeless All Stars had an influence on my sextet writing. Before that I was really trying to figure out how to write for quintet. To me writing for quintet is much more difficult than sextet. You have to figure out what the most important notes are, and the horn melody is always the guide to all of that, quintet-wise. Cedar is a guy that liked more horns.

I tried to think about how I would characterize the way Cedar composes. Nobody knows what a person is thinking of exactly when they're writing. But from the final product, you can just kind of guess at certain things. My thoughts were that his melodies are core generated but informed by his vast knowledge of harmony. Some of his harmonies would be generated by his hip understanding of melody and how to melodically imply hip chord substitutes.

Horn players' tunes are pretty much melodically driven. They have melodies and then they play chords underneath them. I'm not going to say Cedar wrote the chord changes first, because I'm sure it's working together. But his melodies are influenced by the way the chords are moving and by specific things he knows how to do with the voicings.

It's voicing generated. It's harmony generated. At some point there are some melodies that go along with the system. There were also times when hip little chord alterations are suggested by melodic movement.

Cedar's tune "Shoulders" is melodically driven. That's a classic one. A classic line, he built the harmonies around the line. It seems to be in B flat but it's starting on Ab7 chord. I try to think of Cedar, like how can I think of melody and harmony at the same time without leaning toward one or the other, where they're just considered mutually.

Thinking about his tune "Hindsight," I don't know how he conceived of that. Whether he thought of the harmony first, the melody first, or altogether. He had a unique way of putting those two things together. It certainly influenced my writing in that I think of all that stuff at the same time. As a composer, that's a tough thing to do because he could write a lot of tunes that were melodically extreme. Horn melodies. His melodies always had to do with the harmony that would happen underneath. They were pretty melodies just by themselves. They are redundant but they feature different harmonies underneath. You always wonder, what was he thinking of when he did that? Obviously, it seems like the melody's accommodating the harmony, even though it's repetitive. That's when he's changing. I think that's one of his things; he has repetitiveness in the melody in order to accommodate moving chords.

There are other tunes where the melody stays the same, but the chords are moving. Or the melody is in a sequence, but the chords are moving in a different sequence. Everything's moving at the same time.

I tell my piano students when they're going to do a ii-V-I exercise, if they do it chromatically, they can start to hear how some of these tunes are written. And that's how I think Cedar wrote the tune "Clockwise." Without the ii's. He starts with the Vs but they're going down in half steps. That's so Cedar. I don't know anybody else that wrote exactly like he did. There's no one else that played like he did.

Cedar is very much of an intellect among his peers. He could articulate so clearly. Not necessarily clearly to everyone, but in a way that made people think. And it makes us laugh. Back in 1975, people are talking about, "What about all this free music?" I remember Cedar saying something in an interview like, "Well, I don't know about that. I've always been a professional musician." It's great, man. Not saying anything horrible like "I hate those guys. Fuck those guys. They can't play." It was just such a professional way to deal with that question. But true, too. Because he always has been a professional musician. He writes music, he plays written music. He's in professional bands. There's no lying or anything like that. It's an honest answer, but in a way that kind of sends a message about who he is. That is one of the things about Cedar that I will always remember and cherish. I also use it as a guiding principle, because we're all public. If you have something to say, say it in an eloquent way that doesn't perpetuate negativity and come back at you.

This is part of Cedar's genius that I don't know if the world really will ever know. This was one of his skills. He was very intellectually flexible. Obviously, he's very smart. He's very much an intellect. His playing tells you that. But the way he talked about things was also so intellectual, yet at the same time, understandable and relevant.

Cedar was just like you'd expect a fucking genius to be. I don't know how else to say it. He was very private. When he spoke, it would be entertaining. He was in entertainment mode if he was speaking publicly. And by publicly, I mean talking to anybody else. He was just putting on a show. I'll never forget the first time I introduced him to Lizy. He and I were both at the Blue Note for some reason and we actually went and sat with Cedar and Martha. They were just there hanging out and so Lizy and I went to sit and I introduced them to Lizy.

He was very gracious, very nice and everything and said something funny like "Are you sure this is the guy you wanna be hanging out with?" Then he launched into his story. This was the first time he was going to introduce himself to Lizy. He's sitting there, eating his food and he said, "You know, the jazz business is a funny business. I remember when I was a kid and just getting into music, my cousin, he really wanted to get into jazz music. And he was kind of influenced by me, and his father said, "Oh no no no. There's too many drugs involved in that." He wouldn't allow him to go to music school to learn that.

It turns out, years later, he became a pharmacist!" [laughs] He never cracked a smile, he just kept eating in between lines. We literally fell out of our chairs. That endeared Lizy right away. She was like, "Wow, he's a really funny guy" because she didn't know who Cedar Walton was. And I said, "Wait until you hear him play the piano!"

Cedar's sense of humor was always dark and ironic like that story. There was no show business in his sense of humor. And he would just put it out there and then you would either laugh or you wouldn't and that was it. He was really very quiet. But when he would speak, it was always profound.

He was a very difficult person to understand. Obviously, a decent guy. I mean, maybe I was bringing some of that to it because I love this dude. He's a deep guy. So it's not like, he probably wasn't thinking of ii-Vs in alternate keys every minute of his life, obviously. But he was a deep thinker. The guy was a very smart motherfucker, and I always had a sense when he was talking to me that something else was going on.

Ever since Lizy and I have been together, we'd go to the Vanguard on Christmas Eve to hear Cedar. He played the two weeks leading up to Christmas and New Year's. It was our ritual. The last time that Cedar did it was 2012. We went down there with some friends from out of town and we listened to the first set and then we went back and talked to him in the kitchen. Cedar was always very happy to talk to us. We'd have great conversations. Lizy would talk to him for a while too. He seemed to like Lizy. He was cool with her. I remember that last night that I saw him looking healthy. I was telling this friend of ours who was visiting, "You know, we were just sitting there listening to and interacting in the kitchen with fucking Mozart." The fucking genius of this fucking guy. It's hard to explain. I'm shocked at how many people don't realize that, and that he's not more important than he's been.

Sometime, Cedar came off as kind of grumpy [laughs]. That was his demeanor. He was kind of unapproachable and off-standing. But he had a very big heart. There were several times when me and [Mike] LeDonne and Eric [Alexander] would go to see him at the Vanguard during his regular run in December. After the gig, he would hang with us until they kicked us out. He would just be talking music with us. He was the greatest guy that way. He knew we loved him and when he felt comfortable, he would talk.

Another time maybe a couple of years before he passed, he was playing at Dizzy's. It was his quintet with Steve Turre and Vincent Herring. Lizy and I went up there to celebrate our birthdays which are both in October. Cedar and I were in the backroom, and I mentioned that Lizy and I were celebrating our birthdays and asked him if he could play something special. At the beginning of the next set, he came out and played a solo version of "Over the Rainbow." We sat there and Lizy and I were like "Oh my god!" After he played the set, the waiter came over to us and said, "This is on Cedar." It was a three-hundred-dollar bottle of champagne. [laughs]. It was touching. He was a really sweet guy even though he tried to be such a hard ass. I miss him. I still break up about him because I can't believe he's gone. Every time I went to see him play it was like "Ah, this is fucking amazing!" Thank God for recorded music because he's always right there, you can tune in to the best of it.[8]

Mike LeDonne

My first musical experiences with Cedar would be hearing him on those Art Blakey records. Not too long after that I was here in the New York and got to see him playing at Bradley's several times just duo. Milt Jackson's quartet was my favorite band of all time, and I was always there to see the Milt Jackson quartet and every time it would be Cedar in the band. I saw them a lot. I saw Cedar quite a bit during those days. Once I got hooked on Cedar I really couldn't get enough. Every time I went to a record store I went right to the Walton section, [laughs] looking for the new ones.

   Cedar was a huge influence on how I play because we have similar influences. You know he is a prodigy of Bud Powell and so was I. He also has that Texas connection so he's into the blues and so was I. I was into Red Garland and Wynton Kelly and people like that. But what Cedar had that I didn't hear in those other gentlemen was his touch. His touch was so unique to me. Because his sound was so fat and yet had a brightness and a brilliance to it that the older pianists didn't have. And also, he was in that Art Blakey band. The formation of the Blakey band he was in were really the frontrunners of modal music. They aren't talked about in that way but that really was what they were doing. Many of their tunes were about that. Cedar not only had those roots in the blues and in traditional bebop harmony, but he was also leaning into the more modern modal playing. I like his version of it [modal playing] because he didn't sound like McCoy Tyner. He sounded like Cedar when he did it. And everything he did to me, was just a little different. Just different enough. Where he placed his phrases.

It's like that old saying "New Wine in Old Bottles." It's the way he played the things that I heard the others play. But he put them slightly in a different spot and gave them a whole fresh new sound. Plus, the ways he articulated things were so even and rhythmically accurate and bright and so on fire. He had a fiery touch, but it was also super relaxed. And when you watched Cedar play, you saw how relaxed he was. His hands were just a thing of beauty to watch, just how relaxed he was all the time. He never succumbed to being overly hyper and getting too excited. To me, Cedar represented a guy who was always under control. He had so much control. It was amazing. The other thing that really knocked me out about Cedar was the logic that he played with, and he didn't always use a whole lot of notes. Just the right notes. All the time. It seemed like he never made a mistake. I never heard anybody sound so perfect and yet spontaneous. He maintained the spontaneous sound, but every note was like he had pre-written it. There was a kind of a perfection to it that didn't sound dry or pre-thought out or deliberate. It was always fresh but perfect. And I have rarely heard anybody do what Cedar did. The magic of Cedar Walton was that perfection and yet it was always super spontaneous, always fresh, always trying new things. Once I heard a guy playing on that level, it inspired me.

Records like *Bags' Bag* with Cedar playing Fender Rhodes showed me how to play the Rhodes like I had always wanted to hear it. I really enjoyed the fusion sound of Herbie and Chick doing it with a little distortion and different things on it. But when Cedar played it, it was a whole new ballgame. What Cedar showed me is what a Fender Rhodes does. You don't try and play a Fender Rhodes or a Wurlitzer Electric like a piano. You play it like a Fender Rhodes or a Wurlitzer. And Cedar found that! He made his left hand more sparse and it became purely linear in his right hand. And that is like the organ. The organ is very linear 'cause you don't have a comping hand, you have a bass walking hand. Cedar's lines were made for Fender Rhodes for that kind of isolation. You could isolate the lines in his right hand, and they sounded so incredible with a nice fat sound of a good Rhodes. He had his own unique style on that instrument that I've never heard anyone else do. I really don't think he gets his due as far as being one of the absolute top players of Fender Rhodes or electric pianos.

Cedar was a true melodist. This is part of his style as an improviser, too. If you listen to a Cedar Walton solo, you don't just hear bebop lines. You hear development of motivic ideas. His whole thing is isolating a rhythm and putting some notes to it and then hearing that simple little phrase go through the changes in a way that's just like I was saying.

Perfection. Then he'll throw in a bebop line and it's awesome because you've just been taken on this little journey of all these little motifs that are developing and bam, he hits you with some super fantastic bebop line. It's the presentation, it's the programming of his ideas that's so unique. And that's what his tunes are like.

His tunes have very singable melodies, first of all. They're not Charlie Parker heads. They're not 8th note melodies. They're very, very pretty melodies. But they're over unique kinds of changes. They are standard types of changes but like his playing, they're put together in a slightly different way. The arrangement is built right into the tune. You don't even need to make an arrangement. The arrangement is there from the get-go. He isolates rhythms. When you hear "Bolivia" you know and you have that first vamp part, but when you hear the melody, that's a rhythm! [laughs] He makes the rhythm come alive with a pretty melody and beautiful harmony under it. But really, it's more about that rhythm. The shit is always rhythmic like that. All of his tunes. Even "Firm Roots," which is a straight-ahead tune. The melody has very simple rhythms, many of them on the beat. Not so many off the beat rhythms that you might hear a lot of other jazz things sound like. Cedar was a downbeat guy. He put a lot of things on downbeats. When given the chance he's going to put something on the downbeat rather than the upbeat. And this gives it a solid rhythmic core that was like him. I always thought of him as the Rock of Gibraltar. He could do no wrong. This guy is as solid as you get. He's Mt. Rushmore [laughs]. You can't shake this guy. He's never going to screw up and all his stuff is so rhythmically solid that if you can't follow it, you're never going to follow anyone.

There's a simplicity to his music that may throw people off and make them not realize how sophisticated those tunes are. They're so singable. Again like "Firm Roots." It's a very singable melody. And it's kind of a simple melody. But that's not a simple tune to play. [Laughs] That's an ass-kicker!

This is what Milt Jackson loved about him, by the way. He loved his arranging and writing. Not only his playing, but his arranging and writing just pervaded Jackson's group. It just became the sound of Milt Jackson's group. He just let Cedar take over. Because basically it seemed like he could do no wrong. Every arrangement, every tune he came out with was golden! When I went to see him play toward the end, and all of the musicians did, he was only playing his own compositions. And you never felt let down to hear one of those tunes. Whereas sometimes when people play their own compositions, it can feel like there is a repetition about them. He had such a wide scope of tunes that are so completely different but they're all of that same highest perfect level. You're hearing the best compositions back-to-back. You could never be let down. I couldn't hear enough of his compositions. I couldn't wait for the next one when I'd go to see him play!

And his arrangements of standards! Every single standard, he would do the same thing. Even a standard tune, he would approach it from rhythm. And that's what Bags loved. Bags loved arrangements, but he didn't like complicated shit. He liked stuff that played itself and was soulful sounding. That's what Cedar would come up with. But just because it played itself didn't mean it was dumb or overly simple. It just was amazing. He was like a magician in that way. I've never come across anybody who had that kind of style where they could do that kind of stuff. But the other thing with Cedar besides his own tunes is that you could also hear Cedar go play with Freddie Hubbard and play his crazy stuff and Cedar would nail it. No matter what he did. You know it didn't just have to be Cedar Walton tunes. You put anything in front of Cedar and he's going to come up with some magic. He just couldn't do anything else it seemed to me.

You ain't gonna find no bigger Cedar Walton fans than David Hazeltine and Mike LeDonne. [laughs] We always say that since Cedar died, "Aw man, that's our man! What are we gonna do?" We loved him as a person. We got to know Cedar. We got to be friends with Cedar and Cedar became this great guy. He would call me on the phone, and we would talk about T.V. shows and nothing to do with music at all. He was such a sweet guy. After I got over my initial fear or just awe, because let's face it, I was so influenced by Cedar Walton. I must have already transcribed like twenty-five of his solos before I ever got to say a word to him. I'm looking at this guy who I know all this music from and have been so influenced by and I'm looking at him sitting at the table with me and I can't even speak to him. You know? It's like "what do I say?"

Cedar had a bunch of personalities. He'd put on this kind of British persona where he'd be like, "Yes I know it's LeDonne, ok thank you very much" and he'd be doing that. But after a while that thing would drop down and you'd just meet Cedar who was a character. A fun loving, sweet, funny, dude. Yeah, we miss Cedar, boy. There's not going to be another. I'll tell you that.

It's interesting to listen to Dave Hazeltine and see what he did with Cedar. Like how he internalized Cedar and now he's got his own kind of brilliant arranging style that doesn't sound like Cedar but is totally in that ballpark. And all those guys, the One for All guys, they've all got that kind of logic. We've all learned that kind of logic and patience and humility and humor. All of these things that Cedar personified.

I remember seeing an interview Cedar did where he talks about going to see Jazz at the Philharmonic. His mother took him. He said when he heard Hank Jones at Jazz at the Philharmonic, that's what did it. He said, "That's what I want to do, I don't want to be out front, I don't want to be a star, I just want to be perfect in the background." That's what Cedar was about. Never overdo it. Don't overdo it, just always be perfect in the background. Don't be shouting up in the front. I went to so many of his trio gigs, and everybody would clap for Ron Carter and Billy Higgins. But when Cedar would finish a solo, no one would clap! But it's because he's so slick. He would have some kind of slick little thing that would happen right after his solo that took you back to the bridge of the tune. The people were just stunned. "Do we clap or?" He'd have it built in where you didn't have to clap for solos. [laughs] That's Cedar and he never cared about that kind of stuff. He was just up there, Mr. Music. That's it. Pure. There's nobody that I can think of that did what he did.[9]

Bill Charlap

I remember my brother bringing home an album. Now this wasn't what we all think about when we think about Cedar Walton. Most of us think about Cedar and think about his playing with Clifford Jordan or a great Walton trio with Sam Jones and Billy Higgins or something like that, or even with Blakey and the Jazz Messengers. This was Walton's album *Animation*.

Perhaps, maybe for him, a more, if you must say, commercial album, but still, the playing and writing is magnificent. It's perfect with pieces like "Precious Mountain" and "Jacob's Ladder." Cedar played Fender Rhodes on some it and some of it on piano. I knew instantly that this was an absolutely profound musical force when I heard that playing. I had never heard anyone play like that.

The clarity of it, the design of the line, there is not a superfluous note in anything that Cedar played, and the dignity of it, especially on "Precious Mountain," the church-like feeling. The rich, almost prayerful, but jubilant sound that he was making. The powerful sound that he was making at the piano.

Now at the same time, one of my very first gigs, and this had been actually earlier than hearing *Animation*, was playing as pianist with a group called The First Amendment Comedy Troupe on Bond Street in

New York City. They were kind of like Whose Line is it Anyway, or
The Second City, or something like that. They would take suggestions
from the audience, and they would build skits. It was an actors' studio
approach to improvisation. I would underscore whatever they would
do. This gave actors a chance to bring agents down or have people hear
them. Now I realized what was partially going on there. People like
Robin Williams would drop by. It was a happening in New York in the
early '80s. And I was a kid. I was sixteen and I could play anything
I wanted to as people were walking in. I could play anything from Scott
Joplin to progressive rock. And I did. I played pretty much just about
everything. But also underscoring it was kind of like being a silent
movie film pianist. There was an actor, his name was Ashe Harland.
And he made me these cassettes. He would make these cassettes and
they were brilliant because what they were was one tune, a piece, of
some incredibly quintessential forces in the music. They might start
with Horace [Silver] and the Jazz Messengers doing "Room 608" and
then they might go to Lou Donaldson or the MJQ. They might go from
there to the Miles Quintet or the Gerry Mulligan Tentet. Each time
I would get one of those seeds, I would find out who the other players were and then I'd find out everything I could about that player if
I liked them, which in the case of Ashe Harland's taste, which was
particularly perfect, you couldn't go wrong. It was almost the perfect
Jazz History course if you did your homework. One of the things that
was on there was a glorious recording of Art Farmer and Jimmy Heath
doing "Make Someone Happy" and Cedar was on piano. After that,
I collected everything that I could of Cedar.

And again, the clarity, the gorgeous, centered time right in the middle
of the beat, the perfect improvised line, everything about it had such
complete command of the musical elements, almost like Beethoven
or something like that. Because it was, again, so non-superfluous but
strong and all about the music first. Like Beethoven's sonatas, they are
absolutely piano music. There is nothing superfluous in them. They are
all about the composition. Everything had its place.

My generation of players like David Hazeltine, Mike LeDonne, and
Renee Rosnes were all influenced by Cedar in a very powerful way.
There's a reason for that. It's because it was so powerful, and so strong,
and so right, and so correct, that it taught you everything you needed
to know. It was modern, it was rooted in the past and it was looking
toward the future. And there was nothing pretentious.

I got to know Cedar a little bit going on the road with 100 Gold
Fingers. The very Japanese tour of ten piano players that went out a
number of times with different hits, but particularly on that tour was a

wonderful mixture of pianists. It had a nice sort of age with contemporaries and me and Renee Rosnes and Benny Green and Eric Reed. As well as a slightly older group including James Williams and grand masters Kenny Barron, Ray Bryant, Don Freedman, Junior Mance, and Cedar. It was there that I got to know Cedar Walton the man a little bit, who I, of course, felt a little bit like I was looking at a lion. You want to stand, you want to get close to it, because it's so beautiful, but you're a little afraid of, it too. He was so warm. Cedar knew who he was, but he also didn't put on any airs at all. He was very funny. Hilarious! His wit was legendary. He really would make people laugh with his very unique way of expressing himself. Just funny. I remember one time that we had an earthquake, huge earthquake, but we were all in the basement and the whole place started to rock and it was pretty terrifying. This is on the heels of the World Trade Center, and everyone was a little bit nervous. It started to happen and Kenny Barron, as usual, kept his complete cool. Renee intelligently ran up the stairs, and she was quickly on the street level. Most of us just froze. We could have lost a lot of piano players in that one. The earthquake ended and we went on with the gig. Cedar opens the concert, and he plays "My Heart Stood Still." As a typical "Walton-ism." He didn't say anything about it, and you got it or you didn't.

Cedar was a supreme grand master of music of the highest order. He never made you feel that way. No airs whatsoever. Some people who are that grand have some airs about them. Not Cedar. Not at all. The fact that he might have liked anything at all that I did a little was all I needed.

I asked Cedar to play a number of times at the 92nd Street Y. And he did. And I was very honored that he did. We did a concert of Monk's music which included quite an excellent cast of various different players. I'll never forget, when Cedar came out to play. It was Cedar's Monk. He re-conceived the music in Cedar's mold. Didn't lose any of its Monk-ness, but boy did he put an imprint on it that. Even with all those great players and everybody was playing their hearts out, you know as we love Monk's music, and as central as Monk is, here comes Cedar saying, "Hey, listen, there's even more to this. And there's more to this in being a complete artist and finding your way." It was just very moving to me. I know these are things he'd been playing for a long time, and I know he has a specific repertoire of Monk that he loved to play in his way, but it wasn't lost on me.

I remember playing duets with Cedar. He had that way of playing that the composer's mind was there, and his vision was there. Right away, you had something to grab onto that just codified the whole thing. The sound of the piano is very important to me. I remember the first time playing a duet with him, he started "All the Things You Are" and I felt like the guy sitting in front of the speaker in the Maxell commercial. That image! That's how I felt with Cedar's sound. You listen to those things with Blakey. Blakey was making a big sound. And Cedar was cutting through. And that comes from the deep tradition from Joplin through James P. Johnson through Earl Hines, Jelly Roll Morton, Horace Silver. It's all there. This is dance music. And I'm not talking about banging, I'm talking about powerful sound from the piano. And I realized "Oh my goodness. I'm playing football with Joe Namath!" You'd better straighten your back and at least do your very best. I wasn't going to get up there, but I did my very best to match the sound and match the conception. Afterward, I really felt like, "Oh my God," someone just said, "Drop and give me twenty. Now play!"

Cedar is a natural arranger and composer. And the music is always paramount. He was a beautiful accompanist, too. He did some lovely things with Abbey Lincoln, and other things with vocalists like Etta Jones and lots of others. He was a perfect comper. He was part of the rhythm section. He would create things that were both arranged and compositional. He was thinking that way all the time. I think some of the best players really do think that way. Blakey, Paul Chambers, Wynton Kelly, Red Garland, were thinking that way. Everyone's thinking like an arranger.

I appreciated how incredibly intelligent and witty he was. Not that his intelligence wouldn't speak for itself, of course. But the wit? He was hilarious. He really made people laugh. And made people feel good and he uplifted the moment. That's the thing. He really uplifted the moment all the time and you were really happy to see him. He raised you. And I think that's also a piece of his music. He raises you. There's some incredible optimism that's there too. Buoyancy. The music was buoyant. And he was buoyant. And proud.[10]

Benny Green

The first jazz pianists I heard and took notice of consciously were Thelonious Monk, McCoy Tyner, and then Cedar Walton. Thelonious Monk I grew up hearing. My father played the LP of *Monk's Dream* from 1962. I was hearing that album, Thelonious Monk's quartet, every day. McCoy Tyner, I discovered also with my father on a PBS broadcast. He was playing a duet with Sonny Rollins. They were playing "In a Sentimental Mood." I was just totally captivated as a kid when

I saw this broadcast by McCoy's connection with the piano and how personal it was for him.

The next pianist that I heard that really caught my attention was Cedar Walton. My father encouraged me to listen to our local jazz radio station growing up in the San Francisco Bay area here in Berkeley in the '70s. We had a wonderful jazz station at the time called KJAZ based in Alameda. The first sounds of Cedar that I heard was the unforgettable melody of Cedar's "Fantasy in D" ("Ugetsu"). They played it for a station break with Cedar talking. "Hello, this is Cedar Walton. I'm here in the San Francisco Bay area. I was tuning into KAJZ."

I then began, with my limited budget, to go to used record stores and try to find the record by Cedar Walton that had that melody on it. The first record I found and purchased was *A Night at Boomers, Vol. 1*. I fell in love with the melody of "Holy Land" on that album. It still wasn't this elusive "Ugetsu" I'd been searching for. I finally came to it, the song itself, in the form of the Art Blakey album, *Ugetsu*, the original recording of the piece.

I said, "Ah ha. That's that melody." But it still wasn't the version I heard. Years later I realized the version that I was hearing was from Cedar's album *Eastern Rebellion 2* with Bob Berg playing the melody on tenor saxophone, Sam Jones on bass, and Billy Higgins on drums. It was that particular version I was hearing. Regardless, when I first heard it, and now, and for always I can confidently say, there's a sunshine there in Cedar's sound, his melodies and in his intervals, his harmonies, his wit, his tastes.

There's this sunshine that I felt. I felt from Duke Ellington, from Stevie Wonder. It's there in Cedar's music. It's on a human level. No musician's analysis. But on a human level it's so warm. Spiritually. So engaging, so life affirming, so groovy. Just really gives you an attitude and a mood adjustment. It's Cedar's writing, his playing. It's such an expansive gift that he's given all of us to have written and recorded so prolifically while he was here, because there's nothing like that feeling we get. You also get it from all the greats, the sense of connection of the heritage with those who came before him. You feel that. You feel Duke, and Strayhorn, and Red Garland, and Ahmad Jamal, and Wynton Kelly.

In terms of heritage, the whole kind of tradition, if you will, of quotations of musician's playing, making quotes, of other ostensibly older melodies, in their improvised soul. Cedar is a grand master of that. He's right up there with Sonny Rollins in terms of the quotes he makes. That connects listeners in the present who for the most part, don't even know the names of the melodies he's quoting, but you spend something in the witticism of it. You know it's a quote, that he's really connecting us with a lot of love that comes from before. He's one the eternal greats, and we're just so blessed to have the recordings, right? Yes.

Thinking of the Messengers and Cedar, the first two studio records they made on Blue Note in 1961, *Mosaic* and *Buhaina's Delight*, I had a cassette tape with each album on it. It had each full album on each side of the cassette and that was my bible when I was in Betty Carter's band.

I moved to New York in the spring of 1982, at the age of 19, with the specific aspiration of becoming a Jazz Messenger. I'd heard Art Blakey's Jazz Messengers live at Keystone Korner in San Francisco, and I got the whole vision when I saw the band live, even though I had already been listening to their record. I realized I was gonna move to New York and go hear the Jazz Messengers as much as possible, learn their music, be ready to sit in with the band, and show Art Blakey that I was the right man to sit in the piano chair. Show him that musically.

I had that whole vision. The vision was catalyzed, that's testament, to what a strong emanation Art Blakey gave as a leader when I saw him live as a kid. I saw my whole horizon because of him. Betty Carter heard me. I had been in New York for almost a year. She heard me, had me come audition, and hired me at the audition. I began working with Betty after I had been in New York for one year. I had just turn 20, and this was April of 1983. I stayed with her for four years. And, as Betty knew, even going into her band, which was an incredible experience for me. She knew I wanted to be a Jazz Messenger.

So even while I was in her band that was my bible, to speak, in regard to the sextet with Freddie, and Wayne, and Curtis, and originally Jymie Merritt, and eventually Reggie Workman, and Cedar. That '61 band, that record, that was my bible. Literally. I would just listen to that. I would sleep with that. Just again, to this day, I listen to Cedar's notes on those records and the sound he gets from the piano, and I am just fascinated. I listen to Cedar humanly, in a sensual tact in how it makes me feel. The vibration of it. How that affects me.

But then, as a music nerd, more scientifically and analytically as a player, I wonder in the architecture, how does he achieve that? The human effect. It's so subtle and it's so profound with Cedar. More and more, as I get older, I appreciate that part of the magic of any musician's sound, is indeed, in what they consciously choose not to do, as well as what they do. With any true sound that an improvising artist is able to produce, there's a conscious sense of things that they could do, but for a reason, artistically, they're not doing.

I tried to notice that when I listened to Cedar as much as what is the information that he is playing. How, for example, his incredible use of register and orchestration. The kind of pictures. That thing. In preparing to join the Messengers, and I realized when I did join the Messengers, three pianists in particular, leading up to my immediate predecessors which were James Williams and Donald Brown, Johnny O'Neal, Mulgrew Miller, were Horace Silver, Bobby Timmons, and Cedar Walton. I consciously wanted to be an authentic Jazz Messenger. Not just some hot shot who got to be in the band.

For example, Keith Jarrett with the Messengers, we know Keith Jarrett's a master. But it wasn't like he was really a disciple of the Messengers. He was just a really good musician who happened to get in the band because Art was a talent scout. Whereas in my case, I consciously went after wanting to be an authentic Messenger in sound so that Art would want me in the band for musical reasons. Not only can I not imagine me being a jazz pianist, composer, without Cedar's influence, there's no way I could be having this conversation with you right now if not for the link of Cedar and my becoming a Jazz Messenger.

I myself as well as countless people, nameless people, have benefited in our musical careers because of Cedar's contribution. Obviously not by Cedar's alone, because when you say to Cedar, "we're talking about Bud Powell, he's in there, and Monk, and all these people that paved the way for him." And it's so beautiful. There's an interview, in which Cedar mentions something along the lines that people tell him that when they hear his music there's something they can identify there that makes it Cedar. Cedar said that about himself, he felt that his playing simply sounded like a combination of his influences. But we know he's unmistakable to us.

At the end of the day, I asked Woody Shaw once what it was like working with Horace Silver, and Woody Shaw said, "Horace Silver was like a soulful intellectual." And I think of that with Cedar. The craftsmanship of it is just fascinating. But the bottom line, it just feels so good. It's so very, very, in the greatest, truest sense of the word, accessible. And it's in no way dumbed down. It's for the musicians and for the people all at once with Cedar.

I think about Cedar's writing every day. And I wish I could take the listener to so many beautiful places in the course of the thread of one melody and do so, so powerfully, so deeply, with a minimal amount of notes the way Cedar can. And that's just one thing. I appreciate it's not to put a title on the specific unilateral thing that Cedar's influenced me as a writer because, it's not every single song I endeavor to write for whatever specific reason that did this to the particular piece. I think that, just as with my playing, I would love to be able to have some part of something I write be, "More like Cedar." Because, really, I associate Cedar like I do Stevie Wonder. Fundamentally with that sense of sunshine. Inner sunshine.

When you say their name you just instantly relate with that warmth. What is sunshine? What is that? It's this light that quoting Art Blakey, "Washes away the dust of everyday life." It makes you so glad to be alive. Gives you hope, really. Helps you tune into the now and realize what a groovy day this is. I get all that from Cedar and I'd love for my music to not be a self-indulgent exercise but to be something that, through my melodies, can actually bring good life-affirming joys and feelings to people, and not just jazz aficionados. But for a casual listener, who doesn't know about jazz, doesn't know who Thelonious Monk is, doesn't know who Dizzy Gillespie is, could still hear something that I've written and dig it. We can say that of Cedar's writing.

Someone can hear "Bolivia" without knowing anything of the history of the music, and they're going to be tapping their toes, and digging it. And something that "Bolivia" has, as well as a few of Cedar's classics, is that there's these two sections that are like sweet and sour, Yin and Yang, that keep a palette cleanser. Keep rejuvenating one another. With "Bolivia," there's a vamp section. There's a mode and a groove, and a simplicity to it. And there's the more dense section with the chord progression and it's not just one of the two flavors on indefinitely. It's the two seasons. Like night and day. They keep refreshing one another. It's so simple in a really meaningful way.

As a writer, and as a player, I want to keep Cedar's simplicity and his economy, as well as his isms. His particular licks or phrases. Style things. I really want to check into what he doesn't do. Another example of what Cedar doesn't do, if you check the original recording of "Bolivia" from *Eastern Rebellion*, during the vamp section, when Cedar's comping, he only plays white keys. Now, if you gave a chart of "Bolivia" to pretty much any pianist today, and they hadn't heard that recording, or for that matter, keeping it real, they had heard the recording, in real life, you give anyone a chart of "Bolivia" and say, "Play this."

When it comes to that vamp section and it's just something like D-7 for a bar over G pedal, to G13 for a bar, something like that. Imagine then, all the black keys are going to be played in the chorus of that and the chorus of the performance. This isn't about white and black, of course, but what this is about is those white keys. It's C major. And it's, musically, not because he's thinking, "I want to play on this flat surface here that are the white keys," but, musically, again, it's like there's this palette cleanser effect to his writing. That section contrasts all that harmonic movement in the following section.

And so, we're not thinking about that when we're listening to the recording. But there's these magical things going on. He's such a wizard that way and I love, as a scholar of music, as a pianist who's studied music all my life, I just look to unearth these gems and what he's doing. Although he's passed on, the beautiful thing is that his recordings are here. There's no one physically here in person, in the flesh, tapping a student of his music on the shoulder saying, "Hey. Check this out right here. Check out how he does." It's on us to just listen and consider. It's so hip. Unspeakably hip. And so warm. And what makes it so? Because I feel like, as a player, we have a responsibility to learn about music.

While we're in wonder of it and we know that we receive music. We channel music. It comes through us not from us. We want to learn about how to tell a story, and how to paint a picture, and how to touch people. What is it? We hear Shirley Horn. What is it in where she plays the chord? How she phrases. What is it about that that she can create such an enchanting effect upon us? And Cedar is just as deep as I've felt in terms of his emotional range. From any music. From any composer, arranger, player and, again, not to be redundant, how wonderful for us that he's left us this huge body of recorded work to enjoy. For all time. What a gift.

My very, very first opportunity to meet Cedar was in the late '70s. He was playing at the Keystone Korner. He would come to the Keystone Korner pretty frequently. I want to say a couple of times a year if not three times. I would always be there. I had dreams of asking for the lesson and actually getting together with him in some studio, somewhere in San Francisco, and him showing me things. And he'd be all dressed like on the record cover, wearing a suit, and he'd be telling me stuff. That was my fantasy. But whenever I'd actually go to the shows and Keystone Korner, my little heart would start pumping and I'd realize I was terrified to actually speak to him.

Finally on this particular occasion in the late '70s. I had my blue jeans and plaid flannel work shirt on and sneakers. And, I was like, "This is it." I'm just gonna physically make myself walk over, and introduce myself, and ask for a lesson. So, I could see with my eyes plainly that Cedar was talking to an attractive young woman on the intermission. At this point, I was so filled with adrenaline that I just proceeded right up to the two of them, didn't say, "Excuse me," didn't even acknowledge the woman standing there, and I realized I was too scared to say very much.

I couldn't even manage to say, "Hello." I just said, "Do you give piano lessons?" And Cedar, without too much hesitation, about a second or so, he just plainly said, "No." And he went back to talking to the young woman. And I walked away, and my honest thought was, "Wow. I met Cedar Walton!" I thought I was so cool. Fast forward a few years. In the summer of 1982, it was my first couple of months in New York and Cedar and Ron Carter had released a duo recording record called *Heart & Soul*. Their duo was playing at the Knickerbocker Saloon, playing through that same repertoire. Just the two of them.

So, I got there good and early with my little Walkman tape recorder. Snuck it into my down jacket pocket. Got a grapefruit juice which I was just going to nurse for the night and stood behind the piano where you could actually watch.

That evening, along with some of the arrangements from *Heart & Soul*, Cedar played "I Wonder Why," which he's recorded a few times. He played "I Wonder Why" and I knew that I had a recording of him playing it with the Jazztet on an album on the Argo label called *Big City Sounds*. So, this time, this was going to be my second opportunity to meet Cedar. I definitely wanted to go a little smoother than that first one. I'm preparing what I'm going to say this time as they're playing the whole show. When they came off the bandstand I came over and introduced myself by name. I didn't mention the incident at Keystone Korner, and I wasn't dressed much better than I was that time either. I tell them I played the piano and mention "Wonder Why" and how I have a recording of him playing with the Jazztet. That'll show him I'm cool. Right?

I introduce myself. Little nervous but much more grounded than that first time and I just go right into it. I tell them, "I noticed you played 'Wonder Why' and I remember that I have a recording of you playing that with the Jazztet, on an album called *Big City Sounds*." And Cedar looked at me and he said, "I never recorded that with the Jazztet." Instead of letting it go I said, "No. Really," like I'm going to school, Cedar, right? I said, "Really. You did. I have it. It's a record called *Big City Sounds*. It's on Argo. It's with the Jazztet and you guys definitely played 'Wonder Why'." And Cedar, he's getting a little heated, and he says, "I said I didn't record that with the Jazztet ever." Then he said, "Would you excuse me?"

Meanwhile, Orrin Keepnews, the record producer, was there at the Knickerbocker. Cedar went over to the table where Orrin was, and a third person, and got into a conversation. I don't blame him for extricating himself. I went home that night and checked and, indeed it is on that album, *Big City Sounds*, by the Jazztet, and Cedar's the pianist on it. But, more importantly, which I still hadn't really peeped as a young guy, was just having a conversation with the person and I didn't need to push the agenda. It wasn't about whether or not he'd recorded this song. That wasn't as good as that could have gone but it was a notch better than the first meeting.

I used to go to the Village Vanguard during that first year in New York. I had mad cojones back then and on Sunday nights I would ask almost any band leader who had their band there if I could sit in with them. One night, I went and asked Dexter Gordon if I could sit in with him and I bugged him before the show and he said, "Oh, we'll see how it goes. I'll let you know." They played the first show with Dexter's quartet. Magnificent. I bugged him some more on the intermission. "I was talking to you earlier. My name is ...." [DG] "Oh yeah. I remember. You wanted to sit in. You play the piano. As I said, we'll see how it goes." They played the second set and that was it. Two sets. They finished the night. The audience was still there. The applause just kind of dwindled. I was sitting by the side of the drums at the Village Vanguard. Dexter then walks over to me. At this point, he remembered my name because I kept saying it to him. The audience is still there, and he says, "Benny Green." He's standing over me and I'm sitting down, and Dexter was really tall. He's towering over me and I'm just looking up at him. This giant.

He says, "You wanna play the piano?" And I just, sort of, started nodding silently. Then he gestures, his long left arm, toward the piano and he says, "Well, there it is." And I start to freeze up but Dexter doesn't move. He starts laughing. "Ha ha ha ha." Slow and deliberate and I realize, "Whoa. He's calling me out. Are you a real player or do you just want to be able to tell your grandkids that once you sat in with Dexter Gordon? What are you about? Man up." I had to get up and go over to the piano and play. It was do or die. So, Dexter had played "End of a Love Affair." He'd played it that night in the first set. I played this really neat version of it, like a chorus and a half. Dexter stood there the whole time. The audience gave me polite applause. I walked back over, and Dexter said, "Benny Green. You're gonna be alright."

And he walked away. It was hipper than having gotten to play with him. After that I walked over to the bar and there's Cedar Walton.

He had heard the whole thing and watched the whole thing go down. And then Cedar says, "You sound pretty good, young man. What's your name?" And at that point he befriended me.

Fast forward, I'd just go to his shows. Bug him for a lesson and then, finally, in Japan that happened. He invited me to come have a lesson when I was in LA. I was in Japan playing with Ray Brown's trio, and Cedar was in Japan at the same time, and had a night off. He came backstage in the concert hall when I was playing with Ray. Said hello. And on this particular evening Cedar said to me, "Lord Green, you know, you've been asking me for some time for a lesson." He said, "Martha and I have moved out to Los Angeles and the next time you're gonna be out there, I want you to give me a call and we'll get together and have that lesson."

I said, "As a matter of fact, I was going to be in LA about three weeks after that." Which I mentioned to Cedar and he said, "Well, then call me." I was staying at the Hollywood Roosevelt Hotel which was about a forty-five-minute drive wherever it was that Cedar and Martha were living. Cedar came and picked me up and drove us back to their home. When we got to his place, he sat down to the piano. He had me play some. It wasn't Cedar's first time hearing me, though, he knew me over the years. Then Cedar sat down to the piano and said, "Now. Here's what we're gonna do. I'm gonna play, and you watch. Anytime I do something that you want me to explain to you, say "that" and I'll stop and I'll show you what it is I'm doing." Then that's exactly what we did. He just played and I'd be like, "That." He'd slow it down, show me, and explain to me. Have me try it. Open book. I needed to get back to my hotel to prepare and get ready for my shows that evening. And, again, Cedar drove me back to my hotel which meant taking another round trip for him to come back home. And he gave that lesson. Didn't charge me any money and that night he and Martha came to the show.

Being around Cedar, speaking with him and hearing him talk, it was really something. An insight into his music and his playing, in every sense of course, because the man is the music, but just like with his notes, Cedar was very careful in his word selection. Noticeably so. There's a saying in the book of "Don't Sweat the Small Stuff." It says, "You don't have to catch a ball just because it's being tossed at you." Because that's our instinct. Someone throws a ball, "Hey. Catch." Of course, you're going to catch it. You're not going to stop to think, "Hey. I don't have to."

In conversation, Cedar was very much that way. If you would just, casually, unthinkingly, make a slightly unwise choice of words,

Cedar and John Hicks. *Martha Walton collection.*

(l to r) Jackie McLean, Mulgrew Miller, Tommy Flanagan, Cedar, Billy Higgins, and James Williams, 1997. *Martha Walton collection.*

Renee Rosness and Cedar. *Martha Walton collection.*

Cedar and Katelyn Boos, Martha's great niece, 1998.
Martha Walton collection.

Cedar at the piano, 1995. *Martha Walton collection.*

I'm talking subtleties, not something overt, Cedar would not conversationally cosign it. We were on the bus, on a 100 Golden Fingers tour in Japan, and Cedar was talking to us, just holding court. We were just listening. He was talking about his relationship with John Coltrane and how he remembered there were a few concerts when he, Cedar, was in the Jazz Messengers, played as a double bill with John Coltrane's quartet.

Someone else on the bus, another younger person, innocently said, "Well, who would play first?" And Cedar, he thought about it for a while and he said, "I guess we began the shows." And then the same younger person said, "Oh, you guys opened up?" And Cedar said, "No. I wouldn't say, we opened up, but we would play before John would play." And that kind of thing, to me, gives me insight into his choice of notes when he's comping. How very careful and thoughtful he is. Not just going for the obvious. To not ever be on autopilot. Just like he is in conversation. He's that engaged and present minded as a player. Of course, it's one and the same person.

Just being around him and speaking with him showed me a lot about his playing. But it's also in the sound of someone's voice, the rhythm of their speech. It's true. It's very akin to how they play. We all know, anyone who knows anything about Cedar beyond his actual playing, we all know that he had a very, very, as they say, wry wit. Incredible wit. He was just so slick with the double entendres, in a highly unique personal way, very individual. Again, of course it's there in his playing.

I know for a fact, having been around Cedar Walton, that he was genuinely humble. Just to put that into context, I spent more time than I did around Cedar around the great Oscar Peterson, and while Oscar Peterson at all times knew who he was, by all means, and owned it, Oscar Peterson was genuinely humble. He was genuinely humble to Art Tatum, Nat King Cole, and Hank Jones. Genuinely, I saw that. I saw that in Cedar. These grand masters had an absolute humility to their musical forefathers.

To realize that, as simple as it sounds in words, as incredible as his music is. The genius that he is. The voice that he is. The hero that he is to all of us. He definitely was a humble servant of music at the core. And that's just everything to realize about him, I believe. Everything else, I'm so happy to be able to say, he's here for us, for all time, on the record. I never heard any stories from any musicians of Cedar out and out doing someone wrong. Over the years, you have falling outs with people and what have you. I never heard any stories of him burning anybody. That's a lot when you consider how long his career was.[11]

Chapter 14

The Maestro:
The Final Chorus

Baroness Pannonica de Koenigswarter, "Nica," was a friend and patron of many of the great jazz musicians in New York City including Thelonious Monk, Charlie Parker, Art Blakey and many others. In the early '60s she started asking jazz musicians if they could have anything they wanted, what would their three wishes be. Nica's granddaughter Nadine de Koenigswarter published a book with these responses along with many photos taken by Nica from the '60s until her death. While many of the musician's responses are predictable, Cedar's response seemed very authentic and earnest.[1] Here were his answers to the Baroness's question.

1. I don't know how to word this .... I'd like to have immediate access to the world, you know? Anywhere I wanted to go.
2. To have my own band and to be able to swing no matter how I feel. Playing with Art [Blakey] demands that!
3. I wish jazz was accepted like everything else.[2]

Even at a young age, Cedar's responses were foreshadowing what was to come for the rest of his life. He traveled and toured the world as a leader and sideman playing swinging jazz music for all of his adult life. The rhythm sections he was a part of were some of the most swinging groups in the history of the music and many of them have influenced and continue to influence how all jazz musicians play today. Finally, the music that Cedar wrote and arranged, combined with the way he presented himself and his music, created generations of new jazz fans while at the same time cementing himself as an important voice in jazz music.

Cedar continued touring and recording regularly in the 2000s. He recorded frequently for the High Note label as a leader. Titles included *The Promise Land* (2001), *Latin Tinge* (2002), *Underground Memoirs* (2005), *One Flight Down* (2006), *Seasoned Wood* (2008), *Voices Deep Within* (2009), and *The Bouncer* (2011). The final recording Cedar made was with his old friend Houston Person in 2012 titled *Naturally*.[3]

In 2010 he was recognized as a National Endowment for the Arts Jazz Master. On being honored with this award Cedar said, "I'm honored and grateful for being selected for this outstanding award. I consider it an outstanding pleasure as well as being hopeful to live up to this the Jazz Master Fellowship Award."[4] Such a genuine and humble response. One fitting of Cedar, who did not seek spotlight. Whether playing or not, he was about community and family.

In 2009 Cedar began having some health issues. Martha reflects on the time:

> Cedar was always as strong as an ox! When we were travelling, he often carried my luggage and his luggage up and down staircases in train stations and hotels. I never saw him in bed with the flu or a cold. When we were home, he slept a lot (which was well deserved), but he never got sick.
>
> Around 2009/2010, he was complaining about his back hurting. He was losing a few pounds (which was always a good thing to him). We went for our checkups. Cedar's blood work wasn't good, and he was supposed to go to the hospital for a full evaluation the next day; instead, he left for a tour in Japan. The minute he got back, our doctor put him in the hospital, and he was diagnosed with myelodysplastic syndrome ("MDS"). The hematologist assured me that it was a very mild case, and he would have to have an occasional transfusion.

Eventually, it progressed to an early stage of leukemia, which was still going to be manageable.

He lost the battle on August 19, 2013, at 3:05 a.m. His son, Carl, and I were at his side. I was so happy that he was home, in his bed. If he was hospitalized, and I got a phone call that he passed alone, it would have been terrible. This way, I got into bed next to him, held him, talked to him and kissed him, until it was clear that he was gone. It was a beautiful experience.[5]

In the program for Cedar's Memorial Martha wrote:

When I first fell in love with Jazz (several years before I met Cedar), I also fell in love with the people who loved it. I was amazed at how the community (fans, musicians, clubs) took care of their own—someone's mom was dying of cancer in Europe somewhere and couldn't afford to bring her here (non-musician), they were there with a fundraiser; someone's instrument was stolen, they were there; someone was ill and had insurmountable medical bills, they were there. The community bonded together, and whatever the musicians were doing, they would make the time to perform, for free, for their "family."

Now, as always, the community that has been Cedar's and my family for the past 20+ years is coming together again, this time on our behalf. My jazz family has been so supportive—not a day goes by since Cedar's passing that I don't get a call, an invitation, a hug, and of course always a reminder that this music is so full of joy (which, ironically, is why my heart is so heavy since Cedar passed!) I am sure Cedar is smiling, knowing that all of you have been looking after us in his absence!

Not too long ago, I suggested to him that the traveling was becoming too difficult, and maybe he should start taking it easy, maybe, "retire." He looked at me, and without skipping a beat, said, "this is what I do." The subject never came up again, and that is what he did, almost to the very last moment. We came back from France on July 29, and he left us on August 19.[6]

Cedar left us with a lasting legacy of recordings, compositions and arrangements, and countless musicians who honor him daily. He performed and recorded alongside the greatest jazz musicians in the history of the music.

NEA Jazz Masters ceremony; (l to r) George Avakian,
Muhal Richard Abrams, Kenny Barron, Bill Holman,
Bobby Hutcherson, Yusef Lateef, Annie Ross, and Cedar, 2010.
Photo by Tom Pich Photography/NYC.

Cedar performing at the NEA Jazz Masters ceremony, 2010.
Photo by Tom Pich Photography/NYC.

He played on over 200 recordings and wrote many tunes that are still performed and recorded today. Cedar was a major contributor to jazz music and its history for more than fifty years. All the while being remarkably consistent, performing at highest level for his entire professional life. He was a humble giant who was inclusive and supportive of those in his community. Above all, he swung.

Afterword

As the eldest son of jazz pianist Cedar Walton, I always felt like I was one of the luckiest people on the planet. As a kid growing up in Brooklyn, New York, I looked at him as one of the best in the world to be doing that thing he does, and I often had a front row seat to witness and feel that talent. And as an occasional sidekick with him on his some of his countless musical performances and interactions with other musicians, I saw not only the other-worldly, inimitable skill he carried with him wherever he went, but the impact and influence he had on the music and so many of his colleagues in the industry.

So it was natural for me to wonder why he didn't get more "shine," or perhaps the kind of recognition I felt was commensurate with his stature among the giants—I mean, he not only played with virtually all of the other giants, he often led groups, or served as musical director and/or arranger on so many of their projects and tunes. Was it because he never really did much self-promoting or publicizing like others did? Was it his playing style— primarily center of the piano bench, largely emotionless while striding all 88 keys effortlessly throughout his set, no histrionics or facial expressions coinciding with the brilliance on those keys—that didn't call extra attention beyond the music itself that hindered the amount of mainstream love that should've come his way?

As a professional and self-described writer, I thought writing a biography could help, and started on it but couldn't keep that going myself (more on that later). And I stayed close to my father's career and life, still marveling at his playing prowess and how at each performance there was always at least one song or one moment where he did something that just blew me away. I was feeling very appreciative for him for getting some long-awaited accolades during the 2000s, especially his induction as a National Endowment for the Arts (NEA) Jazz Master, considered the Hall of Fame recognition for jazz figures. And I kept hoping to sit Dad down for some biographical conversation as I collected contact info of friends, contemporaries and celebrity fans and admirers for later additions for the book, while also keeping an eye on his declining health and wondering if I'd have enough time left to talk to him.

In the early 2010s he developed a blood disorder that slowed his physical progress, and was often tended to by his beloved wife Martha and others in just enough time, and with just enough prescription meds and supplies to prop him up for his next gigs, so most people didn't know of his struggles for a while. By 2012–2013, his struggles were more apparent, and he just wasn't the same Cedar, or Dad, though his playing was so natural and automatic for him, he was still able to muster up enough skill and energy to keep playing into the summer 2013. When he fell ill during a European gig he had to come home, and his bandstand days were over.

With Martha struggling with home care for him, I came up from North Carolina for a weekend in hopes of spending some time with him while giving her a break from the emotional and physical toll she was dealing with. Imagine trying to get someone to the bathroom at 2 a.m. who is twice your size and weight with no help? Little did I know that after a few days I'd be there to see him take his last breaths, and witness him getting his wings to fly home, away from the horrible pain and discomfort he was experiencing and into Paradise, where he was meant to be all along.

In the years that followed, I started to see and feel even more of the impact of Cedar on the jazz world. Having moved out of the NYC area in 2002, I had been missing out on the local jazz scene, which I felt often set the tone for jazz everywhere else in the United States. This included following and recognizing many of the other pianists and artists making their way in jazz, including those influenced by Cedar. And while I'd become familiar with (& fans of) Bill Charlap, Renee Rosnes, Benny Green and others, I admit I hadn't heard enough of players like Mike LeDonne, David Hazeltine, Eric Reed and Emmet Cohen, all legends in the making that came up behind Cedar. And seeing how so many of them paid tribute to Cedar in their recordings, performances and published (or posted) quotes, it was refreshing to know that my assumptions of his impact were getting validated every day.

I don't remember how I first came to hear Ben Markley's CD, *Clockwise: The Music of Cedar Walton*. I think Ben may have sent me an advance copy, but I was blown away by what I heard. Several of the songs—"Hindsight," "Bolivia" and "I'm Not So Sure"—are my all-time Cedar favorites, so the selection of tunes got me from the jump, and the way he transformed Cedar's arrangements to the big band format without losing the intimacy of the originals was astounding to me. I made sure to reach out to him personally to share with him the excitement and pure joy I felt while hearing, and it became my go-to CD in the car for the rest of the year.

When Ben called me soon after with the idea about this book, my initial skepticism was borne strictly from selfish motives, somehow feeling that as his son, it's my duty to be the one to put this out. But damn, if I hadn't gotten past writing the preface in the past seven years, when the hell was it going to happen? I turned that skepticism to full support pretty quickly, especially after speaking to Ben and feeling a connection with him, a kind of shared passion for Cedar's works, and appreciated that he would be documenting genius and sensibilities he carried that made him who he was. I trusted him when he told me that this project wasn't about the money, it was more about shining a light on one of the true heroes of this American-made treasure we call jazz.

As Emmet Cohen said on his most recent episode of his brilliant weekly YouTube show recorded from his Harlem apartment, "Emmet's Place," his annual Cedar Walton tribute, "Cedar is very important to us, and created a lot of the language of post-Thelonious Monk, Bud Powell and Duke Ellington. We looked to him for 'the way'—the guiding light, and he shows us the way every day." I feel this book has the potential to capture that importance in ways no other previous interview could.

I don't know if it's because I'm biased since I've known Cedar ALL my life, and know or have met so many of those quoted in the book, but this was a true page-turner for me. It is neatly organized in a chronological manner that truly gives us a sense of where he came from, ancestrally and geographically as well as musically. And what better way to introduce each chapter than by titling them with oft-played Cedar compositions?

One of the things that struck me while reading was how consistent his personality and demeanor was with practically everyone he came in contact with. If I read it once, I read it dozens of times: he was direct but not mean; great sense of humor but too bad if you didn't get it; intolerant of bullshit in front of him and either called it out or removed himself from the situation; took the music very seriously but not himself nearly as much. It was how we knew him as a father as well, and they are personality traits my brother and I still try to emulate to this day.

Another thing that struck me was how often and how regular it was for him to show up to watch fellow musicians play and then hang out with them for hours after they played. If I didn't know any better, I'd have thought that's how he spent most of his waking moments, when I knew for a fact that it wasn't—but it was just more than I knew. And it's a beautiful thing, and I can only imagine the feelings that might envelop you as an artist when someone you admire so much shows up to hear you—and then drink with you afterward?!? When we went to hear him play, I now recall usually leaving the club to go home and he stayed behind, but I had to read the book to find out he was really just getting started for the night/morning! I'd no idea that was a regular thing for him!

I found many personal, hilarious moments in this book. My brother Rodney recalls my father calling a popular but awkward Knick player "Spill Jackson" and I hollered. And Curtis Fuller calling Cedar "Mein Comp" was very clever and generated some good chuckles. My favorite is the story Cedar told, and it was retold by David Hazeltine, about his cousin not being allowed to play jazz because of "all the drugs they use," then later becoming a pharmacist instead! The recollections took on an extra meaning because I could vividly picture Cedar saying these things, and that made them feel even funnier.

Dad was hilarious, and reading the stories from the people showed me that, just like we did in the family, when we knew we were going to see Cedar, we expected to hear something very funny. I mean, it was almost an unspoken requirement, and he almost always delivered. It was like that when I'd accompany him to clubs and other places with musicians. It's almost like they'd drop what they were doing to go see him and say "hello," hoping to mine some creatively worded gems from him to laugh at, contemplate for themselves, and in many cases repeat them to others. It reflected a true reverence, or as much reverence as one could have with someone they also found very approachable.

Most of all, this book highlighted many things I did not know about my father, particularly his presence on the jazz scene in New York, Los Angeles, and Europe/Japan. And just about all of it was to my delight, like discovering you had royalty in your family all along and hadn't turned your head to notice it because he never brought any of that royal treatment or expectations home. Suffice it to say, he always seemed to make sure his home was a safe, fun and comfortable environment for him, and we just got right on board.

We lived in a nice, middle class apartment building in the Crown Heights section of Brooklyn in the '60s. The piano in the living room helped to make that room a rehearsal space, an impromptu jam session spot, and a general hang out location in the neighborhood. We often recalled those times when bebop and jazz were becoming popular with young, hip black folks that it was the "hip hop of the day," where the latest slang was created and spoken judiciously amongst each other. Of course, many of those gatherings were enhanced by some pretty good weed, or as my mom used to describe it to me, "the cigarettes without any nicotine to hurt you." My mom and dad were very personable people, and my mom used to produce and organize jazz concerts in Brooklyn, so it was a great place to network. We just loved living there, and the musicians always seemed to have fun when my brother and I were hanging around them.

We had plenty of jazz records in the house, and I used to study them thoroughly, often committing to memory the personnel listings for each Blue Note and other recordings we had. I often created my own jazz "supergroups," writing out jazz bands with some of the best horn players, bassists, drummers and others you could find, and I always had Cedar as the lone pianist. I figured, who else do we need? He can play with all of them!

There were times when I wondered, even as a kid but more so in the many years following, why isn't he getting more recognition for how he plays and his impact on the contemporary bebop jazz scene?

Whatever the reason, I decided as the lone writer of the family that I would take on the monumental task of writing his biography. That decision was further cemented, I thought, by the declaration of my good friend, writing colleague and jazz fan Earl Artis, Jr., who told me that if I didn't write this book about my father that he would never speak to me again. Well, I sure didn't want that to happen, and back in 2008 or 2009 I set out to writing, and started by taking a bus trip from my home in North Carolina to New York City to accompany Cedar each night to the second week of his Christmastime engagement at the legendary Village Vanguard.

It was a glorious week, and I was so mesmerized by the music each night, I never thought to gather any notable quotables from Cedar or anyone else that came to those shows, and there were plenty that came through. I did write a nice foreword to the book, which included my exploits on the Greyhound bus that swore me off bus travel afterward, but that's the last part of that book that was ever written. Thank goodness Ben came along years later to write this, as I'd been out to lunch on my own assignment and never returned!

Look: even though the world has plenty of room for more Cedar-inspired communications—and I may just venture back down that road—this book right here will serve as the quintessential memoir of Cedar for years to come. Well done my friend … or, as Cedar would have bellowed, "OUTSTANDING Lord Markley!!!"

That was kinda fun. Let's do it again sometime!!!

Carl Walton

Selected Awards and Achievements

Cedar arranged the music and played on Etta James's *Mystery Lady: Songs of Billie Holiday*, which won the Grammy Award for Best Jazz Vocal Album in 1995.

Cedar played on Benny Carter's *Elegy in Blue* which won a Grammy for Best Instrumental Solo in 1995.

Cedar played piano or keyboard for the following movies: *Cool Red* (1976), *She's Gotta Have It* (1986), *Round Midnight* (1986).

1985   Black Jazz Music Caucus. Dallas/Ft. Worth, Appreciation of Service in Jazz Education

1987   Certificate of Appreciation, City of New Orleans.

1992   Jazz Arts Service Award

1995   Jazz Personality of the Festival Award. Guinness Jazz Festival. Cork, Ireland.

2004   Living the Dream Mentor Award. Manhattan Country School. New York, NY.

2005   NJPAC's Wachovia Jazz for Teens—Jazz Master of the Year

2010   National Endowment for the Arts Jazz Master

Selected Discography

Kenny Dorham: *This Is the Moment*
Riverside Records OJC CD812-2 [CD]
July 7, 1958; New York

Kenny Dorham: *Blue Spring*
Riverside Records OJC CD134-2 [CD]
January 20 and February 18,1959; New York

J.J. Johnson Sextet: *Really Livin'*
Columbia CL1383 [CD]
March 18,19, 24; New York

John Coltrane Quartet: *Alternate Takes*
Rhino R2-71984 [CD]
March 26; New York

J.J. Johnson Sextet: *J.J. Inc.*
Columbia CK 65296 [CD]
August 1,3, 1960; New York

Clifford Jordan Quarter: *Spellbound*
Reissued as *Spellbound + Starting + Bearcat*
Fresh Sound Records FSR CD 769 [CD]
August 10, 1960; New York

Art Farmer/Benny Golson Jazztet: *Big City Sounds*
Reissued as *The Jazztet-Big City Sounds*
Fresh Sound Records FSRCD 1653
September 16, 19, 20 1960; New York

Wayne Shorter: *Second Genesis*
Reissued as *The Complete Vee Jay Lee Morgan-Wayne Shorter*
Mosaic Box Set MD6-202 [CD]
October 11, 1960; Chicago

Art Farmer/Benny Golson Jazztet: *The Jazztet & John Lewis*
Vogue F 660526 [CD]
December 20-21, 1960 and January 9, 1961; New York

Freddie Hubbard: *Hub Cap*
Blue Note CDP7-84073-2 [CD]
April 9, 1961; Englewood Cliffs

Jimmy Heath All Stars: *The Quota*
Reissued as *The Jimmy Heath Sextet—The Quota + Triple Threat*
Fresh Sound Records FSRCD 859 [CD]
April 14, 20, 1961; New York

Art Farmer/Benny Golson Jazztet: *The Jazztet At Birdhouse*
Reissued as *The Complete/Argo/Mercury/Art Farmer/Benny Golson/Jazztet
    Sessions*
Mosaic Box Set MD7-225
May 15, 1961; Chicago

Clifford Jordon: *Starting Time*
Reissued as *Spellbound + Starting + Bearcat*
Fresh Sound Records FSR CD 769 [CD]
June 14–15, 1961; New York

Art Blakey and the Jazz Messengers: *Mosaic*
Blue Note 8-40856-2 [CD]
October 2, 1961; Englewood Cliffs

Curtis Fuller: *Soul Trombone*
Real Gone Jazz RGJCD 453 [CD]
November 15–17, 1961; New York

Art Blakey and the Jazz Messengers: *Buhaina's Delight*
Blue Note 7-84104-2 [CD]
November 28, 1961; Englewood Cliffs

Clifford Jordan: *Bearcat*
Reissued as *Spellbound + Starting + Bearcat*
Fresh Sound FSR CD 769 [CD]
December 28, 1961 and January 10, 1962; New York

Jimmy Heath All Stars: *Triple Threat*
Reissued as *The Jimmy Heath Sextet—The Quota + Triple Threat*
Fresh Sound Records FSRCD 859 [CD]
January 4,17, 1962; New York

Art Blakey and the Jazz Messengers: *Three Blind Mice*
Reissued as *Three Blind Mice Vol. 1* and *Three Blind Mice Vol. 2*

CDP7-84451-2 [CD] and CDP7-84452-2 [CD]
March 18, 1962. Los Angeles

Blue Mitchell: *The Cup Bearers*
Riverside Records OJC CD 797-2 [CD]
August 28, 30, 1962. New York

Art Blakey and the Jazz Messengers: *Caravan*
Riverside Records RCD-30187
October 23–24, 1926. New York

Freddie Hubbard: *Here to Stay*
Blue Note CDP7-84135-2 [CD]
December 27, 1962; Englewood Cliffs

Freddie Hubbard and His Orchestra: *The Body and the Soul*
Reissued as *The Artistry of Freddie Hubbard/Body and Soul*
Impulse 06025-2780950 [CD]
March 8,12, and May 2; 1963; New York

Art Blakey and the Jazz Messengers: *Ugetsu*
Riverside Records OJC CD 090-2 [CD]
June 16, 1963; New York

Art Blakey and the Jazz Messengers: *Free For All*
Blue Note 7-84170-2 [CD]
February 10, 1964; Englewood Cliffs

Art Blakey and the Jazz Messengers: *Kyoto*
Riverside Records OJC CD 145-2 [CD]
February 20, 1964; New York

Art Blakey and the Jazz Messengers: *Indestructible*
Blue Note 7-46429-2 [CD]
April 15–16, 24, 1964; Englewood Cliffs

Art Blakey and the Jazz Messengers: *Golden Boy*
Blue Note 7-46429-2[CD]
May or June 1964; Englewood Cliffs

Eddie Harris: *Cool Sax from Hollywood to Broadway*
Columbia CS 9095
September 22–24, 1964; New York

Eddie Harris: *Here Comes the Judge*
Columbia CS9681[LP]
September, December 18 1964; New York

Clifford Jordan: *These Are My Roots*
Reissued as *These Are My Roots*
Koch Jazz KOC CD 8522 [CD]
February 1, 17, 1965; New York

Eddie Harris: *The In Sound*
Reissued as *The In Sound/Mean Greens*
Rhino R2-71515 [CD]
August 9, 1965; New York

Milt Jackson: *Milt Jackson at the Museum of Modern Art*
Reissued as *Milt Jackson at the Museum of Modern Art*
Verve 06202517686298 [CD]
August 12, 1965; New York

Joe Henderson Orchestra: *Mode for Joe*
Blue Note 5-80909-2 [CD]
January 27, 1966; Englewood Cliffs

Eddie Harris: *Mean Greens*
Reissued as *The In Sound/Mean Greens*
Rhino R2-71515 [CD]
March 8–9, 1966; New York

Eddie Harris: *The Tender Storm*
Reissued as *The Tender Storm*
32 Jazz 32067 [CD]

Lee Morgan: *Charisma*
Blue Note CDP 59961 [CD]
September 29, 1966; Englewood Cliffs

Blue Mitchell: *Boss Horn*
Blue Note 5-63814-2 [CD]
November 17, 1966; Englewood Cliffs

Lee Morgan: *The Rajah*
Blue Note CDP7-84426-2 [CD]
November 29, 1966; Englewood Cliffs

Milt Jackson: *Born Free*
Verve 525561-2 [CD]
December 15, 1966; New York

Donald Bryd: *Blackjack*
Blue Note 8-21286-2 [CD]
January 9, 1967; Englewood Cliffs

Art Farmet Quintet: *The Time and the Place*
Columbia COL-CD-6870 [CD]
February 8, 1967; New York

Hank Mobley: *Third Season*
Blue Note 97506 [CD]
February 24, 1967; Englewood Cliffs

Lee Morgan: *Sonic Boom*
Blue Note CDP 90414 [CD]
April 14, 28 1967; Englewood Cliffs

Donald Byrd: *Slow Drag*
Blue Note 5-35560-2 [CD]
May 12, 1967; Englewood Cliffs

Art Farmer Quintet: *Art Farmer Quintet Plays Great Jazz Hits*
Columbia CL 2746 [LP]
May 16,23,25, 1967; New York

Hank Mobley: *Far Away Lands*
Blue Note CDP7-84425-2 [CD]
May 26, Englewood Cliffs

Houston Person: *Chocomotive*
Reissued as *Trust in Me*
Prestige 24264 [CD]
June 14, 1967; Englewood Cliffs

Cedar Walton: *Cedar!*
Reissued as *Cedar Walton plays Cedar Walton*
Prestige OJC CD462-2 [CD]
July 10, 1967; New York

Eric Kloss: *First Class Kloss*
Prestige PRCD-24293-2 [CD]
July 14, 1967; Englewood Cliffs

Sonny Criss: *Up, Up and Away*
Prestige OJC CD982-2 [CD]
August 18, 1967

Pat Martino: *Strings!*
Prestige CD 223-2 [CD]
October 2, 1967; New York

Houston Person: *Trust in Me*
Reissued as *Trust in Me*
Prestige 24264 [CD]
October 13, 1967; New York

Lee Morgan: *The Sixth Sense*
Blue Note 5-71065-2 [CD]
November 10, 1967; Englewood Cliffs

Sonny Criss: *The Beat Goes On*
Prestige OJC CD1899-2 [CD]
January 12, 1968; Englewood Cliffs

Charles McPherson: *From This Moment On*
Prestige OJC CD 1899-2 [CD]
January 31, 1968; New York

Lee Morgan: *Caramba!*
Blue Note 8-53358-2 [CD]
May 3, 1968; Englewood Cliffs

Milt Jackson: *Milt Jackson and the Hip String Quartet*
Verve SW 91569 [LP]
May 9, June 3, 17, 1968; New York

Cedar Walton: *Spectrum*
Prestige PRCD-24145-2 [CD]
May 24, 1968; New York

Charles McPherson: *Horizons*
Prestige OJC CD1912-2 [CD]
August 27, 1968; New York

Cedar Walton: *The Electric Boogaloo Song*
Prestige PRCD-24145-2 [CD]
January 14, 1969; New York

Stanley Turrentine: *Another Story*
Reissued as *Stanley Turrentine—The Blue Note Quintet/Sextet Studio Session*
Mosaic Box Set MD5-212 [CD]
March 3, 1969; Englewood Cliffs

Cedar Walton: *Soul Cycle*
Prestige OJC CD-847-2 [CD]
June 25, 1969; Englewood Cliffs

Hank Mobley: *Thinking of Home*
Reissued as *The Complete Hank Mobley Blue Note Session 1963–70*
Mosaic Box Set MD8-268
July 31, 1970; Englewood Cliffs

Art Farmer Septet: *Homecoming*
Mainstream MDCD 720 [CD]
July 15,16, 1971; New York

Houston Person: *Broken Windows, Empty Hallways*
Prestige PRCD-24290-2 [CD]
1972; New York

Curtis Fuller: *Smokin'*
Mainstream MRL 370 [LP]
Early 1972; Unknown

Cedar Walton/Hank Mobley: *Breakthrough*
Cobblestone CST 9011 [LP]
February 22, 1972; New York

Etta Jones: *A Soulful Sunday: Live at the Left Bank featuring the Cedar Walton Trio*
Reel to Real RTRCD002
February 27, 1972; Baltimore

Dexter Gordon: *Generation*
Prestige OJC CD 836-2 [CD]
June 22, 1972; New York

Lucky Thompson: *Friday the 13th: Cook County Jail*
Groove Merchant GM 515 [LP]
October 13, 1972; Chicago

Lucky Thompson: *I Offer You*
Groove Merchannt GM 517 [LP]
1973; New York

Cedar Walton Trio with Clifford Jordan: *A Night at Boomers Vol. 1 & Vol. 2*
Reissued as *Naima*
32 Jazz 32046 [CD]
January 4, 1973

Art Blakey and the Jazz Messengers: *Buhaina*
Blue Note 7-97190-2 [CD]
March, 1973; Berkeley

Art Blakey and the Jazz Messengers: *Anthenagin*
Prestige PRCD-24130-2 [CD]
March, 1973; Berkeley

Gene Ammons & Sonny Stitt: *God Bless Jug and Sonny*
Prestige PRCD-11022-2 [CD]
June 24, 1973; Baltimore

Gene Ammons/Sonny Stitt: *Left Bank Encores*
Prestige PRCD—11022-2 [CD]
June 24, 1973; Baltimore

Milt Jackson Quintet: *Goodbye*
CTI 6038 [LP]
December, 1973; New York

Milt Jackson: *Olinga*
CTI/CBS Associated ZK44174 [CD]
January, 1974; New York

Cedar Walton Trio: *Firm Roots*
Camden Deluxe (E) 74321-610742 [CD]
April, 1974; Rochester

Clifford Jordan: *Half Note*
Steeplechase SCCD 31198 [CD]
April 5, 1974; New York

Sam Jones: *Seven Minds*
Eastwind (Jap) 9015 [CD]
December 21, 1974; Tokyo

Cedar Walton: *Pit Inn*
Eastwind PHCE-2036 [CD]
December 23, 1974; Tokyo

Cedar Walton: *Mobius*
RCA APL1-1009
1975; New York

Cedar Walton: *Beyond Mobius*
FCA Apl1-1435
1975; New York

Art Farmer: *To Duke with Love*
East Wind 9Jap) 32JD-111 [CD]
March 5, 1975; New York

Clifford Jordan Quintet: *Night of the Mark VII*
Muse MCD 5445 [CD]
March 26, 1975; Paris

Clifford Jordan and the Magic Triangle: On Stage Vol 1
SteepleChase (Dan) SCCD 31071 [CD]
March 29, 1975; Amsterdam

Clifford Jordan and the Magic Triangle: On Stage Vol 2
SteepleChase (Dan) SCCD 31092 [CD]
March 29, 1975; Amsterdam

Clifford Jordan and the Magic Triangle: On Stage Vol 3
SteepleChase (Dan) SCCD 31104 [CD]
March 29, 1975; Amsterdam

Clifford Jordan and the Magic Triangle: *Firm Roots*
SteepleChase (Dan) SCCD 31033 [CD]
April 18, 1975; Munich

Clifford Jordan: *The Highest Mountain*
SteepleChase (Dan) SCCD 31047 [CD]
April 18, 1975; Munich

Art Farmer: *Yesterday's Thoughts*
East Wind EJD-3102 [CD]
July 16–17, 1975; New York

Eastern Rebellion: *Eastern Rebellion*
Timeless (Du) CDSJP 101 [CD]
December 10, 1975; New York

Idrees Sulieman Quartet: *Now is the Time*
SteepleChase SCCD 31052 [CD]
February 16–17, 1976; New York

Milt Jackson: *Milt Jackson at the Kosei Nenkin*
Pablo PACD-260-103-2 [CD]
March 22–23, 1976; Tokyo

Milt Jackson: *Milt Jackson At the Kosei Nenkin, Vol. 2*
Pablo PACD-2620-120-2 [CD]
March 22–23, 1976; Tokyo

Milt Jackson & Ray Brown: *Fuji Mama*
West Wind 2054 [CD]
May 3,1976; Tokyo

Art Farmer: *The Summer Knows*
East Wind PHCE-33006 [CD]
May 12–13, 1976; New York

Art Farmer Quintet: *At Boomers*
East Wind (Jap) EW-8042 [LP]
May 14–15, 1976; New York

Art Farmer Quintet: *At Boomers Vol. 2*
Ease Wind (Jap) EW—9054 [LP]
May 14–15, 1976; New York

Clifford Jordan: *The Pentagon*
East Wind (Jap) EW-10002 [LP]
May 17, 1976; New York

Houston Person Quintet: *The Big Horn*
Muse MR5136 [LP]
May 20, 1976; New York

Eastern Rebellion: *Eastern Rebellion 2*
Timeless (Du) CDSJP106 [CD]
January 26–27, 1977; New York

Ray Brown: *Something for Lester*
Contemporary JCD687-7641 [CD]
June 22–23, 1977; Los Angeles

Sam Jones: *Something in Common*
Reissued as *Something in Common*
32 Jazz 32217 [CD]
September 13, 1977; New York

Cedar Walton: *First Set*
SteepleChase SCCD31085 [CD]
October 1, 1977; Copenhagen

Cedar Walton: *Second Set*
SteepleChase SCCD31113 [CD]
October 1, 1977; Copenhagen

Cedar Walton: *Third Set*
SteepleChase SCCD31179 [CD]
October 1, 1977; Copenhagen

Milt Jackson and His Colleagues: *Bag's Bag*
Pablo PACD2310-842-2 [CD]
December 12, 1977 and January 20-21, 1978; Los Angeles

Cedar Walton featuring Freddie Hubbard: *Reliving the Moment: Live at
    the Keyston Korner*
High Note HCD7265 [CD]
December 29–31, 1977 and January 1, 1978; San Francisco

Bob Berg: *New Birth*
Xanadu FDC5190 [CD]
May 12, 1978; New York

Philly Joe Jones: *Drum Song*
Reissued as *Drum Songs*
Milestone MCD-47094-2 [CD]
October 10–12, 1978; Berkeley

Philly Joe Jones: *Advance!*
Reissued as *Drum Songs*
Milestone MCD-47094-2 [CD]
October 10–12, 1978; Berkeley

Johnny Griffin: *Bush Dance*
Galaxy GCD95004-2 [CD]
October 18–19, 1978; Berkeley

Cedar Walton: *Animation*
Columbia Col JC35572 [LP]
1979; New York

Cedar Walton: *Soundscapes*
Columbia COL JC36285 [LP]
1979; New York

Billy Higgins Quartet: *Soweto*
Red (It) 123141-2 [CD]
January 21, 1979; Milan

Cedar Walton: *Charmed Circle: Live at the Keystone Korner*
High Note HCD7303 [CD]
August 14–18, 1979; San Francisco

Cedar Walton: *Cedar's Blues*
Red 123179-2 [CD]
November 15, 1979; Bologna

Billy Higgins Quartet: *The Soldier*
Timeless CDSJP145 [CD]
December 3, 1979; New York

Eastern Rebellion: *Eastern Rebellion 3*
Timeless SJP143 [LP]
December 19, 1979; New York

Billy Higgins: *Bridgework*
Contemporary C14024 [LP]
January 4–5, 1980 and April 23, 1986; Los Angeles

Stanley Turrentine: *Inflation*
Elektra 6R-269 [LP]
February, March, 1980; New York

Stanley Turrentine: *Use the Stairs*
Fantasy FCD-24769-2 [CD]
March, April, 1980; New York

Billy Higgins Quartet: *Once More*
Red (It) 123099-2 [CD]
May 25, 1980; Bologna

Etta Jones: *Save Your Love for Me*
Muse MCD6002 [CD]
August 7, 1980; Englewood Cliffs

Dexter Gordon: *Gotham City*
Columbia Col CK36853 [CD]
August 11, 1980; New York

Houston Person: *Very Personal*
Muse MR5231 [LP]
August 29, 1980; Englewood Cliffs

David "Fathead" Newman: *Resurgence!*
Reissued *David Fathead Newman—Lone Star Legend*
32 Jazz 32014 [CD]
September 23, 1980; Brooklyn

Cedar Walton: *The Maestro*
Reissued *The Maestro*
32 Jazz 32197 [CD]
December 15, 1980; Hollywood

Junior Cook: *Something's Cookin'*
Reissued *Something's Cookin'*
32 Jazz 32095 [CD]
June 12, 1981; Englewood Cliffs

Sonny Stitt: *Just in Case You Forgot How Bad He Really Was*
32 Jazz 32051 [CD]
September, 1981; San Franscisco

Ron Carter/Cedar Walton: *Heart & Soul*
Timeless (Du) CDSOL-6361
December, 1981; New York

Art Blakey: *Art Blakey and the All Star Jazz Messengers*
Baystate (Jap) RJL-8033 [LP]
April 11, 1982; New York

Art Farmer/Benny Golson Jazztet: *Voices All*
East World (Jap) CP38-3020 [CD]
April 24–25, 1982; Tokyo

The Timeless All Stars: *It's Timeless*
Timeless CDSJP178 [CD]
April 28, 1982; San Francisco

Cedar Walton: *Among Friends*
Evidence ECD22023-2 [CD]
July 1982; San Franscisco

Bobby Hutcherson: *Farewell Keystone*
Evidence ECD22018-2 [CD]
July 10–11, 1982; San Francisco

The Timeless All Stars: *Timeless Heart*
Timeless CDSJP182 [CD]
April 8, 1983; Englewood

Eastern Rebellion: *Eastern Rebellion 4*
Timeless (Du) SJP182 [LP]
May 25, 1983; Monster

Etta Jones: *Love Me with All Your Heart*
Muse MR5262 [LP]
September 19, 1983

Woody Shaw: *Setting Standards*
Reissued as *Woody Shaw—The Complete Muse Sessions*
Mosaic Box Set MD7-255 [CD]
December 1, 1983; Englewood Cliffs

Benny Golson: *This is for you, John*
Timeless CDSJP235 [CD]
December 20–21, 1983; New York

Cedar Walton: *The All American Trio*
Baystate (Jap) RJL-8085 [LP]
December 20–21, 1983; New York

Milt Jackson: *Used to be Jackson Vol. 1*
TDK T32Y-1001 [CD]
April 8–9, 1984; Tokyo

Milt Jackson: *Used to be Jackson Vol. 2*
TDK T32Y-1001 [CD]
April 8–9, 1984; Tokyo

Ray Brown Trio: *Bye Bye Blackbird*
Paddlewheel (Jap) K28P-6303
April 11, 1984; Tokyo

Milt Jackson: *It Don't Mean a Thing If you Can't Tap your Foot To It*
Pablo, OJC CD601-2[CD]
July 18, 1984; New York

Cedar Walton: *The Trio Vol. 1*
Red 123192-2 [CD]
March 28, 1985; Bologna

Cedar Walton: *The Trio Vol. 2*
Red 123193-2 [CD]
March 28, 1985; Bologna

Cedar Walton: *The Trio Vol. 3*
Red 123194-2 [CD]
March 28, 1985; Bologna

Slide Hampton Quintet Featuring Clifford Jordan: *Roots*
Criss Cross Jazz 1015 [CD]
April 17, 1985; Monster

Cedar Walton Trio: *Cedar*
Timeless CDSJP223 [CD]
April 19, 1985; Monster

Cedar Walton Quartet: *Bluesville Time*
Criss Cross Jazz 1017 [CD]
April 21, 1985; Monster

Steve Grossman: *Love Is The Thing*
Red (It) 12189-2 [CD]
May, 1985; Milan

Milt Jackson and His Gold Medals Winners: *Brother Jim*
Pablo 2310-916-2 [CD]
May 17, 1985; New York

Frank Morgan with the Cedar Walton Trio: *Easy Living*
Contemporary OJC CD833-2 [CD]
June 12–13, 1985; Glendale

Cedar Walton: *Blues for Myself*
Red 123205-2 [CD]
February, 1986; Milan

Frank Morgan: *Lament*
Contemporary CCD14021-2 [CD]
April 21–22, 1986; Berkeley

The Timeless All Stars: *Essence*
Delos C/CD4006 [CD]
June 25–26, 1986; Berkeley

David Williams: *Up Front*
Timeless CDSJP240 [CD]
October 31, 1986; Monster

Frank Morgan: *Bebop Lives*
Contemporary CCD14026-2 [CD]
December 14–15 [CD]

Steve Turre: *Fire and Ice*
Stash STCD7 [CD]
February 5–6, 1988; New York

The VIP Trio: *Standards Album*
Hibrite (Jap) PCB-0002 [CD]
March 7–8, 1988; Los Angeles

The VIP Trio: *Standards Album Vol. 2*
Hibrite (Jap) PCB-0003 [CD]
March 7–8, 1988; Los Angeles

Milt Jackson: *Bebop*
East-West 90991-2 [CD]
March 29–30, 1988; New York

Cedar Walton: *Plays the Music of Billy Strayhorn*
Discovery DSCD-955 [CD]
September 29–30, 1988; Hollywood

James Clay: *I Let a Song Go Out Of My Heart*
Antilles 422-484-279-2 [CD]
January 29, 1989; Englewood Cliffs

Cedar Walton: *Ironclad*
Monarch MR-1005 [CD]
April 6, 1989; Oakland

Cedar Walton & David Williams: *Off Minor*
Red (It) 123242-2 [CD]
May 18, 1990; Pordenone

Cedar Walton: *As Long as There's Music*
Muse MCD5405 [CD]
July 20, 1990; Englewood Cliffs

Ray Brown: Ray Brown and His West Coast All-Star Giants
GML (Jap) GML-20181 [CD]
September 15–16, 1990; Burbank

The Timeless All Stars: *Time for The Timeless All Stars*
Early Bird (Jap) EBCD-101 [CD]
November 4, 1990; New York

Milt Jackson: *The Harem*
MusicMasters 5061-2-C [CD]
December 10–11, 1990; New York

Freddie Hubbard: *Bolivia*
MusicMasters 5063-2-C [CD]
December 13, 14, 16, 1990; New York

Eastern Rebellion: *Mosaic*
MusicMasters 65073-2 [CD]
December 14, 16, 1990; New York

Sweet Basil Trio: *St. Thomas*
Evidence ECD22161-2 [CD]
February 15, 1991; New York

Sweet Basil Trio: *My Funny Valentine*
Sweet Basil (Jap) ALCR-108 [CD]
February 15, 1991

Diane Witherspoon: *You May Never Know*
Koch Jazz KOCCD-7879 [CD]
June-October, 1991; Hollywood

Kenny Burrell: *Sunup To Sundown*
Contemporary CCD-14065-2 [CD]
June 10–12, 1991; New York

WDR Big Band: *Blues & Beyond*
BHM (G) CD-10285 [CD]
September 14, 1991

Stanley Turrentine: *More Than a Mood*
MusicMasters 01612-65079-2 [CD]
February 13, 1992; New York

Eastern Rebellion/Raymond Court: *In the Kitchen*
TCB (Swi) 9290 [CD]
March 18, 1992; Aarburg

Eastern Rebellion: *Simple Pleasure*
Music Masters Jazz 01612-65081-2 [CD]
June 6–7, 1992; Hollywood

Cedar Walton: *Maybeck Recital Series, 25*
Concord Jazz CCD-4546 [CD]
August 9, 1992; Berkeley

Cedar Walton Trio: *Manhattan Afternoon*
Criss Cross Jazz (Du) 1082 [CD]
December 26, 1992; New York

Milt Jackson: *Reverence and Compassion*
Qwest/Reprise 9-45204-2 [CD]
1993; Hollywood

Steve Grossman: *A Small Hotel*
Dreyfus (F) FDM36561-2 [CD]
March 4, 6, 1993; Englewood Cliffs

Billy Higgins: *Billy Higgins Quintet*
Sweet Basil/Apollon 8003 [CD]
April 18, 1993; New York

Charles Lloyd/Cedar Walton: *Acoustic Masters I*
Atlantic 82583-2 [CD]
July, 1993; New York

Carmen Bradford: *With Respect*
Evidence 22115-2 [CD]
July 23–25, 27, 1993; Los Angeles

Cedar Walton Sextet: *Art Blakey Legacy*
Sweet Basil (Jap) APCZ-8006 [CD]
August 27–28, 1993; New York

Cedar Walton Sextet: *Bambino*
Apollon (Jap) APCZ-8011 [CD]
August 27–28, 1993; New York

Cedar Walton: *You're My Everything*
Sweet Basil (Jap) APCZ-8008 [CD]
September 2, 1993; New York

Milt Jackson: *The Prophet Speaks*
Qwest/Reprise 9-45591-2 [CD]
1994; North Hollywood and Hollywood

Etta James: *Mystery Lady*
Private Music 01005-82114-2 [CD]
1994; Los Angeles

Marchel Ivery: *Marchel's Mode*
Leaning House Jazz No. 1
February 7–9, 1994; Dallas

Eastern Rebellion: *Just One of Those ... Nights At The Village Vanguard.*
Jazz Heritage 513804K [CD]
May 10–15, 1994; New York

Benny Carter: *Elegy in Blue*
MusicMasters 65115 [CD]
May 18–19, 1994; Los Angeles

Sweet Basil Trio: *Never Let Me Go*
Sweet Basil (Jap) TECW-20785 [CD]
September 20, 1994; Englewood Cliffs

Carmen Lundy: *Self Portrait*
JVC 2047-2 [CD]
November, 1994; Hollywood

Tribute to Lee Morgan: *Tribute to Lee Morgan*
NYC Records NYC6016-2 [CD]
December 3–4, 1994; New York

Frank Morgan: *Love, Lost & Found*
Telarc 20 CD-83374 [CD]

Cedar Walton: *Composer*
Astor Place TCD-4001 [CD]
January 9–10, 1996; New York

Cedar Walton: *Roots*
Astor Place TCD-1010 [CD]
January 3–4, 1997; Englewood Cliffs

Eric Alexander: *Man with A Horn*
Milestone MCD-9293-2 [CD]
January 20–21, 1997; New York

Freddy Cole: *Love Makes the Changes*
Fantasy FCD9681-2 [CD]
January 6–7, 1998; New York

Phil Woods: *The Rev And I: Phil Woods Featuring Johnny Griffin*
Blue Note 7243-4-94100-2-2 [CD]
January 10–11, 1998; Saylorsburg

Joe Farnsworth Sextet: *Beautiful Friendship*
Criss Cross Jazz (Du)1166 [CD]
December 11, 1998; Brooklyn

Jackie McLean: *Nature Boy*
Somethin' Else (Jap)TOCJ-68045 [CD]
June 12–13, 1999; New York

Freddy Cole: Merry Go Round
Telarc CD-83493 [CD]
September 8–9, 1999; New York

Roy Hargrove: *Moment to Moment*
Verve 543540-2 [CD]
October 4–10, 1999; Pfeiffer Beach, Big Sur

Cedar Walton Trio: *Mosaic*
Meldac (Jap)MECJ-28102 [CD]
August 23–34, 2000; New York

Cedar Walton Trio & Dale Barlow: *Manhattan After Hours*
Jazz Bank (Jap)MTCJ-1017 [CD]
November 15, 2000; New Jersey

Etta James: *Blue Gardenia*
Private Music 01934-11580-2 [CD]
December 1–2, 2000 and February 25–27, 2001; Los Angeles

Vanessa Rubin: *Girl Talk*
Telarc 83480 [CD]
December 11–13, 2000; New York

Marlene Rosenberg: *Pieces Of ...*
Bassline 200001 [CD]
2001; Chicago

Cedar Walton: *The Promise Land*
HighNote HCD7081 [CD]
March 29, 2001; Englewood

David "Fathead" Newman: *Davey Blue*
HighNote HCD7086 [CD]
May 31, 2001; New York

Larry Coryell: *Cedars of Avalon*
HighNote HCD7093 [CD]
December 4, 2001; Englewood Cliffs

Charles Davis: *Blue Gardenia*
Reade Street 1110 [CD]
February 26, 2002; Brooklyn

Cedar Walton: *Latin Tinge*
HighNote HCD7099 [CD]
June 21, 2002; Englewood Cliffs

Cedar Walton: *Underground Memoirs*
HighNote HCD7119 [CD]
January 11, 2005; New York

Cedar Walton: *Midnight Waltz*
Venus (Jap) TKCV-35349 [CD]
March 18, 2005; New York

Christian McBride: *New York Time*
Chesky JD315 [CD]
January 31, 2006; New York

Cedar Walton: *Once Flight Down*
HighNote HCD7157 [CD]
April 7, 2006; Englewood Cliffs

David "Fathead" Newman: *Diamondhead*
HighNote HCD7179 [CD]
October 23, 2007; New York

Cedar Walton: *Seasoned Wood*
HighNote HCD7185 [CD]
February 1, 2008; Englewood Cliffs

Cedar Walton: *Voices Deep Within*
HighNote HCD7204 [CD]
May 20, 2009; Englewood Cliffs

Cedar Walton Trio: *Song of Delilah*
Venus (Jap) VHCD-1048 [CD]
February 22–23, 2010; New York

Cedar Walton: *The Bouncer*
HighNote HCD7223 [CD]
February 28, 2011; Englewood Cliffs

Piero Odorici: *Cedar Walton Presents Piero Odorici: Piero Odorici With*
    The Cedar Walton Trio
Savant SCD2115 [CD]
May 11, 2011; Paramus

Houston Person: *Naturally*
HighNote HCD7245 [CD]
July 5, 2012; Englewood Cliffs

Acknowledgments

I'd like to express a heartfelt thank you to all those who were willing to contribute to this project. Each person who was interviewed for this book had intimate knowledge of Cedar as a friend, contemporary, or as someone who was influenced by him. Each is worthy of biographies in their own right. I encourage everyone to research each one of these people and the outstanding contributions they have made to jazz. For the purposes of this book, the descriptions are brief and relate to each person's relationship with Cedar Walton.

In order of how they appeared in the book.
William H. Walton, Cousin of Cedar Walton.
James Wilson, Childhood friend of Cedar in Dallas.
Howard Hill, Childhood friend of Cedar in Dallas.
Leon Henderson, Childhood friend of Cedar in Dallas.
Roger Boykin, Dallas musician, first met Cedar in California.
Bobby Bradford, Lincoln High School bandmate and classmate.
Herbie Johnson, Lincoln High School bandmate and classmate.
Ellis Marsalis, Jazz pianist, NEA Jazz Master, first met Cedar in New Orleans when Cedar attended Dillard University.
Houston Person, Saxophonist, first met Cedar in Heidelberg, Germany. Performed and recorded with Cedar often after Cedar returned from the Army.
Lanny Morgan, Saxophonist stained in Germany at the same time Cedar was there.
Jimmy Heath, Saxophonist/Composer/Arranger, NEA Jazz Master, who hired Cedar to record on three recordings in the early 1960s.
Benny Golson, Saxophonist/Composer, NEA Jazz Master, hired Cedar to play in the Jazztet.
John Hackett, Lyricist, met Cedar during his time in LA.
Terence Blanchard, Trumpeter/Composer, member of the Jazz Messengers, Recorded with Cedar.
Brian Lynch, Trumpeter/Educator, member of the Jazz Messengers, performed with Cedar and worked with him in educational situations.

Steve Turre, Trombonist, member of the Jazz Messengers, performed and recorded with Cedar.

Javon Jackson, Saxophonist, member of the Jazz Messengers, performed and recorded with Cedar.

Reggie Workman, Bassist, NEA Jazz Master, member of the Jazz Messengers with Cedar.

Carl Walton, Oldest son of Cedar and Ida.

Fareed Mumin, Brother to Ida, lifelong friend of Cedar.

Rodney Walton, Middle son of Cedar and Ida.

Cedra Walton, Youngest daughter of Cedar and Ida.

Mike LeDonne, Jazz pianist, recording artist.

George Cables, Jazz pianist, recording artist, first saw Cedar play at Slugs.

Jim Harrison, Worked as a publicist for Slugs and Boomers. Also was a music coordinator for Jazzmobile.

Bob Cooper, Club manager of Boomers in New York City.

Louis Hayes, Drummer, NEA Jazz Master performed and recorded with Cedar, including the *Live at Boomers* sessions.

George Coleman, Saxophonist, NEA Jazz Master, original saxophonist in Eastern Rebellion.

Maxine Gordon, Tour manager for Wim Wigt and Alberto Alberti European tours.

Wim and Ria Wigt., Dutch concert promoter and founder of Timeless Records.

Jeff Hamilton, Drummer, recorded with Cedar.

Kenny Washington, Drummer, toured and recorded with Cedar.

Naisha Walton, Daughter of Cedar and Mary Parrish.

Buster Williams, Bassist, performed and recorded frequently with Cedar. Member of the Timeless All Stars.

Ron Carter, Bassist, NEA Jazz Master, performed and recorded with Cedar. Known their performances at Sweet Basil.

Todd Barkan, Club Owner, record producer. NEA Jazz Master. Owned and operated the Keystone Korner in San Francisco and produced many records that Cedar played on.

Tim Jackson, Co-founder of Kuumbwa Jazz and artistic director of the Monterey Jazz Festival.

Jason Olaine, Booking manager for Yoshi's from 1993–1999.

Ralph Moore, Tenor Saxophonist, last saxophonist to play in Eastern Rebellion.

Martha (Sammaciccia) Walton, Wife of Cedar from 1995 to his death in 2013.

Michael Weiss, Pianist, recording artist.

Rufus Reid, Bassist, played with Cedar in all-star band situations in Europe.

Alvin Queen, Drummer, toured with Cedar on multiple occasions in Europe.

Christian McBride, Bassist, played and recorded with Cedar in various situations.

Piero Odorici, Italian saxophonist, toured and recorded with Cedar.

Terell Stafford, Trumpeter, toured abroad with Cedar as part of a *Trumpet Summit* tour.

Roy Hargrove, Trumpeter, Dallas native, recorded with Cedar and played a series of duo concerts at Jazz at Lincoln Center and other domestic locations.

Paula Hackett, Lyricist, collaborated with Cedar on the record, *You May Never Know*.

Willie Jones III, Drummer, toured and recorded with Cedar.

Steve Davis, Trombonist, member of the Jazz Messengers, recorded with Cedar.

Dale Barlow, Australian Saxophonist, member of the Jazz Messengers, played and recorded with Cedar in Europe.

Gianni Valenti, Club owner of Birdland from 1986 till today.

Joe Farnsworth, Drummer, toured and recorded with Cedar.

Jed Eisenman, Artistic programmer, Village Vanguard.

Vincent Herring, Saxophonist, toured and recorded with Cedar.

Larry Clothier, Manager for Sarah Vaughn, Carmen McRae, Milt Jackson, and Roy Hargrove.

George Fludas, Drummer, toured with Cedar.

Harold Maber, Pianist, recording artist and contemporary of Cedar.

Kenny Barron, Pianist, NEA Jazz Master, contemporary of Cedar.

Monty Alexander, Pianist, recording artist and contemporary of Cedar.

Freddy Cole, Pianist, vocalist, collaborated with Cedar.

Eric Reed, Pianist, recording artist, toured with Cedar as part of the 100 Gold Fingers production.

Renee Rosness, Pianist, recording artist, toured with Cedar as part of the 100 Gold Fingers production.

David Hazeltine, Pianist, recording artist.

Bill Charlap, Pianist, recording artist, toured with Cedar as part of the 100 Gold Fingers production.

Benny Green, Pianist, recording artist, member of the Jazz Messengers, toured with Cedar as part of the 100 Gold Fingers production.

Endnotes

Chapter 1

1. W. H. Walton interview by author, October 25, 2021.
2. Ibid.
3. "North Carolina Census Records 1860–1890," North Carolina Genealogy, December 22, 2018, https://northcarolinagenealogy.org/census4.
4. W. H. Walton interview.
5. A written account from a Walton family reunion in 1981 (*The First Reunion of the Walton Family in Bryan, Texas*) says the family originally set out for the Brazos River Valley. Other family members recall stories of the family initially planning to head to California or Oklahoma.
6. *The First Reunion of the Walton Family in Bryan, Texas* (Bryan, 1981).
7. Ibid.
8. Ibid.
9. W.H. Walton interview.
10. Ibid.
11. Cedar Sr. will be referred to as C.A. from here forward.
12. *The First Reunion of the Walton Family in Bryan, Texas* (Bryan, 1981).
13. Walton, interviewed by William A. Brower, "Smithsonian Jazz Oral History Program NEA Jazz Master Interview, October 2 and 3, 2010.
14. Ibid.
15. Obituary of Cedar Anthony Walton, October 9, 1983.
16. Ibid.
17. *The Rice Shock*, Volume II (1921), C. A. Walton Collection.
18. Ibid.
19. Ibid.
20. Golden Weddings, *Dallas Morning News*, September 19, 1982.

Chapter 2

1. W. H. Walton interview.
2. Ibid.
3. W. H. Walton interview.
4. Walton, interviewed by William A. Brower, "Smithsonian Jazz Oral History Program NEA Jazz Master Interview," October 2 and 3, 2010.
5. Ibid.

6. Ibid.
7. Ibid.
8. Ibid.
9. Ibid.
10. Walton, interviewed by Ethan Iverson, "Do the M@Th," March 2010.
11. Walton, interviewed by William A. Brower, "Smithsonian Jazz Oral History Program NEA Jazz Master Interview," October 2 and 3, 2010.
12. Ibid.
13. Daniel J. Nabors, "Darrell, Benjamin Franklin (1863–1919)," TSHA, January 24, 2013, https://www.tshaonline.org/handbook/entries/darrell-benjamin-franklin.
14. W. H. Walton interview.
15. Ibid.
16. James Wilson, interview by author, July 26, 2017.
17. Howard Hill, interview by author, July 25, 2017.
18. Leon Henderson, interview by author, July 5, 2017.
19. Bobby Bradford, interview by author, June 12, 2018.
20. In another account from the Book *Blue Notes*, it is mentioned that David Newman received the nickname "Fathead" because he turned his music upside down in rehearsal because he had it memorized it. Miller saw him doing this and the name "Fathead" stuck.
21. Walton, interviewed by William A. Brower, "Smithsonian Jazz Oral History Program NEA Jazz Master Interview," October 2 and 3, 2010.
22. Bradford, interview.
23. Walton, interviewed by William A. Brower, "Smithsonian Jazz Oral History Program NEA Jazz Master Interview," October 2 and 3, 2010.
24. Pyle, Phillip. "Lincoln High School the Jazz Greats' Alma Mater." *D Magazine*, November 16, 2013. https://www.dmagazine.com/publications/d-magazine/1988/february/lincoln-high-school-the-jazz-greats-alma-mater/.
25. Ibid.
26. Bradford, interview.
27. Herbie Johnson, interview by author, May 29, 2018.
28. Walton, interviewed by William A. Brower, "Smithsonian Jazz Oral History Program NEA Jazz Master Interview," October 2 and 3, 2010.
29. Ibid.
30. Ibid.

Chapter 3

1. Several of Cedar's grade cards from Lincoln High School. Courtesy of C. A. Walton, Dallas Public Library.
2. Walton, interviewed by William A. Brower, "Smithsonian Jazz Oral History Program NEA Jazz Master Interview," October 2 and 3, 2010.
3. Ibid.
4. Ibid.
5. Ellis Marsalis, interview by author, May 1, 2018.
6. Serafin Sanchez, "Denver Jazz History" (thesis, University of Colorado, 2009).
7. Walton, interviewed by William A. Brower, "Smithsonian Jazz Oral History Program NEA Jazz Master Interview," October 2 and 3, 2010.
8. Ibid.
9. Ibid.
10. Walton, interviewed by William A. Brower, "Smithsonian Jazz Oral History Program NEA Jazz Master Interview," October 2 and 3, 2010.
11. Ibid.
12. David Schroeder, "Cedar Walton," chap. 35 in *From the Minds of Musicians* (New York: Routledge, 2018).
13. Walton, interviewed by William A. Brower, "Smithsonian Jazz Oral History Program NEA Jazz Master Interview," October 2 and 3, 2010.
14. Schroeder, "Cedar Walton," chap. 35.
15. D. D. Feder, letter to Cedar Walton, "Denver University Letter," Denver, Colorado: University of Denver, August 27, 1954.
16. Ibid.
17. Walton, interviewed by William A. Brower, "Smithsonian Jazz Oral History Program NEA Jazz Master Interview," October 2 and 3, 2010.
18. Author's transcription of cassette recording of interview with Cedar Walton, interviewer unknown, November 20, 2003, WEAA Baltimore, private collection of Martha Sammaciccia.
19. Ibid.
20. Walton, interviewed by William A. Brower, "Smithsonian Jazz Oral History Program NEA Jazz Master Interview," October 2 and 3, 2010.
21. Walton, interviewed by Ethan Iverson, "Do the M@Th" (March 2010).
22. Walton, interviewed by William A. Brower, "Smithsonian Jazz Oral History Program NEA Jazz Master Interview," October 2 and 3, 2010.
23. Ibid.
24. Ibid.

25. Ibid.
26. Lanny Morgan, interview by author, May 1, 2018.
27. Ibid.
28. Ibid.
29. Ibid.
30. Cedar Walton to Ruth Walton, September 18, 1957, private collection.
31. Ibid.
32. Cedar Walton to Ruth Walton, July 8, 1957, private collection.
33. Walton, interviewed by William A. Brower, "Smithsonian Jazz Oral History Program NEA Jazz Master Interview," October 2 and 3, 2010.
34. Houston Person, interview by author, May 4, 2018.
35. Author's transcription of cassette recording of interview with Cedar Walton, interviewer unknown, November 20, 2003, WEAA Baltimore, private collection of Martha Sammaciccia.
36. Walton, interviewed by William A. Brower, "Smithsonian Jazz Oral History Program NEA Jazz Master Interview," October 2 and 3, 2010.

Chapter 4

1. Cedar Walton to Ruth Walton, September 27, 1957, private collection.
2. Cedar Walton to Ruth Walton, May 22, 1958, private collection.
3. Tom Lord Online Jazz Discography, s.v. "Cedar Walton."
4. Walton, interviewed by William A. Brower, "Smithsonian Jazz Oral History Program NEA Jazz Master Interview," October 2 and 3, 2010.
5. Ibid.
6. Tom Lord Online Jazz Discography, s.v. "Cedar Walton."
7. Walton, interviewed by William A. Brower, "Smithsonian Jazz Oral History Program NEA Jazz Master Interview," October 2 and 3, 2010.
8. Tom Lord Online Jazz Discography, s.v. "Cedar Walton."
9. Ibid.
10. Walton, interviewed by William A. Brower, "Smithsonian Jazz Oral History Program NEA Jazz Master Interview," October 2 and 3, 2010.
11. Marc Myers, "Cedar Walton on 'Giant Steps,'" *Jazzwax*, August 20, 2013, https://www.jazzwax.com/archives.html.
12. Wynton Kelly played piano on one track, "Naima."
13. Ibid.
14. Ibid.

15. Ibid.
16. Lewis Porter, *John Coltrane* (Ann Arbor, MI: University of Michigan Press, 1999), 148.
17. Marc Myers, "Cedar Walton on 'Giant Steps,'" *Jazzwax*, August 20, 2013, https://www.jazzwax.com/archives.html.
18. Ibid.
19. Tom Lord Online Jazz Discography, s.v. "Cedar Walton."
20. Tom Lord Online Jazz Discography, s.v. "John Coltrane."
21. Marc Myers, "Cedar Walton on 'Giant Steps,'" *Jazzwax*, August 20, 2013, https://www.jazzwax.com/archives.html.
22. Ibid.
23. Walton, interviewed by William A. Brower, "Smithsonian Jazz Oral History Program NEA Jazz Master Interview," October 2 and 3, 2010.
24. Tom Lord Online Jazz Discography, s.v. "Cedar Walton."
25. Jimmy Heath, interview by author, September 12, 2017.
26. Walton, interviewed by William A. Brower, "Smithsonian Jazz Oral History Program NEA Jazz Master Interview," October 2 and 3, 2010.
27. "Art Farmer Biography," https://artfarmer.org/art-farmer-biography.
28. Ibid.
29. Ibid.
30. Author's transcription of cassette recording of interview with Cedar Walton, Rhonda Hamilton, date unknown, WBGO, private collection of Martha Sammaciccia.
31. Benny Golson, interview by author, April 23, 2018.
32. Ibid.

Chapter 5

1. Ibid.
2. John Hackett, interview by author, July 5, 2017.
3. Terrence Blanchard, interview by author, June 12, 2018.
4. Brian Lynch, interview by author, September 23, 2018.
5. Steve Turre, interview by author, August, 1 2017.
6. Javon Jackson, interview by author, July 21, 2017.
7. Walton, interviewed by William A. Brower, "Smithsonian Jazz Oral History Program NEA Jazz Master Interview," October 2 and 3, 2010.
8. Tom Lord Online Jazz Discography, s.v. "Art Blakey."
9. Ibid.

10. Walton, interviewed by William A. Brower, "Smithsonian Jazz Oral History Program NEA Jazz Master Interview," October 2 and 3, 2010.
11. Ibid.
12. Ibid.
13. Tom Lord Online Jazz Discography, s.v. "Art Blakey."
14. Ibid.
15. Joe Farnsworth, interview by author, June 5, 2017.
16. *Cedar Walton with Art Blakey and the Jazz Messengers—"That Old Feeling"* (YouTube, 2019), https://www.youtube.com/watch?v=1oITDUn70uY.
17. Todd Barkan, interview by author, June 22, 2017.
18. Slone, Christopher. "Relentless Groove: The Life of Jymie Merritt," *All About Jazz*, June 27, 2009. https://www.allaboutjazz.com/relentless-groove-the-life-of-jymie-merritt-jymie-merritt-by-christopher-slone.
19. Katherine Skinner, "Cedar Walton: An Analytical Study of His Improvisational Style through Selected Transcriptions," dissertation, University of Northern Colorado, 2017, 1–112.
20. Tom Lord Online Jazz Discography, s.v. "Art Blakey."
21. Skinner, dissertation.
22. Reggie Workman, interview by author, June 23, 2018.
23. Christian McBride, interview by author, June 13, 2017.
24. Benny Green, interview by author, August 12, 2018.
25. Alan Goldsher, *Hard Bop Academy: The Sidemen of Art Blakey and the Jazz Messengers* (Milwaukee, WI: Hal Leonard, 2008), 97–100.
26. Ibid.

Chapter 6

1. Carl Walton, interview by author, June 17, 2017.
2. Fareed Mumin, interview by author, June 11, 2018.
3. Rodney Walton, interview by author, May 4, 2018.
4. Cedra Walton, interview by author, May 7, 2018.

Chapter 7

1. Tom Lord Online Jazz Discography, s.v. "Cedar Walton."
2. Ibid.
3. Ibid.
4. Walton, interviewed by William A. Brower, "Smithsonian Jazz Oral History Program NEA Jazz Master Interview," October 2 and 3, 2010.

5. "Eddie Harris," JazzMusicArchives.com, 0AD, https://www.jazzmusi carchives.com/artist/eddie-harris.
6. "Biography," The Official Website of Eddie Harris, 0AD, https://www. eddieharris.com/biography.
7. Katherine Skinner, "Cedar Walton: An Analytical Study of His Improvisational Style through Selected Transcriptions" (dissertation, University of Northern Colorado, 2017).
8. Tom Lord Online Jazz Discography, s.v. "Cedar Walton."
9. Ibid.
10. Also recorded later as "Turquoise Twice."
11. "Turquoise" was also recorded under the title "Turquoise Twice."
12. Joel Harris, "Joe Henderson: A Biographical Study of His Life and Career," dissertation, University of Northern Colorado, 2016.
13. Ibid.
14. Ibid.
15. Ibid.
16. Mike LeDonne, interview by author, June 8, 2017.
17. Tom Lord Online Jazz Discography, s.v. "Cedar Walton."
18. "Sundown Express" was also recorded later under the title "I'm Not So Sure."
19. Bob Porter, *Soul Jazz: Jazz in the Black Community, 1945–1975* (Xlibris, 2016), 229.
20. James Gavin, "Inside Slugs' Saloon, Jazz's Most Notorious Nightclub," *JazzTimes*, April 14, 2020, https://jazztimes.com/features/profiles/ inside-slugs-saloon-jazzs-most-notorious-nightclub/.
21. Ibid.
22. George Cables, interview by author, May 11, 2018.
23. Jim Harrison, interview by author, June 12, 2018.
24. Ibid.
25. Bob Cooper, interview by author, June 12, 2018.
26. Ibid.
27. Gary Giddins, notes to *A Night at Boomers Vol. 1*, LP (1973), Muse MR 5010.
28. R. Walton interview.
29. Tom Lord Online Jazz Discography, s.v. "Cedar Walton."
30. Gary Giddins, notes to *A Night At Boomers Vol. 2*, LP (1973), Muse MR 5022.
31. Louis Hayes, interview by author, June 13, 2017.
32. Cedar Walton to Ruth Walton, December 2, 1975, private collection.

33. R. Walton interview.

34. Michael Wilson, "The Piano's Pull, Day and Night," *The New York Times* (August 29, 2009), https://www.nytimes.com/2009/08/30/nyregion/30routine.html.

Chapter 8

1. Author's transcription of cassette recording of interview with Cedar Walton, Rhonda Hamilton, date unknown, WBGO, private collection of Martha Sammaciccia.

2. *Cedar Walton/Clifford Jordan Quartet* (YouTube, 2017), https://www.youtube.com/watch?v=b7Eq4YPjq1Q&t=130s.

3. *Interview with Cedar Walton and Clifford Jordan* (YouTube, 2017), https://www.youtube.com/watch?v=2b5sQL6VxY4&t=91s.

4. Ibid.

5. George Coleman, interview by author, July 10, 2017.

6. Tom Lord Online Jazz Discography, s.v. "Cedar Walton."

7. Ibid.

8. Colin Larkin, *The Guinness Who's Who of Jazz* (Enfield, Middlesex: Guinness, 1992), 44.

9. Author's transcription of cassette recording of interview with Cedar Walton, Rhonda Hamilton, date unknown, WBGO, private collection of Martha Sammaciccia.

10. Barkan, interview.

11. Barry Kernfeld, "Walton, Cedar," *The New Grove Dictionary of Jazz, 2nd ed., Grove Music Online, Oxford Music Online*, (online version, accessed 20 December 2021, http://www.oxfordmusiconline.com).

12. Wim and Ria Wigt, interview by author, September 22, 2017.

13. Maxine Gordon, interview by author, May 11, 2018.

14. Cedar frequently called his friends "Holmes" like Sherlock Holmes. This was an extension of calling men and women lords and ladies.

15. Ibid.

16. Jeff Hamilton, interview by author, May 23, 2018.

17. Kenny Washington, interview by author, June 12, 2018.

18. "Bologna Jazz Festival 2021–2022," Bologna Jazz Festival, accessed January 3, 2022, https://www.bolognajazzfestival.com/.

19. Barkan, interview.

20. David Williams, interviewed by Ethan Iverson, "Do the M@Th," 2013.

21. Farnsworth, interview.

22. "L'etichetta Italiana per La Musica Jazz," Red Records, November 3, 2021, https://redrecords.it/.

23. Tom Lord Online Jazz Discography, s.v. "Cedar Walton."

24. Ibid.

25. Kenny Barron, interview by author, June 12, 2018.

26. Hamilton, interview.

27. McBride, interview.

28. Eric Reed, interview by author, May 4, 2018.

Chapter 10

1. David Williams, interviewed by Ethan Iverson, "Do the M@Th," 2013.

2. Ibid.

3. Ibid.

4. "Reliving the Moment" was recorded in 1977-78 but was released for the first time in 2014.

5. Ibid.

6. Tom Lord Online Jazz Discography, s.v. "Cedar Walton."

7. Ibid.

8. Buster Williams, interview by author, June 6, 2017.

9. Tom Lord Online Jazz Discography, s.v. "Cedar Walton."

10. Skinner, dissertation.

11. Ron Carter, interview by author, June 12, 2017.

12. Richard Scheinin, "Walton Play for the Love of Jazz, Not for Any," *The Mercury News*, February 28, 1997, 24–24.

13. Tom Lord Online Jazz Discography, s.v. "Cedar Walton."

14. Barkan, interview.

15. Tim Jackson, interview by author, June 14, 2017.

16. Jason Olaine, interview by author, June 8, 2017.

17. Tom Lord Online Jazz Discography, s.v. "Cedar Walton."

18. Ibid.

19. Ibid.

Chapter 11

1. Martha Sammaciccia, interview by author, December 29, 2021.

2. Ibid.

3. Ibid.

4. Ibid.
5. Ibid.
6. Ibid.
7. Ibid.
8. Ibid.
9. Ibid.
10. Ibid.
11. Ibid.
12. Ibid.
13. Ibid.
14. Ibid.
15. Ibid.
16. Ibid.
17. Ibid.
18. Ibid.
19. Ibid.
20. Ibid.
21. Ibid.
22. Ibid.
23. Ibid.
24. Ibid.
25. Ibid.
26. Ibid.
27. Ibid.
28. Ibid.
29. Michael Weiss, interview by author, June 14, 2017.
30. Sammaciccia, interview.
31. Ibid.
32. Ibid.
33. Ibid.
34. Ibid.
35. Ibid.
36. Ibid.
37. Ibid.
38. Ibid.
39. Ibid.
40. Cedar would frequently draw out the "Z" on prize for dramatic effect.
41. Ibid.

Chapter 12

1. Roger Boykin, interview by author, June 12, 2018.
2. Alvin Queen, interview by author, July 24, 2017.
3. Lynch, interview.
4. Turre, interview.
5. McBride, interview.
6. Pierro Odorci, interview by author, April 21, 2018.
7. Terell Stafford, interview by author, July 7, 2017.
8. John Clayton, interview by author, July 16, 2017.
9. Roy Hargrove, interview by author, June 7, 2018.
10. Blanchard, interview.
11. J. Hackett, interview.
12. Paula Hackett, interview by author, July 3, 2017.
13. J. Hackett, interview.
14. P. Hackett, interview.
15. J. Hackett, interview.
16. Willie Jones, interview by author, June 12, 2018.
17. Steve Davis, interview by author, July 26, 2017.
18. Dale Barlow, interview by author, May 9, 2018.
19. Hamilton, interview.
20. Gianni Valenti, interview by author, July 3, 2017.
21. Farnsworth, interview.
22. Vincent Herring, interview by author, June 12, 2017.
23. Washington, interview.
24. Billy Higgin's first record as a leader was titled, "Soweto."
25. Larry Clothier, interview by author, May 29, 2018.
26. Ray Brown, *Something for Lester* (album), 1978.
27. Jackson, interview.
28. George Fludas, interview by author, April 23, 2018.
29. H. Walton, interview.

Chapter 13

1. Harold Mabern, interview by author, May 12, 2018.
2. Barron, interview.
3. Monty Alexander, interview by author, June 21, 2017.
4. Freddy Cole, interview by author, July 10, 2017.
5. Reed, interview.

6. Weiss, interview.
7. Renee Rosnes, interview by author, August 7, 2017.
8. David Hazeltine, interview by author, July 6, 2017.
9. LeDonne, interview.
10. Bill Charlap, interview by author, August 2, 2017.
11. Green, interview.

Chapter 14

1. The exact date of Cedar's response isn't known; it is reasonable to assume from his comment about Art Blakey and the accompanying picture in the book this was in the early 1960s when Cedar was in the Messengers.
2. Pannonica de Koenigswarter, *Three Wishes: An Intimate Look at Jazz Greats* (New York, NY: Abrams Image, 2008), 174.
3. Tom Lord Online Jazz Discography, s.v. "Cedar Walton."
4. "Cedar Walton," Cedar Walton, 2010, https://www.arts.gov/honors/jazz/cedar-walton.
5. Sammaciccia, interview.
6. Martha Sammaciccia, "Memorial Program" (New York City, n.d.).

Bibliography

Archives, Letters, and Collections

Cedar Walton Jr. Private collection of Martha Sammaciccia.

C. A. Walton Collection. Dallas Public Library.

Feder, D. D. Letter to Cedar Walton. "Denver University Letter." Denver, CO: University of Denver, August 27, 1954.

Walton Letters. Private collection of Ruth Walton.

Books, Dissertations, and Theses

Doerschuk, Robert. *88 The Giants of Jazz Piano*. San Francisco, CA: Backbeat Books. 2001.

The First Reunion of the Walton Family in Bryan, Texas. Bryan, 1981.

Gelly, Dave. *Masters of Jazz Saxophone*. London: Balafon Books, 2000.

Goldsher, Alan. *Hard Bop Academy: The Sidemen of Art Blakey and the Jazz Messengers*. Milwaukee, WI: Hal Leonard, 2008.

Harris, Joel. "Joe Henderson: A Biographical Study of His Life and Career." Dissertation, University of Northern Colorado, 2016.

Koenigswarter, Pannonica de. *Three Wishes: An Intimate Look at Jazz Greats*. New York, NY: Abrams Image, 2008.

Lyons, Leonard. *The Great Jazz Pianists: Speaking of Their Lives and Music*. New York, NY: Da Capo, 1989.

Porter, Bob. *Soul Jazz: Jazz in the Black Community, 1945–1975*. Xlibris, 2016.

Sanchez, Serafin. "Denver Jazz History." Thesis, University of Colorado, 2009.

Schroeder, David. *From the Minds of Jazz Musicians: Conversations with the Creative and Inspired*. New York, NY: Routledge, Taylor & Francis Group, 2018.

Shipton, Alyn. *Handful of Keys: Conversations with Thirty Jazz Pianists*. London: Equinox, 2006.

Skinner, Katherine. "Cedar Walton: An Analytical Study of His Improvisational Style through Selected Transcriptions." Dissertation, University of Northern Colorado, 2017.

Magazines and Newspapers

Ansell, Derek. "Cedar Walton Talks to Derek Ansell." *Jazz Journal*, June 2005.

Janowiak, John. "Cedar Walton on Nat 'King' Cole." *DownBeat* 71, no. 7, July 2004.

Lutz, Phillip. "Players: David Hazeltine—Echoes of Walton." *DownBeat Blue & Beyond* 82, no. 2, February 2015.

Micallef, Ken. "Backstage With ..." *DownBeat*, March 2009.

Moorehead, Arthur. "Cedar Walton's Major League Play." *DownBeat* 48, no. 1, January 1981.

"Golden Weddings." *Dallas Morning News*, September 19, 1982.

Neymeyer, Eric. "Cedar Walton and Barry Harris." *Jazz Inside Magazine*, June 2013.

Pyle, Phillip. "Lincoln High School, the Jazz Greats' Alma Mater." *D Magazine*, February 1988.

Salmon, John. "New Stride." *Piano & Keyboard 201*, 1999.

Scheinin, Richard. "Walton Play for the Love of Jazz, Not for Any." *The Mercury News*, February 28, 1997.

Stewart, Zan. "That Latin Tinge!" *JAZZIZ*, May 2003.

Tate, Robert, and Nina J. Hodgson. "Cedar Walton." *Jazz Now*, December 1995/January 1996.

Album Liner Notes

Barkan, Todd. Notes to *Charmed Circle*. CD High Note. HCD 7303.

Berry, Kimberley. Notes to *My Funny Valentine*. CD Evidence. ECD 22120-3.

Bouchard, Fred. Notes to *The Bouncer*. CD High Note. HCD 7223.

Dorn, Joel. Notes to *Three Sundays in the Seventies*. CD Label M. 5711.

Feather, Leonard. Notes to *Cedar Walton at Maybeck*. CD Concord Jazz. CCD 4546.

Feather, Leonard. Notes to *Moanin'*. CD Blue Note. 7243 4 95324 2 7.

Feather, Leonard. Notes to *Mosaic*. CD Blue Note. CDP 7 46523 2.

Feather, Leonard. Notes to *Something for Lester*. CD Contemporary. OJCCD-412-2.

Frigård, Jørgen. Notes to *Second Set*. CD Steeplechase. SCCD 31113.

Gardner, Mark. Notes to *Cedar!*. CD Prestige. LP PR7519.

Gardner, Mark. Notes to *Manhattan Afternoon*. CD Criss Cross.1082 CD.

Giddins, Gary. Notes to *A Night at Boomers Vol. 1*. LP Muse. MR5010.

Giddins, Gary. Notes to *A Night at Boomers Vol. 2*. LP Muse. MR5022.

Gilbert, Mark. Notes to *Love is the Thing*. CD Red Records. 123189-2 RED.

Gitler, Ira. Notes to *Caravan*. CD Riverside. OJCCD-038-2.

Gold, Don. Notes to *Big City Sounds*. CD Fresh Sound. FSR 1653.

Hentoff, Nat. Notes to *Giant Steps*. CD Atlantic. R2 75203.

Jaye, David. Notes to *Cedar Chest*. CD High Note. HCD 6024.

Macero, Teo. Notes to *J.J. INC*. CD Columbia. CK 65296.

McBride, Christian. Notes to *Composer*. CD Astor Place. TCD 4001.

Morgan, Bob. Notes to *Really Livin'*. CD Sony Music Labels. SICJ 78.

Musto, Russ. Notes of *Reliving the Moment*. CD High Note. HCD 7265.

Musto, Russ. Notes to *Just One of Those ... Nights at the Village Vanguard*. CD Music Masters. 01612-65116-2.

Panken, Tedd. Notes to *Roots*. CD Astor Place. TCD 4010.

Porter, Bob. Notes to *Cedar Walton plays Cedar Walton*. CD Prestige. OJCCD-6002-2.

Rogers, John. Notes to *You May Never Know*. CD Ride. RID-CD-18.

Smith, Hank Diamon. Notes to *Night at the Mark VII*. CD Savoy Jazz. SVY 17299.

Walton, Cedar. Notes to *Soul Cycle*. CD Prestige. OJCCD-847-2.

Walton, Cedar. Notes to *The Maestro*. CD 32 Jazz. 32197.

Walton, Cedar. Notes to *Up Front*. CD Timeless. CDSJP 240.

Interviews and Unpublished

Do the M@TH. 2010. "Interview with Cedar Walton." Accessed October 28, 2021. https://ethaniverson.com/interview-with-cedar-walton/.

Do the M@TH. 2013. "Interview with David Williams." Accessed November 1, 2021.https://ethaniverson.com/interview-with-david-williams/.

Walton, Cedar. Interviewed by Unknown. November 20, 2003. FM WEAA Baltimore. Transcription by author.

Walton, Cedar. Interview by Rhonda Hamilton. n.d. FM WBGO Newark. Transcription by author.

Walton, Cedar. Interviewed by William A. Brower. *Smithsonian Jazz Oral History Program NEA Jazz Master Interview*. October 2 and 3, 2010.

Online Databases and Websites

Appelbaum, Larry. "Before & After: Cedar Walton." Let's Cool One, January 17, 2017. https://larryappelbaum.wordpress.com/2011/02/21/before-after-cedar-walton/.

"Biography." The Official Website of Eddie Harris, n.d. https://www.eddieharris. com/biography.

"Bologna Jazz Festival 2021–2022." Bologna Jazz Festival. Accessed January 3, 2022. https://www.bolognajazzfestival.com/.

"Cedar Walton." Cedar Walton, 2010. https://www.arts.gov/honors/jazz/ cedar-walton.

"Eddie Harris." JazzMusicArchives.com, n.d. https://www.jazzmusicarchives. com/artist/eddie-harris.

Gavin, James. "Inside Slugs' Saloon, Jazz's Most Notorious Nightclub." *JazzTimes*. April 14, 2020. https://jazztimes.com/features/profiles/ inside-slugs-saloon-jazzs-most-notorious-nightclub/.

"The Italian label for Jazz Music." Red Records, November 3, 2021. https://redrecords.it/.

Iverson, Ethan. Cedar Walton Interview. Other. *Do the M@Th*, March 2010. https://ethaniverson.com/.

Kernfeld, Barry. "Walton, Cedar." *The New Grove Dictionary of Jazz, 2nd edition. Grove Music Online. Oxford Music Online*. Accessed December 20, 2021. http://www.oxfordmusiconline.com.

Lord, Tom. "Tom Lord Online Jazz Discography." http://www.lordisco.com. Accessed January 2021–December 2021.

Macon, Alex, Alex Macon, Jamey Newberg, Jamey Newberg, Taylor Crumpton, Taylor Crumpton, Tim Rogers, et al. "Lincoln High School the Jazz Greats' Alma Mater." *D Magazine*, November 16, 2013. https://www.dmagazine.com/publications/d-magazine/1988/february/ lincoln-high-school-the-jazz-greats-alma-mater/.

Mueller, Lynne. "Art Farmer 1929-1999 Celebrating His Legacy." https:// artfarmer.org.

Myers, Marc. "Cedar Walton on 'Giant Steps." *Jazzwax*, August 20, 2013. https://www.jazzwax.com/archives.html.

Nabors, Daniel J. "Darrell, Benjamin Franklin (1863–1919)." TSHA, January 24, 2013. https://www.tshaonline.org/handbook/entries/darrell-benjamin-franklin.

"North Carolina Census Records 1860–1890." North Carolina Genealogy, December 22, 2018. https://northcarolinagenealogy.org/census4.

Slone, Christopher. "Relentless Groove: The Life of Jymie Merritt." *All About Jazz*, June 27, 2009. https://www.allaboutjazz.com/relentless-groove-the-life-of-jymie-merritt-jymie-merritt-by-christopher-slone.

Wilson, Michael. "The Piano's Pull, Day and Night." *The New York Times.* August 29, 2009. https://www.nytimes.com/2009/08/30/nyregion/30routine.html.

Video Recordings

Bobby Hutcherson & Cedar Walton—Bolivia. YouTube, 2014. https://www.youtube.com/watch?v=f5P1EypE7Ok.

Bobby Hutcherson & Cedar Walton—Little Sunflower. YouTube, 2014. https://www.youtube.com/watch?v=5B1Cf_OZYw0.

Cedar Walton with Art Blakey and the Jazz Messengers—"That Old Feeling." YouTube, 2019. https://www.youtube.com/watch?v=1oITDUn70uY.

Cedar Walton/Clifford Jordan Quartet. YouTube, 2017. https://www.youtube.com/watch?v=b7Eq4YPjq1Q&t=130s.

Freddie Hubbard with Cedar Walton Trio/God Bless the Child (1992). YouTube, 2010. https://www.youtube.com/watch?v=QO6EhWSD-gU.

Interview with Cedar Walton and Clifford Jordan. YouTube, 2017. https://www.youtube.com/watch?v=2b5sQL6VxY4&t=91s.

OPB New Years '86, Phil Woods with Cedar Walton Trio. YouTube, 2011. https://www.youtube.com/watch?v=h-VEufV7Lks.

Ron Carter & Art Farmer. YouTube, 2014. https://www.youtube.com/watch?v=dbYGS7ht90A.

Walton & Coleman Quartet Live—Umbria Jazz Festival 1976—Part 1 of 3. YouTube, 2017. https://www.youtube.com/watch?v=6Z9FUNATlD4.

Index

E

Earth Wind and Fire (band), 104
Eastern Rebellion (band), 83–91, 95–96, 103, 109, 111, 127, 135, 160, 169,
    248, 251, 283–284, 286, 288, 291–293
Eastern Rebellion (album), 86, 91
Eastern Rebellion 2 (album), 88, 248, 284
Eastern Rebellion 4 (album), 127, 288
Eastern Rebellion/Raymond Court (album), 135, 292
Eisenman, Jed, 185
El Chapultepec (club), 194
El Matador, 118
"Electric Boogaloo Song, The," 76, 280
Elegy in Blue, 180, 273, 293
Elfman, Donald, 168
Ellington, Duke, 15, 23, 30, 51, 87, 119–120, 154, 181, 183, 192, 195, 219,
    223, 232, 248, 269
Ellis, Don, 32
"End of a Love Affair," 254
Erskine, Peter, 224
Evans, Gil, 90

F

Fain, Sammy, 51
"Fantasy in D," 88, 189, 206, 221, 248
  and "Ugetsu," 122, 170, 189, 232, 248
Farmer, Art, 40–41, 43, 52, 95, 112, 116–117, 217, 245, 275–276, 279, 281,
    283–284, 287
Farnsworth, Joe, 94, 169, 171–172, 181–185, 201, 224, 294
"Fatback," 170
"Fathead." *See* Newman, David
Feldman, Victor, 175, 224
Fender Rhodes, 158, 241, 244
Fire and Ice, 158, 290
"Firm Roots," 175, 198, 222, 232, 242
Firm Roots, 88, 95, 282–283
First Amendment Comedy Troupe, The, 244
First Set, 96, 239, 254, 285
Fitzgerald, Ella, 10, 92, 94

"5/4 Thing," 86
Five Points area, 23
Flanagan, Tommy, 37–38, 114, 117, 179, 192, 199–200, 215–217,
    226, 231, 256
Fludas, George, 196
Fort Worth, 9, 193, 204
Foster, Frank, 81
Free for All, 52, 160, 277
Freedman, Don, 246
"From This Moment On," 36, 280
Fuller, Curtis, 36, 46–49, 52, 88, 95, 112, 120, 127, 156–157, 162, 170, 172,
    220, 234, 236, 249, 270, 276, 281

G

Gadd, Steve, 81
Garland, Red, 12, 50, 166, 240, 247–248
Garner, Erroll, 222, 232
Gary, Johnnie, 36
Gehry, Frank, 223
Generation, 112, 225, 281
Germany, 30–33, 35, 72, 102, 153, 182
Gershwin, George, 7
Getz, Stan, 93
Giant Steps, 37–39, 130, 205
Gibbons, Shannon, 167
Giddins, Gary, 78, 80
Gillespie, Dizzy, 11, 23, 32, 37, 39, 67, 163, 251
Girl Talk, 171, 295
Glass Bead Games, 155, 173
Goldberg, Richie, 167
Golden Boy, 74, 277
Golson, Benny, 40–41, 43, 48, 52, 63, 112, 170, 200, 216,
    275–276, 287–288
Gordon, Deborah, 186
Gordon, Dexter, 23, 90, 94, 112, 232–233, 254,
    281, 287
Gordon, Lorraine, 186
Gordon, Max, 185
Gordon, Maxine, 90

Kelly, Wynton, 40, 114, 240, 247–248
Keystone Korner (club), 112, 118–119, 124, 157,
        252–253, 286
Kind of Blue, 59
Kirk, Rahsaan Roland, 118
KJAZ, 127, 248
Kloss, Eric, 76, 279
Knicks (basketball team), 78–79, 140
Koenigswarter, Nadine de, 261
Koenigswarter, Pannonica de, 261
Kuumbwa Jazz (club), 123

L

"Lament," 171, 290
Land, Harold, 112, 170, 236
Latin Tinge, 262, 295
LeDonne, Mike, 68, 75, 120, 225, 240, 243, 245, 268
Lee, Bill, 173
Lee, Spike, 173
Left Bank Jazz Society, 64, 281–282
Legge, Wade, 41
Lewis, Ramsey, 206
Lewis, Victor, 166
"Like Sonny," 39
Lil's (club), 23–24
Lincoln, Abbey, 140, 214, 247
Lion in Winter (film), 121
Lionel Hampton Band, 33
"Little Sunflower," 172
Live at Birdland, 153
Lizy, 238–240
Lord Buckley, 120
Los Angeles Philharmonic, 160
Lovano, Joe, 160
Love Makes the Changes, 122, 294
"Low Rider," 81–82
Lyela tribe, 1
Lynch, Brian, 47, 154, 233–234

M

Vick, Harold, 231
Village Vanguard (club), 65, 74, 114, 135, 170, 181, 185–187, 193, 196,
        202, 218, 239, 254, 272, 293
Vine Street Bar, 168
Vinnegar, Leroy, 75
"Voices Deep Within," 87
Voices Deep Within, 262, 296

W

Walton Jr., Cedar, 1–2, 4–15, 17–18, 21–33, 35–43, 45–57, 59–64, 66–68,
        71–83, 85–91, 93–99, 101–102, 104, 106–109, 111–135, 137–147,
        149–259, 261–265, 267–273, 279–283, 285–296
    Army, 21, 29–33, 45, 71–72, 76, 114, 182
    Baltimore, 33, 64, 281–282
    B. F. Darrell Elementary, 4, 8–9
    "Billy," 5
    birth, 4
    Bologna, 93–95, 143, 286, 289
    Boomers (club), 77–80, 86, 90, 96, 111, 153–155, 203, 226, 248,
        282, 284
    Brooklyn, 28, 60–61, 63–65, 102, 116, 130, 142, 218, 230, 267, 271,
        287, 294–295
    California, 14, 23, 33, 65, 104, 123, 126, 149, 152, 194–195
    Cedartio Waltoni (nickname), 94, 143
    Chicago, 43, 104, 151, 184, 197, 217, 219, 234, 275–276,
        281, 295
    death, 263
    Denver, 23–29, 194–195
    Denver University, 23, 25–27
    Dillard University, 21–22
    European touring, 83, 89, 91
    fusion, 81–83, 85, 205, 241
    Heidelberg, Germany, 32
    Lincoln High School, 8, 10–15, 18, 21
    Los Angeles, 65, 109, 117–119, 140, 163, 169, 220, 222, 255, 271, 277,
        284–286, 290, 292–293, 295
    "Mein Comp," 120, 270
    Monterey Jazz Festival, 123–124
    National Endowment for the Arts Jazz Master, 262, 273